How to Manage International Multidisciplinary Research Projects

How to Manage International Multidisciplinary Research Projects

Edited by

Linda Hantrais

Professor Emerita of European Social Policy, Department of International Relations, Politics and History, Loughborough University, and Visiting Professor, International Inequalities Institute, London School of Economics and Political Science, UK

Edward Elgar
PUBLISHING

Cheltenham, UK • Northampton, MA, USA

Published by
Edward Elgar Publishing Limited
The Lypiatts
15 Lansdown Road
Cheltenham
Glos GL50 2JA
UK

Edward Elgar Publishing, Inc.
William Pratt House
9 Dewey Court
Northampton
Massachusetts 01060
USA

Paperback edition 2022

A catalogue record for this book
is available from the British Library

Library of Congress Control Number: 2022938787

This book is available electronically in the **Elgar**online
Political Science and Public Policy subject collection
http://dx.doi.org/10.4337/9781802204728

ISBN 978 1 80220 471 1 (cased)
ISBN 978 1 80220 472 8 (eBook)
ISBN 978 1 0353 1097 5 (paperback)

Printed and bound in Great Britain by TJ Books Limited, Padstow, Cornwall

Contents

PART II   CASE STUDIES

List of boxes

List of contributors

Jabir Alshehabi Al-Ani is a Senior Research Officer in the Department of Mathematical Sciences at the University of Essex.

Simon Batchelor is Director at Gamos Ltd, Visiting Research Fellow at Loughborough University and Research and Innovation Co-ordinator for the Modern Energy Cooking Services (MECS) programme. His research interests lie in the fields of energy access and low carbon transitions in low- and middle-income countries, mobile telephony, mobile money and social mobilisation.

Julia Brannen FAcSS is Emeritus Professor at the Thomas Coram Research Unit, Institute of Education, University College London. Her research reflects her strong interest in methodology and focusses on the family lives of parents, children and young people, and work–family issues in Britain and Europe, intergenerational relationships, and food in families.

Ed Brown is Professor of Global Energy Challenges in the Department of Geography and the Environment, Loughborough University, UK. His research interests lie in the fields of governance and international development issues, focussing on energy access and low carbon energy technologies and transitions, questions of transparency and corruption, and financial globalisation.

Ben Campbell is Lecturer in the Department of Anthropology at Durham University, UK. His research interests span environmental anthropology, culture and sustainability, low carbon energy transitions, indigenous knowledge and development, conservation and social justice, with a particular focus on Nepal and the Himalayas. He has led research projects on Modern Energy Cooking Services (MECS).

Jon Cloke was co-founder of the Low Carbon Energy for Development Network (LCEDN) and network manager for Understanding Sustainable Energy Solutions (USES) programme, based at Loughborough University. He has also worked as an NGO consultant to different non-government organisations including the UK-based NGO Practical Action developing policy documents for guiding strategy.

John Connolly is Professor of Public Policy in the School of Education and Social Sciences at the University of the West of Scotland. His research centres on the areas of health security governance, multi-level public sector reform and evaluation. He works across interdisciplinary boundaries to inform public policies at multiple levels of governance.

Joni Cook is the Communications Officer for the Modern Energy Cooking Services (MECS) programme, having previous managed communications for the Low Carbon Energy for Development Network (LCEDN) in the Department for Geography and Environment, Loughborough University, UK. Her research addresses physiological and evolutionary questions of plant ecology.

Nicole Denier is an Assistant Professor in the Department of Sociology at the University of Alberta.

Emmanouil Detsis is an astrophysicist by training and certified project manager by practice. He has delivered several EU framework programme projects for the European Science Foundation over the past decade, specialising in interdisciplinary projects.

Lei Ding is a Doctoral Candidate in the Department of Mathematical & Statistical Sciences at the University of Alberta.

Karen Duke is Professor of Criminology and Co-Director of the Drug and Alcohol Research Centre at Middlesex University. She specialises in research on drugs policy and the interfaces with the criminal justice system, and stakeholder analysis of addictions policy and young people and substance use prevention and treatment practices.

Linda Hantrais FAcSS is Professor Emerita of European Social Policy at Loughborough University, UK, and Visiting Professor at the London School of Economics and Political Science, UK. Her research interests span international comparative research theory, methods, management and practice, with particular reference to public policy and institutional structures.

Minna van Gerven is Professor of Social and Public Policy in the Department of Social and Public Policy at Helsinki University. Her research interests are in qualitative social science research, including comparative social policy, welfare states, social security and services in Finland and other EU member states.

Fiona Henriquez is Professor of Parasitology in the Institute for Biomedical and Environmental Health Research at the University of the West of Scotland. She works at the interface of medical and environmental sciences, focussing on the emergence of antimicrobial resistance in the environment and the development of mitigation strategies for disease prevention.

Shenggang Hu is a doctoral student and Assistant Lecturer in the Department of Mathematical Sciences at the University of Essex.

Yang Hu is Senior Lecturer in Sociology and Data Science in the Department of Sociology at Lancaster University.

Karen D. Hughes is the Alex Hamilton Professor in the School of Business and Professor of Sociology in the Faculty of Arts at the University of Alberta in Canada. She has published widely on issues relating to work, organisations, and labour markets, with specific interests in gender, work, and entrepreneurship, inclusive economies, and economic and technological change.

Andrew Hursthouse is Professor of Environmental Geochemistry in the Centre for Environmental Research at the University of the West of Scotland. In his research, he applies an earth-systems approach to transport/behaviour of pollutants in the environment (air quality, land degradation, remediation, and aquatic biogeochemistry), evaluating impact on ecosystems and for human health.

Ron Iphofen FAcSS is an adviser to the European Commission, European Research Council, and to government and independent research agencies across Europe. His is internationally recognised for his expertise on research ethics and scientific integrity, and for helping to maintain professional standards in research.

Bei Jiang is an Associate Professor in the Department of Mathematical & Statistical Sciences at the University of Alberta.

Linglong Kong is an Associate Professor and Canada Research Chair in Statistical Learning in the Department of Mathematical & Statistical Sciences at the University of Alberta.

Alla Konnikov is a Post-Doctoral Research Fellow in the Department of Sociology, Faculty of Arts, at the University of Alberta in Canada. Her research interests are located at the intersection of labour force inequality, gender and ethnic relations, focussing on gender and ethnic AI-driven bias and strategies for its mitigation.

Aygen Kurt-Dickson is Research and Innovation Strategy Manager at the London School of Economics and Political Science, UK. She is an expert facilitator for interdisciplinary and collaborative research projects. Her role involves strategy development in research and knowledge exchange funding, and connecting social science-based research to innovation for impactful outcomes.

Tuuli Malava is a Research Assistant and Master's student in social and public policy at the University of Helsinki, Finland. Her research interests include statistical methods, labour market policies and activation.

Merita Mesiäislehto is Senior Researcher at the Finnish Institute for Health and Welfare in the Ministry of Social Affairs and Health (THL), in Finland. Her research interests include comparative welfare state mechanisms, social security systems and minimum income, social and economic inequalities, vulnerable groups and their labour market situations.

Rebecca O'Connell is Reader in the Sociology of Food and Families at the Thomas Coram Research Unit, Institute of Education, University College London. Her research focusses on the social anthropology and policy relevance of research on food practices among children and families in the UK and Europe, using international comparative mixed and multi-methods approaches.

Tiina Randma-Liiv is Professor of Public Management and Policy in the Ragnar Nurkse Department of Innovation and Governance at Tallinn University of Technology, Estonia, and a member of the Estonian Academy of Science. Her research interests focus on comparative and transitional public management, public administration reforms, e-participation and small states.

Irina Rets is a Research Associate at the Management School of Lancaster University, UK, with research interests covering topics related to inclusion and technology-enhanced learning. She is conducting research for the BIAS project at Lancaster University, looking into the fair use of AI in the organisational context.

Peppi Saikku is Research Manager at the Finnish institute for Health and Welfare, Ministry of Social Affairs and Health, Helsinki, Finland. Her research interests are cross-sectoral policies and services for vulnerable groups.

Long Seng To is Joint Director of the Centre for Sustainable Transitions: Energy, Environment and Resilience (STEER) at Loughborough University, UK. She holds an Engineering for Development Research Fellowship funded by the Royal Academy of Engineering, and she chairs the Solar Subgroup of the UN Expert Group on Resource Management.

Monideepa Tarafdar is the Charles J. Dockendorff Endowed Professor in the Isenberg School of Management at the University of Massachusetts Amherst, US.

Betsy Thom is Professor of Health Policy and Co-Director of the Drug and Alcohol Research Centre at Middlesex University, UK, and an honorary professor, Department of Psychology and Behavioural Sciences, at Aarhus University, Denmark. Her research focusses on socio-cultural and public health aspects of alcohol and drug use and the criminal justice system.

Antje Wiener FAcSS is Professor of Political Science and Global Governance at Hamburg University, Germany, and an elected By-Fellow of Hughes Hall, Cambridge University, UK. Her research centres on international relations theory, specialising in contested norms and climate justice, and calling for a more inclusive and pluralistic approach informed by multi-thematic and multidisciplinary perspectives.

Dengdeng Yu is an Assistant Professor in the Department of Mathematics at the University of Texas at Arlington.

Preface

RATIONALE FOR THE BOOK

Interest in international multidisciplinary research has escalated in a post-pandemic world that is facing major societal challenges, not least the global threat of climate change. In this context, the need for a guide to the management of scientific collaborations that cross national boundaries and bridge disciplinary divides is both timely and apposite.

This book primarily targets mid-career academic and non-academic researchers across the disciplinary spectrum in a wide range of international settings who are preparing to manage international multidisciplinary projects. The insights it provides will also be of interest for established researchers in the UK, Europe and further afield, who are seeking to expand their knowledge and experience of research project management.

A particular focus of the guide is the contribution of social and human scientists to the management of complex projects. In the 1990s, researchers in the social sciences and humanities were drawn into the European Commission's framework programmes as junior partners in collaborations with the 'natural' sciences. In the early twenty-first century, social scientists were able to take full advantage of having their own socio-economic funding stream to expand their international networks and hone their skills at working across cognate disciplines. UK researchers, especially social scientists, gained a strong reputation for their expertise and attainments in the European research arena both as partners and as project coordinators. In 2016, when the UK voted to leave the EU, social scientists were found to have benefitted to a greater extent from the EU funding and capacity building opportunities provided by the European Union's programmes and European Research Council awards, compared both to other scientists in the UK and to social scientists in other EU member states. Their experience in managing international projects has been invaluable in preparing this guide.

During the same period, developments in science policy, at national and European levels in favour of a more 'integrated' approach to research funding and programmes created new challenges and opportunities for multidisciplinary researcher collaborations. The Horizon 2020 (2013–2020) and Horizon Europe (2021–2027) European programmes, for example, emphasised the importance not only of adopting an integrated multidisciplinary approach to research but also of demonstrating economic, social and cultural impact from EU-funded programmes. These developments in Europe required innovative forms of cooperation enabling UK social scientists to retain and build on their international reputations. The future achievements of researchers in the international arena depend not only on this proven capacity to work cross-nationally but also on their ability, irrespective of their own disciplines, to collaborate effectively with researchers in other disciplines to promote international methodological learning and knowledge exchange.

THE BOOK'S AIMS AND OBJECTIVES

Managing multidisciplinary international collaborations requires skill sets that focus on mutual understanding between disciplines and cultures, willingness to foster communities of practice based on relations of parity, trust and cooperation, and readiness to learn from other research traditions. Drawing on worked examples of international multidisciplinary research collaborations, this guide aims to improve understanding of, and responses to, the many challenges arising in research that crosses disciplinary, national and cultural boundaries. More specifically, it seeks to accompany project managers and team members through the process of developing and applying strategies that will enable them to bridge what are often deep-seated disciplinary and cultural divides, thereby assisting them in implementing effective integrated approaches to the design and delivery of high-quality, high-value research across disciplines, sectors and societies.

STRUCTURE OF THE BOOK

The three introductory chapters provide an overview of the theory, methods and practice of managing international multidisciplinary research projects, focussing on the challenges confronting research leaders and team members, and the solutions adopted in real-life situations. The authors draw on their own first-hand experience and publications, and on accounts provided by researchers at varying stages in their careers in different international and disciplinary environments, to analyse and document the research management process. The chapters refer readers to the ten illustrative case studies, presented in the second part of the book, featuring different types of projects on a range of topics, whether funded by international institutions, national research councils or government departments.

Chapter One: Exploring the complexities of international multidisciplinary project management

The first chapter tracks the growing complexities of international multidisciplinary research project management through the postwar period to the present day. By reviewing the development of research programmes that extend across national borders and disciplinary groupings, involving potentially incompatible theoretical, conceptual and methodological approaches, the author explains why coordination of international multidisciplinary teams has become such a complicated and demanding process. The chapter explores the shifting meanings of international and multidisciplinary research and their implications for project management. It raises salient issues that are addressed in subsequent chapters and in the case studies, associated with the contextual backgrounds of researchers; the language and epistemic communities to which they belong; the socio-economic and political environments impinging on the phenomena under analysis; the institutional frameworks and constraints within which researchers are operating; the agendas of national and international funding agencies; and the interface between researchers and their multisectoral stakeholders.

Chapter Two: Launching into an international multidisciplinary project

Drawing on examples from the illustrative case studies, the second chapter examines the vast array of complex overlapping tasks entailed in collaborative research across national borders and disciplinary boundaries, many of which need to be carried out simultaneously and cumulatively. The chapter focusses on the early stages in the process covering the issues to be considered when deciding whether to respond to a funding call; when navigating institutional regulations, including financial rules, incentives and expectations of sponsors and stakeholders; and when preparing and submitting a research proposal, securing appropriate funding and negotiating a budget, including the institutional requirements of participating researchers, and the constraints they impose. In addressing the question of access to external funding, the authors review the implications of different funding mechanisms when selecting a project manager, building a multidisciplinary research team with appropriate skill sets and experience of international cooperation, and when planning subsequent stages in the research.

Chapter Three: Managing the research process

Drawing further on the illustrative case studies and the chapter authors' own experiences, the third chapter focusses on the challenges of conducting international multidisciplinary research projects once funding has been secured and appropriate structures and procedures have been established. The chapter offers guidance on managing the research process when working with partners from different disciplinary and national research cultures, showing how funders' requirements, the composition of research teams, and mix of disciplines and cultures impact on the research design and methods. Consideration is given to communication and engagement strategies adopted both internally between team members, and externally with funders and other stakeholders, including policymakers, academic institutions and the wider public. The chapter concludes by reviewing and synthesising the lessons learnt from the real-life experiences of the case study project coordinators who managed international multidisciplinary research programmes and projects, and of the team members who participated in small and large-scale collaborations.

Linda Hantrais

Acknowledgements

The editor would like to thank, firstly, the co-author of Chapters Two and Three, Julia Brannen, as well as the authors of the case studies and their team members for contributing to this guide by critically analysing their experiences of the international multidisciplinary research process, and their many funders for supporting the research on which the case studies are based. In some instances the accounts were written while projects were ongoing, in others when the research was in its final stages, and in two instances when the case study authors were able to reflect on their experiences several years after completing the projects they describe. Most of the authors were juggling their time between meeting the deadlines for the book and answering the demands of full-time academic positions, while coping with complicated working arrangements and family responsibilities during the pandemic.

The editor is also grateful for the advice and assistance provided during the planning and drafting phases of the book by the many colleagues who were convinced of the value and timeliness of the guide, in particular the members of the UK national Academy of Social Sciences' core International Advisory Group, which she chairs. In addition to Julia Brannen, who co-authored two of the chapters and one of the case studies, Ron Iphofen and Antje Wiener, as corresponding authors of case studies, they include Chris Caswill, Peter Elias, Dave Filipović-Carter, Ulrich Hilpert, Ashley Thomas Lenihan, Susanne MacGregor and Judith Phillips, who actively supported the proposal and its realisation. The constructive comments and encouragement received from Roger Benjamin, Anne Corbett and Gabi Lombardo were much appreciated.

Linda Hantrais

PART I

INTRODUCTORY CHAPTERS

1. Exploring the complexities of international multidisciplinary project management

Linda Hantrais

INTRODUCTION

In less than a century, three major societal changes have affected the ways in which research has been defined, conceptualised, funded, conducted, assessed and disseminated:

- Postwar internationalisation and the progressive scaling up of different forms of cross-border and cross-cultural research collaborations
- The gradual erosion of disciplinary boundaries and hierarchies, stimulating the development of new cross-disciplinary subfields and multidisciplinary research partnerships
- The growing emphasis on achieving value for money and proven impact in the context of budgetary constraints and ubiquitous technological innovations

These changes were accelerated in the 2000s by the global financial and climate crises, Brexit and the COVID-19 pandemic, which added to the complexities of effectively managing international multidisciplinary research projects. They also amplified the demand for large-scale interdisciplinary collaborations to tackle societal challenges.

INTERNATIONALISATION OF THE RESEARCH LANDSCAPE

For centuries, scientific research has been international: from the wandering scholars in medieval universities; through the Renaissance when 'travel really meant education' (Meyerhardt, 1915); to the Nobel Prize winners of the twentieth century; the launch, in 1984, of the European Union's Framework Programmes for Research and Technological Development (FPs); and, in

1996, of the Marie Skłodowska-Curie Actions as the EU's flagship funding programme for doctoral education and postdoctoral training of researchers. By the early decades of the twenty-first century, large-scale international research collaborations were recognised as being key to solving the world's societal problems, bringing both risks and opportunities for research teams, and accelerating the need for scientists to hone the skills required for cooperating effectively in international environments.

Framing International Research Collaboration in the Twentieth Century

In the early postwar period, pressures intensified to rebuild societies, economies and diplomatic relations through international research cooperation. For example, the Centre Européen pour la Recherche Nucléaire (CERN) was established in 1954 as a large-scale world-class physics research facility in Switzerland with 12 founding member states. The vision of the European and North American scientists who spawned the project was both 'to stop the brain drain to America that had begun during the Second World War, and to provide a force for unity in post-war Europe' (CERN, 2021). Switzerland was chosen to host CERN because of its political neutrality and its concern to create 'safeguards against the misappropriation of scientific research results for military purposes' (Info Swiss, 2017). Today, CERN has 23 member states and, since its founding, some 12,000 scientists representing 120 nationalities are known to have contributed to its activities. As one of the largest multinational collaborations in the world, CERN has had to address the enduring problems of international research associated with language barriers, national research funding contributions, locational issues, researcher mobility and skill shortages.

In 1959, following the founding of the European Economic Community in 1957, the Statistical Office of the European Communities (Eurostat, 2021) began issuing agricultural and labour force statistics that had been collected in countries with widely differing statistical traditions (Desrosières, 1993). Eurostat would go on to serve as an essential data source for European-level comparisons between countries and regions.

Another early influential example of the postwar internationalisation of research was the establishment in 1963 of the European Centre for the Coordination of Research and Documentation in the Social Sciences in Vienna (Petrella & Schaff, 1974). The Vienna Centre was founded under the auspices of the United Nations Educational, Scientific and Cultural Organisation (UNESCO) as an independent international non-governmental agency funded by ministries, academies of science and research councils in 21 countries. In the context of the Cold War, the Centre was to serve largely as a discursive forum for the meeting of different research traditions and schools of thought in eastern and western Europe and, as its name implies, to facilitate the exchange of social science knowledge and documentation.

As positivism and the survey tradition became more dominant in the English-speaking social sciences, much of the early path-breaking methodological literature on international research emanated from the United States (Armer & Grimshaw, 1973). Single-nation research teams developed their own concepts, methods and analytical procedures (typically large-scale surveys) without seeking the cooperation of researchers in the societies they were studying. The implicit objective was to use foreign societies to test the validity of theories established at home, and to demonstrate the superiority of the western model of economic and political development.

The working practices of the Vienna Centre marked an important shift away from this 'asymmetrical', 'imperialist' or 'colonialist' model of international research, critically referred to as the 'safari' approach (Szalai, 1977, p. 69), in favour of a more 'symmetrical' or 'equitable' paradigm. The Centre's model depended on constructive interchange with team members in the participating countries, and their active involvement in project design and delivery (Grootings, 1986) (cf. AMR, BIAS). All national groups were expected to be equally represented and engaged throughout the research process, requiring the Centre to develop the management skills of project administrators.

Despite the provision of grants from international organisations to support the Vienna Centre's running costs, national teams depended, in practice, on very different financial, material and human resources, and scientific expertise. Ideological divisions meant that they did not share the same objectives, theoretical underpinnings or conceptual frames. The Centre's east–west projects incorporated several nation states united by a common topic of study. They were not designed to be necessarily or deliberately comparative in that their primary objective was not to conduct systematic cross-national comparisons of phenomena in more than one temporal or spatial socio-cultural setting (Hantrais, 2009). In the cold-war climate of the 1970s and 1980s, many east–west collaborations resulted in parallel, often decontextualised, descriptive studies conducted by researchers in and on their own societies, adopting different approaches to data collection and interpretation. This tradition is still evident in much of the allegedly international or comparative research today when outputs take the form of a series of parallel national monographs, or edited collections of contributions, in which only the introduction and conclusion may present post hoc comparisons and syntheses of findings.

Already in the 1980s, the experience of participating in international research projects at the Vienna Centre had demonstrated that the larger the number of eastern and western countries involved, the lower the level of agreement about basic research paradigms. In this type of project, the organisational structure was likely to be bureaucratic (Grootings, 1986). By contrast, the smaller the number of countries and the more they shared research approaches, the more likely it was that cooperation would be intense and productive throughout the research process (cf. FFP, POLKU). The outputs of such studies were also usually of a higher theoretical, methodological and substantive quality. These early observations foreshadowed some of the challenges associated with project scale and scope in international studies that would become more salient in subsequent years (cf. CLICCS, LCEDN).

A decade after the establishment of the Vienna Centre, in 1974, the European Science Foundation (ESF, 1974) was created in Strasbourg on the initiative of a joint committee of European science research councils representing the Netherlands, Finland, Norway and Sweden, together with the UK's Royal Society. The ESF assembled 16 national scientific research councils and institutions from eight of the then nine EC member states, plus Austria, Denmark, Finland, Greece, Norway, Sweden, Switzerland and Yugoslavia. The councils worked in conjunction with the Commission of the European Communities, the Council of Europe and the Organisation for Economic Co-operation and Development (OECD).

The ESF was designed to operate as a non-governmental, internationally oriented, non-profit association. Member research councils and, later, national academies contributed to the budget according to a scale based on the net national incomes of their countries. The main objectives of the ESF were to advance cooperation in basic research, promote mobility of researchers, assist the free flow of information and ideas, and foster the harmonisation of the research activities supported by member organisations. Concerted actions and collaborative schemes were created to facilitate the sharing of existing national infrastructures, albeit on a much smaller scale than CERN, and to contribute to the assessment and execution of projects, and the provision of specialised services and grants.

ESF administrators worked closely with scientific committee chairs to overcome barriers due to structural differences in the ways that national research councils operated, particularly regarding funding mechanisms and assessment procedures, which would continue to be problematic in the management of projects relying on multiple sponsors owing to their different priorities (cf. LCEDN). In 1998, the Foundation launched their EUROpean COllaborative RESearch (EUROCORES) scheme as a networking tool (ESF, 2015). The scheme was designed to allow the research community to take the initiative in proposing topics for scientific investigation and activities, and to encourage international cooperation and scientific synergy in nationally funded projects. Subsequently, the EUROCORES were opened to partners from anywhere in the world with the aim of creating the critical mass considered essential for scientific excellence.

When the European Commission launched its framework programmes (FPs) in the mid-1980s (see Annex 1.1), the symmetrical approach to cooperation was, almost routinely, adopted in the management of its international projects and networks. The first FP (1984–1987) focussed on activities that would contribute to the definition or implementation of Community policies. In 1983, the European Council agreed: 'To define a common Community strategy in the field of science and technology, setting out the scientific and technical objectives to be pursued at Community level together with selection criteria for Community action, relative priorities and financial indications'. The aim was to promote international research cooperation on a larger scale than was possible for individual member states, while strengthening the cohesion of the common market and establishing uniform standards across the then ten member states. FP1 identified what were to become recurring themes, reflecting the EU's and member states' changing preoccupations and priorities over the next 40 years (cf. AMR, B–SET, CLICCS, LCEDN): promotion of agricultural and industrial competitiveness; management of raw materials and energy resources, and escalation of development aid; improvement of living and working conditions; and the development and effectiveness of the Community's scientific and technical potential.

Subsequent FPs and other EU research programmes, with their ever-increasing budgets and the greater socio-economic, cultural and political diversity of participating EU member states, expanded the scope of European research activities. The focus shifted progressively to the applications of new technologies (cf. TROPICO), human capital and mobility, social objectives (cf. EPPIC), European added value and, importantly for this volume, building research capacity. Accordingly, provision was made in FP4 to cover the socio-economic conditions for international scientific and technical cooperation as well as the training and mobility of researchers. The Marie Skłodowska-Curie Actions were launched in 1996 to support EU researcher transnational mobility fellowships. Cooperation was extended to international organisations in third countries outside Europe: for example, the National Science Foundation in the United States and the National Institute of Science and Technology Policy in Japan.

Following the signing of the Maastricht Treaty on European Union in 1992, and the Treaty of Amsterdam in 1997, with five more member states the EU consolidated its treaty obligation with respect to international research and technological development in the following terms:

[The Union] shall support their [member states'] efforts to cooperate with one another, aiming, notably, at permitting researchers to cooperate freely across borders and at enabling undertakings to exploit the internal market potential to the full, in particular through the opening-up of national public contracts, the definition of common standards and the removal of legal and fiscal obstacles to that coopera-tion. (Treaty on the Functioning of the European Union, 2012, title XIX, article 179)

FP5 for the period 1998–2002 was designed to respond to the major socio-economic challenges facing Europe, rather than the world, at that time. The programme focussed on a limited number of research areas that combined technological, industrial, economic, social and cultural aspects. Management procedures were streamlined by creating four thematic programmes and three horizontal programmes. One of the horizontal programmes endorsed the international role of community research (INCO 2) and was allocated 3.18% of the programme's budget. As the EU enlarged, applicants for framework pro-gramme funding were required to involve at least two different member states, or one member and one associated state. They were also expected to ensure that less favoured member states were well represented, and that candidate countries would be progressively integrated into EU-funded projects.

Scaling up International Research Collaboration in the Twenty-First Century

The growing complexity of large-scale European research collaborations revealed underlying tensions and conflicts both within EU institutions and between different levels of governance (Chou & Gornitzka, 2014). The drive towards international research was bolstered in 2000 by the creation of the European Research Area (ERA), as 'a single, borderless market for research, innovation and technology across the EU' (European Commission, 2000). The aim was to make Europe 'the most competitive and dynamic knowledge-based economy in the world capable of sustainable economic growth ... and greater social cohesion' (European Parliament, 2000).

ERA could be interpreted as an attempt to reconcile competing visions of knowledge and integration pressures within and from beyond the EU. While ERA served to make international research collaboration yet more multi-layered and complex, it also provided scope for multiple and often conflicting interests. In this context, and in preparation for the enlargement of the EU by adding a further ten member states in 2004, including eight from central and eastern Europe, FP5 was able to build on the experience of the Vienna Centre and the ESF to integrate countries with very different research cultures, without being constrained by national budgetary limitations. From the perspective of the European scientific community, the launch of ERA marked a milestone in the internationalisation of research. By building up a critical mass of continent-wide researchers and creating large-scale infra-structures for multilateral initiatives, supported by the European Strategy Forum on Research Infrastructures (ESFRI, n.d.), which was launched in 2002,

ERA served as an impetus to foster more effective cross-border cooperation. The 'big science' model was moving centre stage with its implications for the management of international research.

FP6 (2002–2006) presented the ultimate goal of ERA as 'the integration of the EU's research at local, regional, national and international level'. The programme confirmed the scaling up of the EU's international goals by funding larger projects of longer duration, requiring more distributed management procedures. Two new instruments were introduced: integrated projects (IPs) and networks of excellence (NoEs). Both these tools were designed to ensure a strong degree of managerial autonomy for the consortia implementing them, as well as a critical mass of expertise and resources by incorporating a minimum of six member or associated states. In addition, the IPs' large-scale activities were to be conducted, where possible, as public–private partnerships to help mobilise significant financial, material and human resources around designated objectives, in response to the European Commission's growing concern to deliver value for money and impact, while demonstrating accountability of public funds.

The launch of the European Research Council (ERC) in 2007 was designed to shift the balance away from non-scientific factors in the selection criteria for large-scale project funding. In the FPs, resources had been concentrated on thematic priorities, requiring specific mixes of countries in an attempt to achieve an 'equitable' distribution of funds between member states, irrespective of country size and economic capacity. ERC's mission was 'to encourage the highest quality research in Europe [and beyond] through competitive funding and to support investigator-driven [bottom-up] frontier research across all fields, on the basis of scientific excellence' (European Commission, 2007). Importantly, as with the Marie Skłodowska-Curie Actions fellowships, not only could individual award holders of any nationality choose the EU member or associated state where they wanted their awards to be hosted, provided that 50% or 30%, depending on the scheme, of their time was spent in an EU or associated country; they could also select researchers of any nationality with whom to work, and their own research topics (cf. FFP). In 2020, successful applicants were being hosted both by the then 27 EU member states, and by Iceland, Israel, Norway, Switzerland, Turkey and the UK (notwithstanding Brexit).

FP7 reiterated the fundamental objective of encouraging European researchers to stay in or return to Europe, while also seeking to stimulate intersectoral mobility and attract researchers from other parts of the world to Europe. The Horizon Europe programme (FP9, 2021–2027) for research and innovation confirmed the strategic importance of international cooperation in the widest possible sense by focussing on access to the latest knowledge and the best talent worldwide; business opportunities in new and emerging markets;

and science diplomacy to influence and enhance external policy (European Commission, 2021a). After a period characterised by introspection and parochialism during much of the twentieth century, Horizon Europe acknowledged the need for multilateral research and innovation initiatives requiring worldwide international cooperation as the most effective way to tackle universal challenges in a context of industrial competitiveness. The societal challenges of the twenty-first century – climate (cf. CLICCS), health (cf. AMR, B–SET, EPPIC), food, (cf. FFP), energy (cf. LCEDN) and water (cf. AMR), exacerbated in the 2000s by the financial and health crises – justified the pooling of international scientific resources to tackle the global burden and achieve wide-reaching impact (European Commission, 2021a).

PATHWAYS TO MULTIDISCIPLINARITY

While the internationalisation of research was proceeding apace, in the early twentieth-first century traditional disciplinary silos were more gradually opening up. Incentives to develop multidisciplinary research collaborations stimulated reflection about disciplinary boundaries and questioned disciplinary hierarchies, reviving age-old debates about the classification and status of the sciences (Cogswell, 1899).

These recurrent debates about developments in disciplinary classifications justify the attention paid in a guide to scientific training and project management for several reasons. Firstly, the 'reorganisation of knowledge' has increasingly been driven by the urgent need for innovative research from across disciplines to tackle the global societal challenges of the twenty-first century. In a communication issued in 2003, for example, the European Commission emphasised the need to overcome disciplinary boundaries within the educational sphere in the following terms:

> … we see the academic world having an urgent need to adapt to the interdisciplinary character of the fields opened up by society's major problems such as sustainable development, the new medical scourges, risk management, etc. Yet the activities of the universities, particularly when it comes to teaching, tend to remain organised, and more often than not compartmentalised, within the traditional disciplinary framework. (Commission of the European Communities, 2003, p. 8)

Secondly, the implications of efforts to loosen up disciplinary boundaries are far reaching for the funding and management of collaborative research partnerships within and between countries. Thirdly, the impetus given to the big science model, the symmetrical paradigm and distributed administrative structures in recent decades requires researchers from different disciplinary, institutional, sectoral and cultural backgrounds to learn to work together effectively throughout the research process if they are to achieve common objectives in the context of the fourth (digital/technological) revolution (Hantrais & Thomas Lenihan, 2021).

Revisiting Disciplinary Boundaries

Recurring debates, which were being rehearsed during the 1970s and 1980s, especially but not exclusively in the social sciences, have drawn attention to the potential for cross-fertilisation and complementarity between disciplines (Benjamin, 1982, in the United States; Nießen & Peschar, 1982, in Europe). They also reawakened awareness of the long-term negative repercussions of institutionalising disciplinary structures in American and European universities in the nineteenth century (Rothblatt & Wittrock, 1993). The rekindling of interest in multidisciplinarity and interdisciplinary integration in more recent decades foregrounded the role played by different epistemologies in collaborative research projects, creating both opportunities and challenges for researchers, funders, stakeholders and project managers (Hantrais, 2009).

Already in the literature of the late nineteenth century, classifications of the sciences had been a topic of philosophical speculation and debate (Cogswell, 1899). Distinctions were periodically made and critiqued between abstract and concrete, physical and psychological or material and mental sciences; between theory and practice, description and explanation, deduction and induction; and between methods and content. Based on the precursor of natural philosophy as the study of the natural and physical world, six main sciences were identified in early debates: mathematics, astronomy, physics, chemistry, biology and sociology.

Many new disciplines and subdisciplines were emerging in the eighteenth and nineteenth centuries to cater for technological innovations in agriculture, industry and service professions. The question posed at that time, and since then, was whether these new technologies deserved a place in traditional university curricula by providing dedicated professional education and training (Brosan, 1972; Torstendahl, 1993). And if so, how did existing scientific structures need to be adapted to accommodate and promote the technological innovations required in industrial societies?

Responses to these questions were largely determined by national philosophical and ideological conceptions of the roles traditionally ascribed to universities. Hitherto, European universities had been broadly defined as places of learning for cultural disciplines and other scholarly activities independent of government control (Rothblatt & Wittrock, 1993). The incorporation of technology into the scientific landscape intensified the growing distinction between useful or utilitarian knowledge, which was already being made between theology, law and medicine on the one hand, and natural philosophy as captured in the natural sciences on the other hand, together with history, literature and the arts (Torstendahl, 1993). These transformations intensified the interest, for analysts of the philosophy and history of science, in exploring further, and understanding more thoroughly, the intersectionality and complexity embedded in scientific classifications, and the ethos underpinning them in different national research cultures.

The ways in which countries met these technological challenges would shape their approach to multidisciplinary research for centuries to come. Within Europe, at the one extreme was France, where the state responded by creating specialised training institutes for professional careers in engineering, independently from the universities. The first *grandes écoles*, as they came to be called, were formally established in the 1790s. Their mission was primarily to train civil engineers in the service of the state under the control of relevant government departments (Graves, 1965).

Today, most engineering *grandes écoles* span mathematics, engineering, physics, chemistry, economics, as well as humanities and social sciences. As elitist and competitive selective professional training institutions, the mission of the *grandes écoles* was not to undertake scientific research, but they soon became, and were to remain, important scientific players for their multidisciplinary work on innovation, exemplified by the Centre de Sociologie de l'Innovation at the École des Mines (Akrich et al., 1988). The success of the *grandes écoles* in producing the country's top engineers at the forefront of technological innovation severely inhibited the capacity of the university sector to develop expertise in this area of scientific inquiry, heralding its demise for over a century in the competition for national and international resources.

At the opposite end of the spectrum from France, Germany adopted a different approach, which was also to have long-lasting repercussions for research structures, albeit not to the detriment of universities. From the outset, technological and academic education in the arts and sciences were closely integrated in the nineteenth century (Torstendahl, 1993). The German system supported the emergence of new disciplines and research specialisms in Humboldtian institutions by stimulating a holistic and humanistic approach to science and learning, which would serve as a model for other northern European countries. Universities became a bastion for technological integration, which more than a century later would favour Germany's university researchers in the competition for large-scale multidisciplinary research networks (cf. CLICCS). The Humboldtian model was adopted by countries such as Estonia, where the Tallinn University of Technology continues actively to promote 'research-based learning and teaching, academic freedom, creative and critical thinking' combined with 'an entrepreneurial and practical mindset' (Randma-Liiv, 2021) (cf. TROPICO).

The UK represented yet another configuration, involving a more gradual transformation of higher education to accommodate technological research. From humble beginnings in the early nineteenth century, it was not until the final years of the Second World War that attention focussed on ways of remedying the deficiencies revealed in British industry by 'the shortage of scientists and technologists who can also administer and organise, and can apply the results of research to development' (Percy, 1945, p. 5). The wartime Conservative–Labour coalition government's debate over the relative merits of providing research-based technological training in universities or in technical colleges was to continue through much of twentieth century.

Sustaining and Blurring Disciplinary Divides

A hierarchy of scientific institutions was emerging within Europe during the twentieth century with more or less porous borders, largely mapping onto the disciplinary divides that had been set centuries earlier, but with the addition, in the postwar period, of prestigious non-profit multidisciplinary research institutes such as the Max-Planck-Gesellschaft (2021) in Germany.

In the 1960s, under the auspices of the OECD (2015), a team of national experts in research and development (R&D) set out to respond to the demand among policy analysts and decision-takers for documentation on the level and nature of both human and financial resources that different countries, regions, firms and institutions devoted to R&D. In what came to be known as the Frascati Manuals, the distinction, though heavily contested at different times, is retained in the component activities of R&D between basic and applied research. The manuals show how this distinction operates across and within disciplines irrespective of the institutions in which they are located (OECD, 2015, section 2.5). By illustrating comprehensively the difficulties of classifying research activities and assigning them to different institutional settings, the manuals provide helpful pointers for project leaders when they are selecting international multidisciplinary team members, and the countries with which they will be working, in understanding and reconciling culturally determined contributions to the research (cf. AMR, TROPICO).

In countries such as France, institutionally based disciplinary divides remained difficult to bridge due to decisions taken in earlier centuries to train the nation's elites in specialised institutions separately from the universities. The demise of French universities was exacerbated in 1939 when the Centre National de la Recherche Scientifique (CNRS, 2021a) was established for researchers from all disciplines. CNRS laboratories creamed off many of the internationally renowned scientists from the universities by developing activities in areas of research that were not 'popular' in universities (CNRS, 2021b). Even in the 2010s, following moves to draw CNRS researchers into universities, French holders of European Research Council (ERC, 2021) awards were more likely to cite their CNRS rather than their university affiliation.

As student numbers rocketed, particularly in the social sciences and human-ities, the incessant state-driven educational reforms of the 1950s and 1960s further constrained the potential for French universities to pursue integrated research programmes. Partly to reduce pressures on student numbers in the universities, in 1966 *instituts universitaires de technologie* (IUTs) were estab-lished to provide short-cycle forms of higher education. They offered applied vocational, rather than professional, training for jobs outside academia. The reform of French higher education in 1971 instituted disciplinary divides by assigning universities to either the natural or social and human sciences. The scientific community in the universities was ill prepared to join the inter-national competition for resources and status to carry out multidisciplinary research when opportunities arose at the turn of the twenty-first century, the more so in a context where technology was still considered as no more than an outcome of research rather than a core research discipline (Moulier-Butang, 2015).

In the UK, by contrast, a hierarchy of universities emerged but with porous borders, enabling autonomous institutions to develop different strengths in research, learning and knowledge creation in their chosen disciplines in a com-petitive environment. Colleges of advanced technology (CATs) were created in 1956, originally under the control of local education authorities, to provide vocational training in technological subjects. In 1966, ten CATs became auton-omous national institutions with university status, funded by the Department for Education. The UK polytechnics, which were also founded in the 1960s, along similar lines to the IUTs in France, challenged the categorisation of knowledge as a good held by universities (Brosan, 1972). They offered applied professional education and training in advanced engineering and applied science subjects, to which social and human sciences were added. Research in polytechnics was perceived as being essentially oriented to problem-solving, whereas research in universities maintained 'an intrinsic value as an activity independent of the results achieved' (Brosan, 1972, p. 46). The polytech-nics operated under a separate funding and degree-awarding regime, the Council for National Academic Awards, until they too became universities in 1992, and belatedly joined the competition for international multidisciplinary cross-sectoral research funding and management (cf. EPPIC).

Meanwhile, the Russell Group (2021) of research-intensive, world-class universities (24 in 2021), established in 1994, was seeking to optimise the conditions in which world-leading research and education would flourish, and to ensure their social, economic, cultural and intellectual impact. The group consolidated their historic standing in the higher education and research hierar-chy, in some cases by encouraging mergers between institutions with different disciplinary specialisms, exemplified by the fusion between the University of Manchester and the Manchester Institute of Science and Technology in 2003.

The shift towards multidisciplinary collaboration at EU level in the 2010s and 2020s came at a time when national governments were also promoting and funding an integrated approach to projects within their research communities. The 2016 UK Government (2016) White Paper on *Higher education: Success as a knowledge economy,* published on the eve of the Brexit referendum, argued for 'a greater focus on cross-cutting issues that are outside the core remits of the current funding bodies, such as multi- and inter-disciplinary research, enabling the system to respond rapidly and effectively to current and future challenges' (UK Government, 2016, box 3.3). The establishment in 2018 of UK Research and Innovation (UKRI, 2021a) brought together the seven existing disciplinary research councils, Research England, which supports research and knowledge exchange at higher education institutions in England, and the UK's innovation agency, Innovate UK (cf. B–SET).

This framework is closer to the model of Germany's overarching multi-disciplinary research council, the Deutsche Forschungsgemeinschaft (DFG, 2021c), which funds all academic and science-related activities of nationwide relevance conducted by universities and their cooperation partners. DFG has its origins in the Weimar Republic as an emergency fund to support German scientific and scholarly research. The council was re-launched in 1951 as a self-governing body to channel federal and state funds to universities.

In 2005, the federal government and German states launched a universities excellence initiative, which was designed to strengthen research at German universities and enhance their global appeal. The excellence strategy, adopted in June 2016, consisted of two funding lines: clusters of excellence, developed and implemented by DFG, to support project-based funding in internationally competitive fields of research at universities or in university consortia; and the German Council of Science and Humanities, which advises the German government, and is responsible for developing and implementing support for universities of excellence (DFG, 2016).

The DFG's initiative aims to enhance the research strategies and profiles of German universities by pursuing the successful development of a strong research culture across disciplines and sectors (cf. CLICCS). The UK and German cases elucidate the relevance of information about the different funding sources for research by discipline for the management of international multidisciplinary research collaborations. At the time of the Brexit referendum in 2016, UK government funding for the life sciences, engineering and physical sciences had been rising, whereas it was declining for the social sciences, arts and humanities. Engineering and physical sciences relied heavily on their research councils, as did the life sciences (cf. AMR), which were also well supported by UK charities. The arts and humanities were almost solely dependent on their research council, whereas UK social sciences had been the main beneficiaries of EU funding (Hantrais & Thomas Lenihan, 2016).

The success of UK social sciences (and humanities) in the competition for awards, particularly for ERC (2021) funding, was confirmed by data for 2020, attributable in part to the pre-Brexit legacy. This success also meant that they would most likely be adversely affected if this funding source was compromised, unless they engaged fully in multidisciplinary projects at both national and international levels drawing on their experience and their proven expertise in managing international collaborations particularly in policy-relevant research (cf. EPPIC, LCEDN, PRO-RES).

FROM THEORY TO PRACTICE IN INTERNATIONAL MULTIDISCIPLINARY RESEARCH: THE CASE OF SOCIAL SCIENCES

In the European Commission's early research programmes, social sciences were an add-on rather than an integral component in international multidisciplinary projects. In FP4 (1994–1998), social scientists were given an opportunity to demonstrate their capacity to work effectively and productively in the management of research projects that cross national and disciplinary boundaries within the wide range of social science disciplines. Despite considerable opposition within the Commission, both regarding the level of funding and programme content, a dedicated Targeted Socio-Economic Research (TSER) stream was launched under FP4, followed by a key action for Improving the Socio-economic Knowledge Base in FP5. Commission officials had wanted funding to be concentrated on the Joint Research Centre (JRC, 2007), which was originally established under the Euratom Treaty in 1957 to promote nuclear safety and security in Europe. The TSER management committee created a historical precedent by rejecting the Commission's proposed work programme for FP4 [personal communication]. A coalition of representatives from Germany, the Nordic countries and the UK was able to draft a work programme designed to develop a shared knowledge base for research into the socio-economic challenges facing Europe. The programme opened up new opportunities for social scientists to cooperate not only across national borders but also across epistemological boundaries, while remaining within the broad confines of the social and human sciences.

While the TSER stream was being rolled out under FP4 at the turn of the century (European Commission, 1999), the Directorate-General for Research (DG RTD) was looking for ways of consolidating opportunities for social scientists and for providing evidence of impact from their interdisciplinary work. DG RTD decided to cluster together several projects and networks under FP5 within the social sciences. Their aim was to maximise European added value within a given area, and establish the critical mass needed to find effective solutions to what were recognised as complex multidisciplinary problems. The Commission was not concerned about methods, except insofar as the research community would be able to demonstrate that it was contributing to methodological advancement and refinement, thereby ensuring greater reliability of data. Project teams were expected to show that they could generate and exploit high-quality replicable data, while also improving access to datasets that other researchers could use as an empirical basis for theory building and scientific explanations in comparative analysis.

During the lifetime of FP5 (1998–2002), with DG Research under instructions to work more closely with the policy DGs to demonstrate value for money, impact and policy relevance of EU-funded research, the Commission organised a series of 'dialogue workshops'. The intention was to implement an integrated approach towards research fields, identifying complementarities and improving multidirectional communication between researchers and stakeholders. The dialogue synthesis papers reporting on the workshops were multi-focussed insofar as they targeted researchers, policymakers, civil society organisations, economic actors and the media. The authors of these syntheses were directed to make proposals for improving the dialogue between research, policy and society at large and, in doing so, to explore issues of interdisciplinarity (Marchipont, 2003, p. vi).

Drawing on this experience and working with the Commission's policy DGs, DG Research commissioned a series of 20 social science policy reviews in 2003 (Guy, 2004). The authors of the reviews were tasked with identifying policy directions in some 300 funded projects and networks, which had not necessarily been designed to investigate how research can inform policy. The Commission only partially succeeded in creating the post hoc synergy they were seeking. But the reviewers were able to flag the potential for developing an integrated approach towards research fields capable of offering more effective solutions to complex multidisciplinary problems.

The findings from the reviews lent support to the proposition (irrespective of the funding source) that the combination of methods within and across projects and networks can result in the production of more reliable datasets, methodological innovation and a more sensitive appreciation of epistemological diversity (cf. BIAS, B–SET, CLICCS, FFP, POLKU, TROPICO). They also demonstrated the importance of adopting an integrative approach throughout the research process. Building on these precedents, by scaling up the size of international collaborations in the integrated networks and networks of excellence, FP6 and FP7 sought to encourage multidisciplinary activities across disciplinary fields orientated towards long-term policy objectives, rather than concentrating on precise predefined results without policy relevance, as had long been the case in previous FPs.

Although the social sciences and humanities, to a more limited extent, continued to have 'their own proper space within FP7', the European Research Advisory Board (EURAB, 2005, p. 5), chaired by Helga Nowotny, who was to become president of the ERC in 2010, argued for 'a much stronger and more deliberate integration of SSH [social sciences and humanities] into the whole scope and objectives of FP7'. The report stressed the importance of the contribution of these disciplines not only in their own fields but also in the delivery of science and technology programmes.

The complex multi-faceted nature of the topics selected for the societal challenges in Horizon 2020 (FP8, 2013–2020) meant that embedding social and humanities research across the programme would be essential to maximise the returns to society from investment in science and technology. Their contribution was initially ignored until a 100,000-signature petition forced the European Commission to introduce a societal challenge [personal communication]. Challenge six addressed Europe in a changing world, covering inclusive, innovative and reflective societies. Opportunities were then built into the programme for social and human scientists not only to collaborate closely with science, technology, engineering and mathematics (STEM) in the search for solutions to major societal challenges, but also to enable them to partner with other researchers and practitioners in the social sciences (European Commission, 2014).

Horizon 2020 reiterated the importance that the EU attributed to the adoption of an integrated multidisciplinary approach to research while demonstrating the economic, social and cultural impact from EU-funded programmes. In the absence of a dedicated funding stream, topics were flagged where social sciences could contribute, ranging across the societal challenges, information and communications technologies (cf. TROPICO), nanotechnologies, advanced materials, biotechnology, advanced manufacturing and processing.

Annual monitoring reports were commissioned to track progress in integrating social sciences and humanities in the programme. The conclusions in the fifth report for projects funded in 2018 echoed those of previous editions (Kania & Bucksch, 2020) in finding that integration needed to be based on a deeper cross-sectoral 'holistic' approach, covering the entire cycle of the research process:

> … from the drafting of calls and topics, through the preparation of conceptual proposals, the composition of project consortia, to the selection and evaluation of projects by evaluators with clear SSH expertise. In addition, the goals in terms of societal impact should be explicitly set out in the topics, in project proposals and in their implementation reports. (Kania & Bucksch, 2020, p. 66)

To fill the void created by the refocussing of European research in both Horizon 2020 (FP8) and Horizon Europe (FP9), the European Alliance for Social Science and Humanities (EASSH, 2019c) was formally constituted in 2015, when Horizon 2020 was being planned, explicitly 'to promote learning and research in the social sciences and humanities (SSH) as a resource for Europe and the world, and to engage with policymakers and research funders in support of the social sciences and humanities'. In its responses to the consultation on Horizon Europe, EASSH (2019a) strongly supported the case for a revised methodology for monitoring interdisciplinary integration, while also suggesting how impact assessment of projects and programmes under Horizon Europe could be improved.

A position paper from European Cooperation in Science and Technology (COST, 2017, p. 3), an EU-funded, intergovernmental framework, argued that: 'Multidisciplinary research often results in discoveries and innovations that, in turn, will help the European Union to realise its ambition to boost jobs, economic growth, investments, and improve the quality of life of its citizens and the environment.' The paper clearly set out the objectives that it recommended for Horizon Europe (FP9): the programme should have 'a multidisciplinary character', ensuring the 'defragmentation of knowledge', and fostering 'excellent collaborative, transdisciplinary [but not explicitly interdisciplinary], bottom-up research undertaken by networks' (COST, 2017, pp. 2–3).

MANAGING SCALE AND COMPLEXITY DURING CRISES

In the context of the demands to scale up international collaboration and the reorganisation and integration of knowledge, researchers have been under increasing pressure to respond to the demands of international and national organisations by adapting their way of working. The need for research leaders capable of delivering effectively and efficiently managed international multidisciplinary research projects was further intensified in the 2000s by the global financial and climate crises and, in the UK, by Brexit. The global health crisis of the early 2020s, combined with the urgent need to find solutions to climate change, brought recognition that, in the digital age, technological innovations could best be achieved through worldwide multidisciplinary scientific collaborations (Hantrais & Thomas Lenihan, 2021).

With a new European Commission installed at the beginning of the year, the EU announced the relaunch of the European Research Area (ERA) in September 2020. The European Commission Press Corner (2020) reported that: 'Europe is currently facing significant societal, ecological and economic challenges that are aggravated by the coronavirus crisis. Research and innovation is [sic] therefore crucial in addressing these challenges, delivering on

Europe's recovery and speeding up the twin green and digital transitions.' Fortuitously, or with foresight, the Horizon Europe (FP9) research programme for 2021–2027 had identified 'areas of intervention' which would continue to be key to meeting the global challenges of health, inclusive and secure societies, digital and industry, climate, energy and mobility, food and natural resources (cf. AMR, BIAS, CLICC, LCEDN, FFP, TROPICO).

The relaunch of ERA was accompanied by a timely White Paper from the European Strategy Forum on Research Infrastructures (ESFRI, 2020). The role of ESFRI was presented as key in facilitating 'the cross disciplinary research and the exploitation of data interoperability to produce new science to tackle new societal challenges' (ESFRI, 2020, p. 7).

The pandemic accelerated the adoption of digital technologies in some areas where uptake had stalled or was only slowly progressing, such as data collection techniques, online working, learning and social interconnectedness. Innovations in artificial intelligence, robotics and machine learning played a major role in responding to the epidemiological, biomedical, and socio-economic challenges raised by the pandemic (Kritikos, 2020). These new challenges required the scaling up of production, fast-tracking of digital supplies, and construction of online platforms and video-conferencing products. They confirmed the need for multiskilling and for appropriately trained scientists to build on and exchange their knowledge and experience (cf. BIAS, B–SET), and to learn to work productively across national, sectoral and disciplinary barriers to shape and diffuse technological innovations in a socially positive, sustainable and equitable manner during the pandemic and beyond. Importantly, the pandemic brought to the fore the major role played by scientists from all disciplines and sectors (universities, research institutes, government departments, industry and not-for-profit organisations) not only as researchers and innovators able to pool resources but also as advisers to governments, and as communicators with the wider public.

ANNEX 1.1

Framework Programmes (FPs) for Research and Technological Development

FP1 1984–1987

Council resolution of 25 July 1983 on framework programmes for Community research, development and demonstration activities and a first framework programme.

https://cordis.europa.eu/programme/id/FP1-FRAMEWORK-1C

FP3 1990–1994

Framework programme of Community activities in the field of research and technological development, 1990–1994.

https://cordis.europa.eu/programme/id/FP3-FRAMEWORK-3C

FP4 1994–1998

Specific programme of targeted socio-economic research, 1994–1998.

https://cordis.europa.eu/programme/id/FP4-TSER

FP5 1999–2002

Fifth RTD Framework Programme, 1998–2002.

https://cordis.europa.eu/programme/id/FP5

FP6 2002–2006

Multiannual Framework Programme 2002–2006 of the European Community for research, technological development and demonstration activities aimed at contributing towards the creation of the European Research Area.

https://cordis.europa.eu/programme/id/FP6

FP7 2006–2013

Seventh Framework Programme of the European Community for research and technological development including demonstration activities (FP7).

https://cordis.europa.eu/programme/id/FP7

FP8 2014–2020

Horizon 2020 Framework Programme.

https://cordis.europa.eu/programme/id/H2020-EC

FP9 2021–2027

Horizon Europe, the EU research and innovation programme (2021–2027) for a green, healthy, digital and inclusive Europe.
https://op.europa.eu/en/web/eu-law-and-publications/publication-detail/-/publication/93de16a0-821d-11eb-9ac9-01aa75ed71a1

2. Launching into an international multidisciplinary project

Linda Hantrais and Julia Brannen

INTRODUCTION

Academic researchers have long been aware of the implications for their future career paths of decisions taken early in their studies to pursue certain fields of investigation. These choices come into play not only when they are planning doctoral and postdoctoral studies, and applying for positions in academic or research institutions, but also during their careers when they are seeking project funding and becoming involved in project management and delivery. Mid-career social scientists, and even more so human scientists, know that they are likely to be at a disadvantage in terms of access to resources and status when they are competing with natural scientists and when their performances are being assessed by the same criteria. They may face greater challenges in adapting to structural changes in an international research landscape where the organisation of knowledge continues to be dominated by the natural sciences (Gilbert, 2016). But, as illustrated by the case studies in this book (see Table 2.1), which are all authored by social scientists, they may also be better equipped as a result of their training in these disciplines to analyse the cooperative research process and to find solutions to the many issues that arise.

In collaborative research that combines international and multidisciplinary structures, the potential for complexity intensifies not only for research managers but also for members of research teams. Although the issues to be addressed in multidisciplinary research are similar to those in international projects, the combination of these two types of scientific inquiry brings additional layers of complexity, reinforcing the importance of training and of learning from experienced researchers. The authors of the case studies in this guide were invited to scrutinise the different stages in the research process, from the decision to embark on an international multidisciplinary project, through research design and data collection, to the analysis, interpretation and dissemination of findings. They were asked to explain how they sought to overcome the many

Table 2.1　　　*Case studies featured in the guide*

Acronym	Project title	Corresponding author
AMR	**A**nti**M**icrobial **R**esistance in the real world	John Connolly
BIAS	**BIAS**: Responsible AI for labour market equality	Karen D. Hughes
B–SET	The **B**loomsbury **SET**: **S**cience, **E**conomics, **T**echnology	Aygen Kurt-Dickson
CLICCS	**CLI**mate, **C**limatic **C**hange and **S**ociety	Antje Wiener
EPPIC	**E**xchanging **P**revention practices on **P**olydrug use among youth **I**n **C**riminal justice systems	Betsy Thom
FFP	**F**amilies and **f**ood in hard times [**F**amilies and **F**ood **P**overty]	Rebecca O'Connell
LCEDN	**L**ow **C**arbon **E**nergy for **D**evelopment **N**etwork	Ed Brown
POLKU	Different pathways to employment [Eri **POLU**illa työllisyyteen]	Minna van Gerven
PRO-RES	**PRO**moting integrity in the use of **RES**earch results	Ron Iphofen
TROPICO	**TR**ansforming into **O**pen, **I**nnovative and **CO**llaborative governments	Tiina Randma-Liiv

Note: **Bold** indicates components of acronyms.

hurdles that they encountered along the way and to reflect on lessons learnt from their experiences.

Drawing on the case studies presented in this volume, Chapters 2 and 3 examine the vast array of complex overlapping tasks entailed in conducting collaborative international multidisciplinary research, many of which are carried out simultaneously and cumulatively. This chapter considers the very early stages in the process. It begins by addressing the issues associated with different research structures and environments when deciding whether and where to seek external funding. The case study authors describe how they secured appropriate funding, and how they managed the many requirements of different funders. In commenting on the criteria applied in the assessment of European and national research funding programmes, they refer to the growing importance of policy relevance, accountability and value for money. The case studies show how funders' requirements affect the composition and working practices of research teams representing various mixes of cultural and disciplinary backgrounds, and how different funding mechanisms impact on international cooperation.

PREPARING TO MANAGE RESEARCH IN
INTERNATIONAL MULTIDISCIPLINARY SETTINGS

All the case studies present programmes and projects that had been carefully planned and developed, often over several years as a result of the coordinators' previous involvement in international multidisciplinary networks. Given the focus of their research, the very large research consortia in the B–SET, CLICCS and LCEDN programmes required partners from a wide range of disciplines capable of bringing different perspectives and insights to bear on the issues being studied.

The founder members of the LCEDN programme initiated their idea for what was to become an extensive international multidisciplinary network at a workshop held in 2010 under the auspices of the UK Energy Research Centre (UKERC, 2021). Their meeting place scheme was launched jointly in 2004 by three UK research councils: engineering and physical sciences (EPSRC), economic and social research (ESRC), and natural and environment research (NERC). The workshop brought together academics from diverse disciplines across the UK, interested in engaging with the low carbon agenda by building bridges between existing pools of expertise in the energy and development fields. The B–SET team organised two sandpits and networking events to encourage researchers from different disciplinary backgrounds to prepare project bids for their initiative under Research England's Connecting Capability Fund, and the CLICCS coordinators spent two to three years planning their proposal for what was, in the first instance, a seven-year programme.

Research funders have long sought to develop training for work in international research across cultural and disciplinary boundaries. The European Commission, for example, funded a series of dialogue workshops during the lifetime of the Fifth Framework Programme (FP5, 1999–2002) to enable researchers from different disciplines to exchange views on methodologies and provide guidance on how to formulate research questions and inform public debate, policy formation and implementation (Marchipont, 2003). Between 2003 and 2007, the European Science Foundation (ESF) supported a programme of integrated workshops and seminars to train social scientists in the quantitative skills needed for the analysis of complex social scientific data, such as pan-European datasets, with the aim of advancing comparative quantitative social science (Mohler, 2007).

Research councils have been proactive in initiating international cross-disciplinary collaborations. For example, between 2010 and 2012, ESRC funded an award under its researcher development initiative to pilot a series of workshops, resulting in a web tool (Restore) for international social research training under the auspices of the National Centre for Research Methods

(NCRM, 2014). Training workshops were subsequently delivered in higher education institutions and other venues in the UK and elsewhere in Europe.

For more than a decade in the UK, EPSRC (2021) operated their 'sandpit model', involving intensive five-day residential interactive workshops for 20–30 participants, who committed to engaging in a carefully structured process designed to cover a range of tasks. The workshops included activities to assist researchers from different disciplinary cultures in defining the scope of the issue; agreeing a common language and terminology among researchers from diverse backgrounds; sharing understanding of the problem across participants' expertise; using creative and innovative thinking techniques in break-out sessions to focus on a problem; and turning sandpit outputs into research projects.

On a smaller scale, other UK research councils have used 'speed-dating' events to encourage collaborations across disciplines, exemplified by a joint call launched in 2015 by ESRC in conjunction with the Biotechnology and Biological Sciences Research Council (BBSRC). The two councils organised a much shorter and less highly structured workshop, resulting in eight interdisciplinary projects in the area of social and behavioural epigenetics. These innovative, collaborative projects aimed to understand the complex interactions between social phenomena, human biology and behaviour, as well as the impact of early life experiences on future health.

ESRC subsequently formulated five lessons for collaborative research that could be applied across cultures and disciplines. Researchers were advised to consider why they and their research partners wanted to collaborate; to establish (competing) accountabilities; to identify their collaborative approach and the implications for the shape of their collaboration; to discuss money, time and resources with their partners; and to reflect on the scope for legacy from their collaboration.

With the support of UK Research and Innovation (UKRI) and funding from Research England, in 2021 the UK Centre for Postdoctoral Development in Infrastructure Cities and Energy (C-DICE, 2021) launched a four-year programme to leverage the capability of 18 leading research-intensive universities. The consortium is managed by Loughborough University together with Birmingham and Cranfield Universities, in partnership with leading companies and other stakeholders. The programme is designed to harness significant UKRI, university and industry investment in facilities and doctoral training. The aim is to build the advanced skills required to create a pipeline of world-class talent capable of tackling global issues that demand a major interdisciplinary research effort. By participating in multidisciplinary teams, postdoctoral researchers, primarily at an early career stage, are given an opportunity to gain multidisciplinary and cross-sector skills and expertise, to generate novel solutions to societal challenges, and to win seed-corn funding for their projects.

The case study authors describe how their programmes and projects provided on-the-job international and multidisciplinary training and mentoring for mid-career researchers to gain experience from their association with real-life projects. Research assistants and fellows were given responsibility for carrying out reviews of the literature, implementing mixed, innovative and less familiar methods for conducting fieldwork in interdisciplinary projects, and for managing sub-projects.

SECURING FUNDING FOR INTERNATIONAL MULTIDISCIPLINARY PROJECTS

Postwar internationalisation and the progressive scaling up of different forms of cross-border and cross-cultural research collaborations, in combination with the gradual erosion of disciplinary boundaries and hierarchies, both stimulated and hampered the development of new cross-disciplinary subfields and multidisciplinary research collaborations. These changes were shaped by, and contributed to, the institutional structures within which research was being funded and conducted in the twenty-first century. Research funding arrangements were being forged between universities, public, private, and third sector institutions, involving the negotiation of budgetary arrangements, and requiring accountability to funders. As more diversified sources of funding were sought to match the scale and complexity of global societal challenges, cross-sectoral partnerships were extended across countries, and efforts were intensified to bridge disciplinary divides.

This section covers the issues to be considered by project managers when deciding whether to respond to a funding call; when navigating institutional regulations, financial rules, incentives and funders' expectations; when appointing a management team; and when preparing and submitting a research proposal, securing appropriate funding and negotiating budgets. The section explores the concepts of multi-, trans- and interdisciplinarity in funders' call guidance, schemes and annual plans. The authors consider the expectations of sponsors and stakeholders, the constraints they impose, and how their requirements are interpreted by applicants, professional brokers and independent reviewers. They examine how project managers deal with issues of co-funding, budgetary cuts, changes in rules, and the impact of external disruptions; and how they meet the institutional requirements of participating researchers.

Navigating Funding Sources for Multidisciplinary Projects

Although the EU had become a major source of funding for international networks and projects by the early twenty-first century, it was not the only potential source of funding for international and/or multidisciplinary research. Despite attempts to harmonise funding schemes, national and international project funders continue to have their own priorities, requirements and expectations when drawing up calls for proposals, selecting and financing research programmes.

Already in 1998 when the ESF (2015) launched the EUROCORES scheme, it had to navigate between its disciplinary standing committees to accommodate and pool resources from national research councils and academies with different conceptions of project funding and research agendas. Funding for awards had to be agreed by national research councils and disciplinary panels that were not necessarily using the same scientific criteria and were not responsible for the same combinations of disciplines. As a result, disparities persisted in the levels of funding received and in the requirements of different sponsors (Hantrais, 2009).

Chapter 1 documented the momentous changes that were wrought to research structures during the twentieth century and endorsed in the early decades of the twenty-first century. The push towards multidisciplinarity, particularly in the European context, did not supplant deeply embedded cultural traditions and hierarchies of knowledge inherited from earlier times. Nor did it replace the preferences in research communities for different types of project, or funding schemes for single-discipline proposals. The UK's ESRC, for example, continues to recognise that, although 'many of the most pressing research challenges are interdisciplinary in nature, both within the social sciences and between the social sciences and other areas of research', the Council remains 'committed to the support of excellent research within a single discipline' (ESRC, 2021b) (cf. BIAS).

In the wake of the 2008 financial crises, national and international funders increasingly required that the projects they were supporting should demonstrate value for money, accountability and impact, thereby emphasising the central role that these criteria would play in project assessment and management, alongside multidisciplinary and policy relevance. Due to path dependencies, researchers in some countries and disciplines were better prepared than others to seize new opportunities for collaborations by adapting and extending their approaches in what had become an ever more competitive research arena. Here, UK scientists already had an advantage, as argued in the 1990s in a comparison with French researchers (Tennom, 1995). British researchers were portrayed as being driven by the market demands of productivity, 'maximum output for minimum input', motivating them to become entrepreneurs. They were more likely than their French counterparts to concentrate on applied policy-relevant research and the 'user interface', and they were accustomed to applying for external funding and delivering value for money, which served them well in accessing international grants. From a French perspective, the British approach to research was instrumental at the expense of science.

Within countries, similar issues arose when disciplinary research councils were adapting their working practices to accommodate multidisciplinary projects. Traditionally, UK research councils were, for example, structured around six categories of disciplines, with what could be considered as relatively 'porous borders' between cognate disciplines due to their cross-cutting and cross-fertilising, yet distinct, epistemologies. The six categories encompassed: arts and humanities, biotechnology and biological sciences, economic and social sciences (initially incorporating 14 disciplines ranging from anthropology to politics and statistics) (cf. BIAS, LCEDN), engineering and physical sciences, medical research, and natural environment (cf. AMR). Within these groupings, quasi-disciplines were emerging, including criminology (cf. EPPIC), education, management, cultural and gender studies (cf. BIAS) in the social sciences and humanities, or biomedical engineering and public health in medical and environmental research (cf. AMR).

When disciplinary-based research councils were brought together in 2018 to form a new organisation, UK Research and Innovation (UKRI, 2021a), a seventh council for science and technology facilities was added, designed to operate world-class research infrastructures in the UK. A stated aim of UKRI was to increase integrative cross-disciplinary research through its own global (grand) challenges research fund, reflecting, and in line with, the European Commission's strategic goals for the sciences. To this end, UKRI (2021b) created a cross-council remit agreement committed to supporting an enhanced culture of interdisciplinary and multidisciplinary research in the UK, drawing together insights and approaches from one or more research disciplines, without disadvantaging researchers who worked across disciplinary boundaries (cf. AMR).

Unlike most other European countries, a large proportion of the competitive international funding received by the UK is channelled through the university sector (Royal Society, 2016a). The research environment and performance of UK universities are regularly assessed both individually and collectively every four or five years in a peer review process, using discipline-based criteria. A research excellence framework (REF, 2021) determines a discipline-based hierarchy of research quality for university researchers with consequences for government funding support and other resources. Special provision was made for 'interdisciplinary' research in 2021, in response to the findings from a review of the REF as applied to the university sector in 2014 (Stern, 2016). This independent review, commissioned by the Minister of State for

Universities and Science in the Cameron government, revealed that 'interdisciplinary work was disadvantaged ... through the disciplinary "silos" embodied in the Unit of Assessment panel structures'. The author stressed that:

> Interdisciplinary approaches and collaboration between institutions and other sectors can enhance both the academic and socioeconomic creativity and impact of research. Furthermore as universities increasingly commit to addressing complex, intrinsically difficult 'Grand Challenges' of global importance there is a clear recognition that such issues and problems require a range of different perspectives that interdisciplinarity and collaboration can foster. (Stern, 2016, p. 14)

The review prompted the creation of an interdisciplinary research advisory panel to ensure 'the fair and equitable assessment of all research submitted to the assessment exercise' (REF, 2021).

The changes associated with the status of the UK as a third country following Brexit created an additional complication for UK researchers at a time when the EU was also increasingly emphasising multidisciplinarity in its funding programmes, and thereby reducing opportunities for researchers in some disciplines. Under the 2020 Trade and Cooperation Agreement (TCA), the UK was to contribute to, and participate in, EU research programmes as an associated country, at least for the duration of Horizon Europe (FP9) (European Commission, 2021b). The conditions with which the UK was to comply, and under which non-compliance would result in suspension, were set out at length in the TCA (EUR-Lex, 2021, part five). They included free movement of researchers and access to services, and exclusion from any activities where experts or evaluators are appointed on the basis of nationality, causing considerable concern in institutions that had hitherto recruited and trained disproportionately large numbers of international students and researchers (Royal Society, 2016b), and for project managers in receipt of European awards (cf. PRO-RES).

Despite persistent rigid and hierarchical disciplinary boundaries, French funding and assessment procedures were also being progressively adapted to accommodate and facilitate a more integrated approach to disciplinary working. This shift was necessary if French researchers were to be motivated to participate in EU-funded programmes (PRO-RES, TROPICO). In 2020, the French Agence Nationale de la Recherche (ANR, 2021) funded and assessed 37 research themes in public organisations, including universities and research institutes. Thirteen assessment panels were established to deal with transversal themes and bilateral projects covering cross-disciplinary challenges and integrating issues from various scientific fields. Scientists recruited to the French Centre National de la Recherche Scientifique (CNRS, 2021b), located in universities and research centres in France and abroad, continue to be assessed individually and collectively by disciplinary panels. In 2021, provision was made by ministerial decree for 'interdisciplinary' work, identifying more than 50 possible combinations of disciplines.

The United States affords another model for multidisciplinary research funding and structures. The National Science Foundation (NSF, 2021), as an independent government agency, supports fundamental and applied research, as well as education in all the non-medical fields of science and engineering. Life sciences and medicine fall outside the NSF's remit and are funded primarily by National Institutes of Health (cf. PRO-RES). The NSF identifies ten areas, many of which involve hybrid disciplines and activities, ranging from computer and information science and engineering, through environmental research and education, integrative activities (including evaluation), and international science and engineering (infrastructures and international partnerships, networking and multi-team international collaborations), to social, behavioural and economic sciences. The National Centre for Science and Engineering Statistics and the Office of Multidisciplinary Activities oversee intersections with other science and engineering fields and assist with seeding new multidisciplinary and interdisciplinary activities for the future.

Accessing Funding for International Multidisciplinary Projects

A majority of the projects featured in this guide (see Table 2.2), both small and large, were dependent on national research councils, which often serve to channel government funds (AMR, BIAS, B–SET, CLICCS); others were directly funded by national governments (POLKU). Most of the LCEDN funding came directly from the UK government, with support from research councils in some cases. The B–SET programme was unusual: as one of the first awards made under a new scheme launched in 2017 by Research England (2021), the aim was specifically to develop research collaborations in UK higher education institutions.

Of the programmes and projects in receipt of European funding, two fell within the remit of the Horizon 2020 (FP8) programme (PRO-RES, TROPICO), one on a shared cost basis (EPPIC); the FFP project was a fully costed European Research Council (ERC) Starting Grant. As a coordinating and support action, the funding provided for PRO-RES was not strictly speaking for conducting research. Rather, it was intended to support activities such as networking, exchanges, and transnational access to research infrastructures.

Research councils, national governments and the European Commission offer two main types of project funding – responsive and programme awards – in most cases to support work that fits with their priority areas. Responsive funding is researcher driven, allowing greater freedom of choice concerning topics and the composition of research teams, exemplified by ERC awards for individual researchers at different stages in their careers (FFP). Each of

Table 2.2   Project funding and assessment

Project	Funding organisations	Duration	End date	Amount
AMR	UK Research Council (Natural Environment Research Council, NERC) World Bank in kind	3 years	2023	£793 290
BIAS	UK/Canada Research Councils (Economic and Social Research Council, ESRC; Social Sciences and Humanities Research Council of Canada, SSHRC)	3.5 years	2023	£508 000 (UK) and $460 000 (CDN)
B–SET	Research England (UKRI), Connecting Capability Fund (CCF)	3.2 years	2021	£4.96 million
CLICCS	German Research Council (Deutsche Forschungsgemeinschaft, DFG) Hamburg University host institution	7 years	2026	€46.56 million
EPPIC	European Commission Health Programme Consumers, Health, Agriculture and Food Executive Agency (CHAFEA)	3 years	2020	€599 511 (partners 40%)
FFP	European Commission (European Research Council, ERC) University College London host institution	5 years	2019	€1.371 million
LCEDN	UK government departments (BEIS, DECC, DfID, FCOD) Research councils (EPSRC, ESRC, NERC)	2 × 5 years	2022	£100 000 to £40 million
POLKU	Finnish government Prime Minister's Office, Ministry of Health and Social Affairs Netherlands and UK partners in kind	1.5 years	2022	€149 919
PRO-RES	European Commission Horizon 2020 (FP8)	3.5 years	2021	€2.8 million
TROPICO	European Commission Horizon 2020 (FP8) DG Connect; partners in kind	4.5 years	2021	€4.9 million

these funding bodies specified their own priorities and criteria for assessing proposals, selecting projects for awards, supervising the research process and evaluating outcomes. Except for the ERC award, all the projects featured in this guide were submitted following calls for proposals to work on topics identified by the funders. Irrespective of the funding source and mode, all the proposals addressed recurring themes, reflecting contemporary preoccupations and policy priorities relating to global societal challenges. The authors of the case studies stress the importance, in international multidisciplinary programmes where the topic is defined by the funders, of discussing its relevance and meaning for different institutions, cultures and disciplines.

Not only were the topics defined by the funders in most of the case study projects (Table 2.1), but also the overall methodological approaches to be applied in addressing them. Research councils explicitly encourage applications for research that 'combines disciplinary approaches, research focused on advancing scientific theory, and research aimed principally at developing practical applications' (ESRC, 2021b). The research that they fund is expected to demonstrate 'one or more of innovation, interdisciplinarity and impact', where 'impact' is increasingly 'an essential component of research proposals and a condition of funding' (ESRC, 2021b) (BIAS, B–SET, LCEDN).

NERC (2021a) supports discovery science and strategic research, and provides capital funding for new technologies, equipment, infrastructure and facilities (AMR). Within UKRI, councils work together at the boundaries of their remits to avoid gaps in funding. For example, NERC (2021a) specifies its support for research collaborations that involves working internationally with funding organisations in other countries, including the National Science Foundation in the United States, the Research Council for the State of São Paulo in Brazil (FAPESP), and the Fonds National de la Recherche in Luxembourg.

The BIAS project was funded jointly by research councils in Canada and the UK. Research England's Connecting Capability Fund (B–SET) was designed 'to share good practice and capacity internally across the higher education sector, forge external technological, industrial and regional partnerships, and deliver the Government's Industrial Strategy priorities' (Research England, 2021). While incentivising university collaboration in research commercialisation through high-performance knowledge exchange in UK universities, award holders were required to deliver the government's policy aims, as well as accountability and value for money.

Research councils provide applicants with online notes advising them how to write a good research proposal (ESRC, 2021a; SSHRC, 2021) (BIAS), while offering guidance for reviewers and moderators (NERC, 2021b) (AMR). Research England's (2021) guidance notes for applicants supplied a list of funding criteria to be met, including scale of funding, number and appropriateness of partners, and institutional buy-in (B–SET). In Germany, the Deutsche Forschungsgemeinschaft (DFG, 2021b) 'supports projects from all areas of science and the humanities and especially promotes interdisciplinary cooperation among researchers' (CLICCS). DFG does not provide dedicated funding for international cooperation projects, but various schemes are designed to integrate international researchers and intensify international cooperation, as explained in their extensive 'How to ...' guides for applicants (DFG, 2021a).

The European Commission (n.d.) publishes online manuals providing extremely detailed and complex guidance and rules for applicants for EU funding (cf. FFP, PRO-RES, TROPICO). In addition to national research offices in Brussels, many universities and research institutes have their own research offices to assist with the preparation and completion of applications, especially with regard to budgets. University College London (UCL, 2021), for example, provides a researchers' toolkit, with guidance for the principal investigators on 'management of the project within the terms and conditions of their funding and in line with associated UCL policies; adherence to Funder reporting requirements; and timely communication of significant project changes/developments' (cf. FFP). Institutions may also conduct an internal assessment of proposals before allowing them to be taken forward.

National government departments support large international multidisciplinary research programmes and networks that have been built up over a number of years and are contributing to the body of knowledge about global challenges, such as energy and international development (LCEDN). They often work in conjunction with other funding bodies across divergent branches of academia and policymaking (Brown et al., 2018). National government funders may also support small-scale projects involving much simpler application procedures on narrowly defined research topics with shorter time frames and less international input (POLKU).

Meeting Funders' Requirements

The case study authors describe how their proposals were shaped by the requirements of funders, and how they dealt with the issues that arose in matching schedules and remaining within budgets. They were invited to comment on what different funders considered as legitimate costs for personnel, infrastructure, administration, travel and institutional overheads. Projects funded by national research councils acknowledged the generosity of the financial support they received and the relatively unproblematic nature of the relationship with their funders. In their case study, the AMR authors provide a detailed account of the allocation of NERC funding for fieldwork and laboratory costs, which were a central feature in their project. The budget did not give rise to any issues since the project team was familiar with the funders' guidelines for their discipline. Nor did the BIAS team encounter any problems with managing the bilateral award they received from the Canadian and UK research councils for similar reasons.

For innovation and commercialisation purposes, the Connecting Capability Fund scheme, which supported the B–SET programme, required not only collaboration between universities but also with industry, public and third sector partners. When the proposal was being prepared, the team sought and secured pledges for their involvement as end users and potential match-funders in the programme. Since the scheme was the first of its kind, the funder did not initially provide explicit detailed guidance, which meant that the applicants had more flexibility when writing the proposal. But they found that more negotiations and discussions were needed with the funder once the bid was in the pipeline for awards.

The CLICCS consortium had spent several years planning their proposal to DFG and were thoroughly versed with their procedures and requirements. The large-scale funding enabled them to consolidate a complex multisectoral hub combining multidisciplinary research groups within a single university, drawing on the expertise of a range of affiliated leading science institutions located in Hamburg.

The FFP award holder appreciated the advantages of ERC starting grants in providing early/mid-career researchers with control over a substantial budget subject to relatively few constraints. The administrative difficulties encountered during the early stages of the project were the result of the institution hosting the award being absorbed into one of London's largest colleges (UCL).

Some case study authors comment on the problems of working within prescribed budgets. The POLKU cases study illustrates the challenge of conducting fieldwork in a low-cost government-funded project, which they attribute in part to the research coordinators' decision to take the initiative in collecting new data, and to do so using a more ambitious approach than that required by the funder. The research team also wanted to include theoretical development in their academic outputs. These aspects made the proposal more attractive for the funder since they maximised value for money given the limited funding for the programme. But the coordinators had to rely on the goodwill of their partners in agreeing to collaborate in the project using their own resources.

The EPPIC case study describes the issues raised in their project by the fact that European funding covered only 60% of the total budget, leaving the partners to cover the other 40% from their own resources. This model derives from the EU concept of partnership, with matched funding provided by national governments via universities. Over time, in the UK it has come to mean that projects receive inadequate funding, unless they are able to raise funds from other sources. In both the EPPIC and POLKU projects, the authors acknowledged at the outset that they would have to accept the additional burden as the price to pay for carrying out what they considered to be important aspects of the research not covered by the main funders. This motivation did not prevent the project leaders from feeling that they had been overly ambitious in offering too much for the work contracted, and, in the cases of EPPIC, PRO-RES and TROPICO, from needing to request a no-cost extension to complete the work in the proposal.

Examples are given in the case studies not only of problems raised by budgetary constraints, but also of the amount of flexibility project coordinators had in renegotiating schedules and transferring funds between different budget heads due to changing circumstances. Because the funders were flexible in allowing virements between categories in the original allocation, the EPPIC coordinators were able to manage within budgetary constraints. Other project coordinators identify areas where, due to unforeseen external disruptions, most notably caused by the pandemic, they were able to make savings. For example, by arranging online meetings during the pandemic, they cushioned pressures on their budgets (AMR, PRO-RES, TROPICO).

Assessment of Project Proposals

The assessment of international multidisciplinary programmes and networks has long been recognised as problematic, to the extent of calling into question the validity of the peer review process. In its advice for research that crosses different disciplines, UKRI (2021b) seeks to reassure researchers that 'peer review is fair and appropriate for projects that span across the research remit of two or more council research remit domains', thereby avoiding 'the "double jeopardy" of parallel processes within each of the councils involved'.

Research funders are frequently criticised for not taking sufficient account of disciplinary specificities in recruiting review panel members and for not adapting their criteria accordingly (EASSH, 2019b; Kania & Bucksch, 2020). These concerns apply not only to assessments of research proposals but also to interim and end-of-award reports. Funding organisations continue to have difficulty finding evaluators equipped with the necessary knowledge and skills to understand the different cultural and intellectual styles, and epistemologies associated with the disciplines involved.

The TROPICO project illustrates the problem of working not only across disciplines but also across EU directorates with different priorities and criteria. The European Commission's Directorate-General for Research and Innovation (DG RTD) was collaborating with the DG for Communications Networks, Content and Technology (DG Connect), who were more interested in the ICT aspects of the proposal. Although the quality of the research on the topic of e-governance by an essentially public administration team was highly rated, the proposal did not initially pass the threshold for the disciplinary mix and was placed on the reserve list. When funding belatedly became available, the proposal was nonetheless selected for an award, and the experts in political science who undertook the mid-term review were satisfied with the capacity of the project team to fulfil the funders' requirements in the absence of dedicated ICT expertise.

PROJECT COORDINATION AND MANAGEMENT

Today, the model that celebrates the work of the research 'leader' is in the ascendant in a context where the nature of the scientific enterprise and the role of universities and how they see themselves in the world have fundamentally changed (Brannen, 2021). Most of the highest-impact work is carried out by research teams, often very large teams, as is almost always the case in international multidisciplinary research. Large teams are challenging for research managers, especially given the spread of partners across countries and disciplines.

The scale of the networks and programmes required of twenty-first century researchers to meet global challenges has meant that professional research administrators are increasingly being recruited to ensure efficient management of large international multidisciplinary projects. Few of the case studies in this volume had negotiated funding to cover the costs of employing a full-time professional manager or administrator. The role played by project coordinators was, therefore, key to the success of the research when judged by the ability of research teams to achieve the aims and objectives set out in their proposals.

Recruiting Coordinators and Managers

Already in the 1970s, team size had become an issue for project management. The larger the team and the more complex its organisation, the greater was the likelihood of the management structure being bureaucratic (Grootings, 1986), and of the need to employ professional managers irrespective of their disciplinary backgrounds (ESF, 1974).

The practice of appointing professional research managers from disciplinary and sectoral backgrounds distinct from those of the project team has interesting precedents. Andrew Sors, the head of social sciences and humanities in the DG RTD when the Targeted Socio-Economic Research (TSER) strand was being established in the 1990s (European Commission, 1999), held a UK doctorate in materials science and had early career experience as a research engineer in the chemical industry. He went on to become head of science and technology at the European Commission's delegation to India and then rector of the Collegium Budapest Institute for Advanced Study. Writing in 2017, he continued to advocate a pragmatic approach to research communities, aware of the 'legitimate expectations from those who fund the research – especially in the public sector'. He also acknowledged the tensions that arise between funders and researchers as a result of the need to respect their autonomy while demanding innovation and the 'creativity of research that might not always have a "successful" outcome' (Pohoryles & Sors, 2017, p. 1).

As in the past, in most of the projects featured in this book, principal investigators and coordinators also acted as executive managers. Leaders of projects, both large and small, require intellectual and methodological expertise that can bring each part of a complex project together. Since they already have onerous tasks to perform, including administrative and financial responsibilities, they appreciate being able to delegate at least some managerial tasks to team members or to a professional administrator, either in the host institution(s) or by appointing a dedicated administrator or manager externally. The case studies illustrate how institutional support varies within and across countries, as the FFP principal investigator (PI) found when her host institution in the UK was absorbed into a much larger institution. The EPPIC project coordinators were able to rely on supportive infrastructures for project management, financial control and legal advice in their home institution.

The BIAS project employed a part-time administrator. The principal investigators, who had training in statistics in China and in management in India, shared the management tasks between them and with the co-investigators, whose disciplinary interests spanned management and mathematics, sociology and computing science. The author of the B–SET programme, as a steering group member, and research and innovation strategy manager at her home institution, coordinated the funding proposal, by acting as a bridge between research development and innovation activities. The B–SET programme was initiated and delivered by a team of professional managers, who organised their own calls for projects and selection procedures. In recruiting the project management team, the programme's PI was looking for individuals with generic competencies of project management and significant multidisciplinary programme management experience, as well as an understanding of financial management, commercial markets, and event organisation.

The decision adopted by ESF to restructure its activities in 2016 and to establish Science Connect reflected growing recognition of the need to appoint professional research managers, irrespective of their contributing disciplines, who understand, and are able to handle, the priorities of funders and the issues involved in meeting their requirements, including financial management (ESF, 2021). The Science Connect coordinator for the PRO-RES project on research ethics, funded by the European Commission, who was an astronomer and space scientist, took over many of the bridging roles with funders and stakeholders, thereby enabling the project coordinator to concentrate fully on the scientific tasks.

BUILDING AN INTERNATIONAL MULTIDISCIPLINARY RESEARCH TEAM

A primary task of project coordinators from any discipline is to build a research team. The case studies show how funders' requirements impact on the composition of research teams across disciplines and countries, and how the mix of disciplines and cultures can influence the subsequent conduct of the research (see Table 2.3). Authors were asked to justify their selection of team members, taking account of their contextual backgrounds and the requirements of funders; the language and epistemic communities to which they belong; different theoretical and methodological approaches and research traditions, as well as extra-scientific factors such as the socio-economic and

Table 2.3   *Composition of international and multidisciplinary project teams*

Project	Countries and (nationalities)	Disciplines
AMR	**UK**, India	biochemistry, bioengineering, environmental science, geochemistry, social sciences
BIAS	**UK, Canada** and US (global)	computing, management, mathematics, sociology, statistics
B–SET	**UK**, Africa, Middle East, Asia	biological sciences, economics, medical anthropology, public health, technology, veterinary science
CLICCS	**Germany**, global	computing, earth systems, geophysics, meteorology, physics, political science, sociology
EPPIC	**UK**, Austria, Denmark, Germany, Italy, Netherlands, Poland	anthropology, criminology, health policy, psychology, social policy, sociology
FFP	**UK**, Norway, Portugal	anthropology, sociology, statistics
LCEDN	**UK**, Africa, South America	anthropology, civil engineering, economics, electrical engineering, environmental science, human/political geography, social policy, sociology
POLKU	**Finland**, Denmark, Netherlands, Sweden, UK	economics, law, public policy, social policy, sociology
PRO-RES	**UK**, Belgium, Croatia, Estonia, France, Greece, Italy, N. Ireland	business ethics, computer science, economics health sciences, marine biology, nanotechnology, international relations, life sciences, philosophy, physics, psychology, research ethics, social science, sociology
TROPICO	**Norway**, Belgium, Denmark, Estonia, France, Hungary, Netherlands, Spain, Wales	public administration

Note: **Bold** indicates project lead country.

political environments impinging on the phenomena being analysed; the institutional frameworks and constraints within which researchers are operating; the agendas of national and international funding agencies; the innumerable assessment procedures that researchers must undergo; and their interface with multisectoral stakeholders.

Selection of Countries

Some projects had a robust scientific rationale for selecting partners from particular countries. For example, since the POLKU project was to have a specifically comparative dimension, partners were selected because their countries represented contrasting approaches to welfare provisions for unemployed people in Europe. The FFP project wanted to compare the arrangements for children to access adequate nutritious food in low-income families in three contrasting welfare regimes. In the European-funded Horizon 2020 projects, the particular mix of countries was justified by the need to include a geographical range of regions representing different sets of characteristics (PRO-RES, TROPICO).

In the AMR project, the selection was determined by the funders' call for projects investigating research questions designed to address environmental issues in regions in the world most affected by a specific problem. The BIAS project was developed in the context of a joint funding programme between research councils in Canada and the UK under their artificial intelligence initiative, and compared the impacts of AI in the two countries. The B–SET programme was interested in recruiting project partners from anywhere in the world as long as they contributed to the programme's key aims. The CLICCS programme was international in that it treated the global challenge of climate change from a German perspective. Although members of the consortium had lived and worked in different regions of the world, no other countries were directly represented among the partners.

An issue that frequently arises in international projects is how to deal with ethical approval, institutional and legal requirements across countries. Ethical considerations are most salient in projects involving human or animal subjects, in-depth interviewing and observational methods. The PRO-RES project on integrity in the use of research results in non-medical science had a central interest in ethical issues, and the ways in which they have been addressed in different research communities. The project partners included experts in business and research ethics, several of whom had worked together to produce guides to ethical practices (Iphofen, 2020).

Many institutions now have their own research ethics committees. Research councils, in particular, require attention to be paid to ethical issues in the projects that they fund. The lead country is often expected to ensure that ethical standards are met. None of the case studies reported problems with gaining ethical approval for their research, although instances were cited where potentially difficult situations had to be resolved (EPPIC, FFP).

Disciplinary Mixes of Partners

Analysts of the factors determining the success of international partnerships have long recognised that teams are more likely to collaborate effectively if their members have worked together in the past and share similar intellectual traditions (Galtung, 1982), conceptual frames of reference and complementary methodologies, as well as psychological proximity, compatible socio-economic and political structures and ideologies (Rose, 2003). In multidisciplinary research, factors such as flexibility and openness, and closeness between disciplines can also facilitate cooperation. In the European Commission's flagged projects in Horizon 2020, social and human scientists were, for example, more likely to be selected to participate in, and coordinate, projects in areas where successful integration depended on disciplinary proximity (Kania & Bucksch, 2020).

Even when the choice of countries is based on a sound scientific rationale, practicalities may prove more significant in determining the selection of team members. The authors of the case studies refer to the importance of choosing partners with whom team members had already worked in each other's countries, or who had met at conferences, or through wider networks. Being able to call on pre-existing relationships was often critical, especially in projects of short duration where no time was available to establish new connections (POLKU), and where core funding would not cover all partners (EPPIC). Prior knowledge meant that coordinators were conversant with the skills, competences and personality traits of their collaborators and with the impact of their cultural and disciplinary backgrounds on mutual understanding of the issues and concepts associated with the project topic, working methods and institutional expectations (LCEDN). The B–SET consortium had already established a local network of professional research managers in the Bloomsbury area of London before the call was announced, and most of the CLICCS consortium researchers worked at Hamburg University or at another institution in the same city.

Many of the case study authors commented on the importance of working in teams of researchers with analogous and cognate disciplinary affiliations and backgrounds, who could more easily apply 'symmetrical' or 'equitable' approaches to project management (Grootings, 1986). The BIAS case study describes how project coordinators were able to adopt a flat organisational structure for developing shared understandings across disciplines, ensuring that all the team members were fully involved in decisions about working practices and outputs, even though some team members were new to the collaboration.

The AMR case study author commented on the caution exercised by the coordinators based in the UK, the lead country, to avoid any hint of 'colonialism' in a project involving partners in India with different skill sets with whom they had already collaborated. The PI of the FFP project emphasised the value of the shared interest of the core team members in methodological expertise and development.

The EPPIC case study demonstrated the advantages of including researchers from cognate and hybrid disciplines within the social sciences, with whom they had previously collaborated in European projects. Despite the coordinators' best efforts to include specialists from non-social science disciplines to satisfy the funders' requirements, most of the members of the TROPICO team had backgrounds in public administration, which, like many of the social sciences, is a hybrid discipline (Hustedt et al., 2020). Not only was the team able to meet the requirements of the funders in carrying out the research on the digitalisation of governance, but they also found that researchers in their discipline, with whom they had worked previously, particularly in Eastern European countries, welcomed the opportunity to be associated with an EU-funded project and its outputs.

The BIAS project, which was funded by two social science research councils, affords an example of how sociologists were able to collaborate with computational scientists to extend their understanding of concepts that were central to the project. The project members homed in on its acronym after prolonged discussions among team members about the meaning they attributed to the concept in an international interdisciplinary project seeking to understand the role of artificial intelligence (AI) in reproducing gender and ethnic inequalities (biases) in labour market processes that are increasingly digitalised.

3. Managing the research process

Linda Hantrais and Julia Brannen

INTRODUCTION

A major aim of this guide is to accompany project managers and team members through the process of developing and applying strategies that will enable them to bridge what are often deep-seated disciplinary and cultural divides when undertaking international multidisciplinary research. An associated aim is to assist research coordinators in implementing effective integrated approaches to the design and delivery of high-quality, high-value research across disciplines, sectors and societies by improving their understanding of the many challenges they face.

The successful launch of an international multidisciplinary programme or project was shown, in the previous chapter, to depend on the selection of team members with an appropriate mix of skills and competences, and on the establishment of the necessary structures and processes for conducting the research, as set out in the funding proposal and agreed at the outset with the sponsors. This chapter focusses on the real-life experience of carrying out international multidisciplinary research projects and the lessons that can be learnt from the process. Drawing on the ten case studies, the chapter illustrates how decisions taken in the early stages of projects determine the research design and methods, engagement with team members and diverse stakeholders, dissemination strategies and, ultimately, the assessment of longer-term tangible and intangible societal impacts resulting from collaborations.

The case study authors were invited to reflect, with their teams, on both the positive and negative lessons that they had gleaned from their experience. The chapter concludes with a synopsis of the lessons learnt by project managers and coordinators about how to manage international multidisciplinary research projects most effectively. The advice proffered should be of value not only for academic and non-academic researchers at key milestones in their careers, but also for more established researchers seeking to expand their knowledge and experience of managing multidisciplinary research projects in the UK, Europe and further afield.

RESEARCH ORIENTATIONS, DESIGNS AND METHODS

In developing an international research project design and selecting suitable methods, account must be taken not only of the choice of countries and disciplines, and related research traditions, but also of extra-scientific factors. The theoretical or pragmatic appropriateness of the rationale for the research design is shaped by the legal requirements in the countries, societies, cultures and institutions where the research is being conducted, giving rise to potential conflicts of interest, issues concerning data protection, permissions, libel, intellectual property rights, procurement, confidentiality and informed consent, particularly when in-depth interviews are being undertaken. Depending on the disciplinary mix, these extra-scientific factors can have different implications for the time schedule of the research, its design, data collection, analysis, interpretation and validation of findings.

The ten illustrative case studies in this collection represent a variety of approaches to research design and methods (see Table 3.1). This section shows how decisions about these central components in the research process were negotiated and implemented by project coordinators and their research teams.

Developing the Research Design

In the past, the research coordinator or core national coordinating team would design the project alone and then issue instructions for its implementation (Grootings, 1986). Today, it has become customary in international multidisciplinary projects, and even more so in resolutely interdisciplinary projects, for core team members to develop the research design jointly and to agree on common research questions and equivalent conceptualisations. This collective approach to research design means that attention must be paid to the preferences, or predispositions, for certain epistemological approaches related to different intellectual styles and research cultures that are known to reinforce barriers to effective international cooperation (Galtung, 1982). In international collaborative research, the cultural and 'touristic bias' associated with the orientations and preferences of researchers in particular research settings has long been a concern for team coordinators (Warwick & Osherson, 1973). Operating within international teams provides a powerful test of 'objectivity' if the potential bias created by national research cultures and epistemological traditions is to be overcome.

Although none of the case studies addressed the issue of researcher bias directly, the discussion to which the term gives rise was thoroughly rehearsed by the BIAS team members with their varied disciplinary backgrounds when

Table 3.1   *Research designs and strategies used in the case studies*

Project	Work packages	Research design	Research methods
AMR	4	systematic spatial survey and analysis	mapping and tracking, fieldwork, laboratory testing
BIAS	2	interdisciplinary mixed method	qualitative interviews, modelling, testing, simulation
B–SET	[30]	knowledge exchange	issuing project calls, selecting, assessing and funding research projects
CLICCS	[4+14]	large-scale spatial/temporal multi-methods	qualitative, observations, modelling, synthesis
EPPIC	4	comparative multi-methods	scoping survey, literature review, interviews, focus groups, workshops
FFP	[3]	systematic multi-level comparison mixed methods	literature reviews, secondary analysis of national data, documentary analysis, semi-structured interviews, photo elicitation, questionnaires and food budget standards
LCEDN	[3+13]	large-scale international multidisciplinary network	landscape mapping, participant observation, focus groups, qualitative interviews, practical project development, practical actions, workshops
POLKU	5	systematic comparison multi-methods	systematic literature review, secondary analysis of international statistics, documentary policy analysis, evaluation studies, vignettes, microsimulation
PRO-RES	9	systematic review	in-person/online dialogue workshops, interactive action plans, stakeholder consultation, virtual platform, case studies
TROPICO	11	systematic multi-level comparison multi-methods	joint case study protocol, literature review, mapping, documentary analysis, semi-structured interviews

Note: [ ] indicates (sub)projects within case studies.

they were considering their project title. The BIAS case study illustrates the importance of team members being tolerant of the paradigms of their colleagues and agreeing on how each discipline and its methodology can contribute to explaining the phenomena under study. Without referring to researcher bias, the PRO-RES consortium had to overcome the difficulty of generating productive discussion and exchange of ideas and experience between research team members who considered themselves to be strongly wedded to a single research paradigm. The author of the CLICCS case study describes how a public call was put out to recruit researchers not only familiar with the required conceptual, empirical and methodological approaches, but also with open-mindedness towards interdisciplinary research, and the ability to draw on different fields of study and relevant disciplines.

Irrespective of the number of partners and coordinators, the level and duration of funding, and country and disciplinary mix, all the case studies described in this guide adopted research designs specifically to deal with the complexity of working in international multidisciplinary teams. Some were deliberately interdisciplinary (AMR, BIAS, B–SET, CLICCS, LCEDN) in that they set out to ensure that the different disciplines they included contributed to conceptual understanding and knowledge exchange. Others, or sub-projects within them, were systematically comparative (EPPIC, FFP, POLKU, TROPICO) in that they selected country participants representing certain characteristics and ensured that the same methodologies were applied consistently.

As demonstrated by the B–SET, CLICCS, LCEDN and TROPICO case studies, in larger-scale programmes, the work needs to be broken down into manageable portions. In planning research designs, much internationally funded research is shaped by the organisation of the project's methodology into 'work packages', or 'sub-projects', specified in the funding proposals and allocated to small teams with relevant expertise. The work package structure was introduced in the EU's framework programmes in the early 2000s to enable research teams who were located in different countries to work on separate components of a project either in parallel or sequentially (cf. PRO-RES).

This approach to research design has the advantage of ensuring that each of a project's research questions can be closely matched with a set of research methods. For mid-career researchers, being able to lead a work package or sub-project offers an opportunity to gain valuable experience of project management. The authors of the CLICCS and TROPICO case studies describe in more detail the design and methods used in the specific work packages and sub-projects for which they were responsible, while setting them within the context of the wider study. The B–SET programme was designed to create a strong research and innovation base with international connectivity for knowledge exchange and technology transfer by initiating and funding a series of smaller-scale (sub-)projects to develop and deliver testing, prototyping and modelling of low-cost portable diagnostic tools and technologies in a broad range of areas and countries.

A potential disadvantage of this type of project design is that the practicalities of the approach may necessitate undue effort being devoted to the process of linking different work packages, at the risk of losing sight of the overall intellectual aims of the project (EPPIC). The CLICCS consortium incorporated a cross-cutting sub-project in their design to ensure interdisciplinary cohesion across its three intertwined research themes. Another way to address the issues associated with large team size and complex research structures is to institutionalise 'bridging' roles that connect and coordinate the programmes' activities and work packages (BIAS, PRO-RES).

From Research Design to Methods

The concentration of funding support on big science has prompted, if not forced, the non-natural sciences to adopt methodological pluralism and to overcome paradigmatic divides and entrenched theoretical positions anchored in particular epistemologies (Brannen, 1992; Bryman, 2008; Hantrais, 2009). Together with the growth of multidisciplinarity and interdisciplinarity, these factors have led to the use of a combination of methodologies, to which many of the case studies testify, with implications for project management.

As Table 3.1 shows, most of the programmes and projects discussed in the case studies involved complex research designs that, in turn, required different types of methods for data collection. In part, this approach reflects the diversity of their research questions together with the fact that different disciplines were involved in addressing these questions from their own vantage points, and by employing their particular expertise (B−SET, LCEDN, PRO-RES).

If team members resolve to use different types of data collection methods, for example, face-to-face or telephone surveys, or in-person or online interviews, other matters need to be decided, especially whether to prioritise quantitative or qualitative approaches, the ordering of different methods and the ways different types of data are integrated (Brannen, 2005; Bryman, 2008). The most challenging problems identified by researchers trained in quantitative approaches, and relying on high-cost infrastructures, as most widely used in natural and STEM sciences, largely involve the availability, reliability, replicability and comparability of data. By contrast, many of the difficulties encountered in projects and networks adopting qualitative approaches, as is more usual in the social and human sciences, relate to potential subjective bias, differences in understandings of concepts and cultural contexts, and in interpretations of data (Hantrais, 2009).

Within different paradigms, the issues that have to be addressed in conducting international multidisciplinary research may be more obvious for qualitative approaches precisely because qualitative research is so closely concerned with meaning and the cultural embedding of phenomena. The potential 'value bias' of researchers, due to their sociocultural, ideological and epistemological orientations, surfaces in the phases of conceptualisation, data collection, analysis and interpretation. Research teams have to find ways of avoiding skewed case selection and flawed interpretation of data that could ultimately affect the outcomes of the research.

The case studies used different combinations of methods to counter potential risks of researcher bias. The BIAS and PRO-RES projects, for example, describe how concepts were thoroughly discussed in team meetings, then tested and modified in relation to each context before being implemented. Many combinations of methods are commonplace and uncontentious: literature reviews, documentary analysis and some primary data collection are widely used to describe and understand the contextual features of the phenomena under study. Such contextualisation, as practised in the mixed-methods or multi-methods research designs and applied in BIAS, EPPIC, FFP, POLKU and TROPICO, is essential in comparative interdisciplinary research when the aim is to compare data across contexts and to understand what accounts for differences and similarities between contexts (Brannen & Nilsen, 2011; Hantrais, 2009).

Given their careful research designs that take account of the specificities of social context, qualitative approaches have the advantage that they may throw light on the significance of quantitative data, as amply demonstrated by the FFP and POLKU projects. In FFP, a mixed methods research design was agreed in which a large-scale dataset was analysed to identify which types of families were most at risk of food poverty in each country, before conducting qualitative research with different types of low-income families. In the project's qualitative country cases of households, the aim was to examine the differences that local and family contexts made to alleviating food poverty and to set them in relation to national-level quantitative data. POLKU carried out a thorough review of data about national social security systems to identify similarities and differences before embarking on qualitative studies. Both projects employed less common research methods. FFP used photo-elicitation interviews, in which young people took photographs of food and eating in their everyday lives and discussed them with the researcher at a later visit. Researchers took photographs of 'kitchen tours', which prompted further questions. POLKU organised vignettes with experts in local social security and public employment service administration in small, medium and large cities to reveal process-related issues concerning unemployment.

Irrespective of the methodological approach adopted, the key concepts involved in international research are frequently influenced by disciplinary cultures. As the authors of the EPPIC case study report, terminology in the field of youth justice and substance use varied even within the social sciences. The authors comment on the importance of taking the time to embed non-judgmental or non-stigmatising language into the research process. Conceptualisation also risks being influenced by national politics, ideologically driven preferences of sponsors and interests of stakeholders; these contextual factors were analysed systematically by the author of the TROPICO case study.

While issues of conceptualisation are by no means absent in quantitative project designs and their implementation, they tend to be magnified in qualitative studies if conceptual understandings and interpretations among international team members diverge, for example owing to linguistic differences or differential access to contextual knowledge. Conceptual matters are particularly challenging in comparative social policy research because different national policies, for example social security provisions, are not only subject to change but also include and exclude different social groups (POLKU). A potentially useful scientific by-product of differences in intellectual styles, research traditions, ideologies and cultures is that researchers, as well as the environments within which they are trained and work, can become objects of comparative study in their own right, as illustrated by the survey carried out among team members in the BIAS project.

A notable feature of the FFP, LCEDN, POLKU and TROPICO case studies is that their projects were intended to offer transferable policy solutions. In the FFP and POLKU projects, a combination of different methods was critical in allowing project teams to answer the broad sets of questions posed in the research proposals, providing both country-specific knowledge and, in the case of POLKU, systematic comparative analysis of relevant characteristics of different welfare arrangements and services. The aim in FFP was to provide a multi-layered explanation of food poverty. In both projects, the potential for direct comparison was, however, noted as a major obstacle that a mix of methods helped to overcome. To fulfil the aims of the POLKU project, categories of groups covered by social security and unemployment benefits had to be extended to ensure comparability, whereas in FFP particular groups had to be excluded from the international survey analysis, due the lack of strictly comparable data.

The TROPICO sub-project adopted a multi-level analytic research design, based on a comparative contextualised approach to examine e-participation practices and to identify drivers and barriers that contribute to the success of these initiatives at national, organisational and individual levels, and to assess their transferability to other policy contexts. The PRO-RES project's resources and ethics framework were designed to be delivered to a range of levels applicable to non-medical research from undergraduate to funded professional research agencies.

The LCEDN programmes of research on low carbon energy and international development, funded by the UK government and research councils, afford an interesting example of an interdisciplinary (geographers, civil engineers, social anthropologists) multiscalar cross-sectoral networking approach, involving practical action projects in different low-income countries. The authors demonstrate how they exploited opportunities for linking disciplines and enhancing systemic complexity by cross-fertilising it with innovations taking place in the private sector. They highlight linkage possibilities in disciplines not often seen working together (Brown et al., 2018). They argue that the value of this perspective lies as much in how to persuade project designers, research councils and government funders, policymakers and the private sector to devote equal attention to this kind of transcalar interdisciplinary way of working as it does to analysing financial models.

COMMUNICATION, ENGAGEMENT AND DISSEMINATION

In small- and large-scale international multidisciplinary research projects, effective internal and external communication is essential if project managers and coordinators are to achieve their objectives and meet the expectations and requirements of their funders, institutions and team members. At the proposal stage, applicants are required to present communications, engagement and dissemination strategies that they have agreed with their teams, in the knowledge that their work will be monitored and assessed throughout the research process, and that they will be held responsible for any shortcomings in the results that they produce. Each of the case studies considers communication, engagement and dissemination strategies within research teams as well as externally with funders, stakeholders and audiences in different countries and sectors. In some cases, a work package, or transversal sub-project, was devoted specifically to these strategies (AMR, CLICCS, EPPIC, TROPICO).

Communication within Project Teams

A sine qua non for successful international collaborations suggested by the case study authors concerns open and regular channels of communication between team members. While previous collaborations could facilitate communication, past practices need to be reviewed, especially when applying them in large research programmes (LCEDN). In projects that were launched before the pandemic, internal discussions were initiated essentially via in-person workshops to prevent and resolve research-related misunderstandings. When the pandemic struck in early 2020, much contact moved online. Throughout the research process, time needed to be allocated for planned and unplanned synchronous communication, both in-person and remotely. Such meetings enabled research coordinators to maintain a high level of engagement among team members; to discuss conceptual and technical issues; and to test and modify their approaches in different cultural settings before they were implemented.

Bilateral team meetings needed to be carefully scheduled in the AMR and BIAS projects to take account of different time zones: the UK and India, and

Canada, the UK and the US, respectively. Given the large number of partners and countries represented in the PRO-RES consortium and their project design, the project manager needed to ensure that participants could express themselves fully during meetings via breakout groups and reports back to plenaries. Focussed and actionable information flows were maintained by circulating minutes, notes and reports. Reactions to newly discovered information were resolved by initiating an extensive offline iterative process, or by calling a new meeting.

Effective communication was maintained throughout the FFP project by keeping all team members updated with minutes of meetings and listings of actions agreed. Time was scheduled during face-to-face meetings for socialising, including sharing food, the topic of the research, to ensure successful collaboration.

The BIAS case study authors stressed the central importance of adopting a flat organisational structure for developing formal and informal intra- and interdisciplinary communication. This structure allowed for flexible on-demand meetings. Individual team members, with a solid understanding of the concepts and methods used in different disciplines, took responsibility for bridging the communication gap between the groups.

Communication across international teams in a large-scale project was shown to be closely linked to the incremental building of knowledge from the research. As the CLICCS case study reports, each year, a group of its researchers from the various sub-projects together summarise the ongoing findings with reference to the cluster's leading research question. Given that the project was running for seven years and was directed towards identifying drivers to, and away from, climate change, this reporting arrangement played an important role in the whole research process by sustaining team cohesion.

External Communication with Funders

External funders usually require annual monitoring reports to track progress and/or mid-term meetings or events at which project teams demonstrate how they are meeting the aims and objectives agreed in the original research proposal. Despite the structures put in place by funding bodies to promote and support multidisciplinary working, adoption of the big science model continues to be reflected in the application of assessment practices and criteria. The European Commission, for example, regularly synthesises data from the assessment of the programmes that it funds. The fifth report on projects funded in 2018 under the Horizon 2020 programme, which financed PRO-RES and TROPICO, focussed on the integration of social sciences and humanities. The authors found that integration needed to be based on a deeper cross-sectoral 'holistic' approach, covering the entire cycle of the research process, to the selection of evaluators with clear expertise in social science and humanities (Kania & Bucksch, 2020, p. 66).

The TROPICO project illustrates the problems of assessing multidisciplinary proposals: the Commission was not satisfied initially that the project team met the disciplinary criteria in the call, whereas the mid-term assessors, who shared the political science and public administration expertise of the project coordinators, delivered a more positive assessment of the team's work.

EPPIC was one of the few projects that had been completed when the case studies in the guide were being written, which meant that its final report had been evaluated. The external assessors were all experts in areas covered by the project. They had been appointed by the funders while the project was being delivered and had been kept informed about its actions. They attended one partner meeting and the final EPPIC conference, and were involved in the interim evaluation at 18 months as well as the final evaluation. Their assessment was based on a survey among the partners and on interviews with all the researchers.

The budgets for international projects routinely cover the costs of meetings and events, including participation in advisory groups, as provided for in research proposals. The case study projects set up advisory boards (BIAS, FFP, EPPIC, PRO-RES), steering groups (B–SET, POLKU) and, as in the case of TROPICO, both academic and practitioner advisory boards, to provide timely advice and support. Advisers representing different stakeholders attended meetings with team members and commented on their strategies and reports. The aim was generally to promote a broader consensus and fuller engagement with project issues raised by the researchers. Advisers also provided useful links with networks and stakeholders, particularly in the policy environment. In the case of the AMR project, the World Bank's in-kind contribution performed these roles.

The BIAS project included ten experts on its advisory board from industries that they were studying and from academia. The project team communicated with them via digital tools (email and virtual). In the course of their project, the TROPICO team members were able to benefit from direct input from the IT units in government agencies and local government offices that they were studying, and which were represented in project 'summits' together with e-government practitioners, who also participated in the project's advisory board.

The EPPIC advisory group was set up to include representatives from prominent international organisations in their field of study: the European Monitoring Centre on Drugs and Drug Addiction (EMCDDA); the United Nations Interregional Crime and Justice Research Institute (UNICRI); and the funding body (CHAFEA). Board members were selected for their expertise and knowledge about quality standards and interventions within the criminal justice system and provided useful links to wider networks. They attended all face-to-face partner meetings and were consulted by email as necessary on specific issues. In addition, each country established its own national advisory group to provide feedback on interim findings to the research partners.

The PRO-RES advisory board included the vice-chair of the International Network for Government Science Advice (INGSA). He was able to provide a forum for policymakers, practitioners, academies and academic researchers, in which they could share experiences, build capacity and develop theoretical and practical approaches to the use of scientific evidence in informing policy at all levels of government.

The steering group played a central role in the B–SET project. The principal investigator and the chair of the group spent the first six months setting up the programme's consortium agreement, developing partnerships, arranging the governance structure, and issuing the first call for project grants. Each partner institution had a named academic champion and at least one institutional representative on the steering group whose members guided the programme delivery, identified gaps and issues in building further collaborations, and approved dissemination and impact.

Engagement with Policy Stakeholders

By promoting international cooperation, integrating international and disciplinary approaches, and extending and refining the evidence base, the case studies show how international researchers, in their capacity as knowledge brokers, can enhance the policymaking process and reveal insights that may have relevance beyond their original contexts. By opening opportunities for adaptive and iterative policy learning across nations and disciplines, they contribute to scientific inquiry, international understanding, and the extension and deepening of the knowledge base in contemporary societies. By sharing contextualised knowledge across jurisdictions, researchers can contribute to a deeper understanding of policy-informed evidence leading to the formulation of innovative policies (Hantrais, 2009).

Discussion of evidence-based policy, or the relationship between evidence and policy more widely, which is not always explicitly developed in the case studies, raises questions concerning the hierarchies of evidence favoured by research and policy communities (Hantrais et al., 2015). In general, social science evidence has tended to be less appealing to policymakers than evidence from the natural sciences because the methods used by social scientists do not appear to offer the same degree of certainty; because they raise issues of complexity that are perceived as being at odds with naive empiricist orientations; or because social science is regarded merely as 'common sense'. In their role as knowledge brokers, project coordinators and managers show how they work across national and disciplinary boundaries using their sound knowledge and understanding of different policy processes, as well as the socio-economic, cultural and political systems of the countries serving as comparators (cf. EPPIC, FFP, LCEDN, POLKU, TROPICO).

Politicians may not be the only users of policy research. Governments also commission research, both directly and through national research councils (cf. AMR, B–SET, CLICCS, LCEDN, POLKU). Publicly-funded research, especially that commissioned by governments, is increasingly expected to demonstrate policy relevance and impact, as demonstrated in the EU's framework programmes (see Annex 1.1). In recognition of the importance of communicating the findings from publicly-funded projects to policymakers, the media and the wider public (emphasised by the pandemic), project managers and coordinators have, of necessity, become skilled in conveying the messages distilled from their research to different audiences, including in representational formats that are readily accessible and timely for policymakers (cf. EPPIC, FFP, PRO-RES, TROPICO). Some researchers become trusted policy advisers, but at the risk of neglecting more academic outputs that have become so important to national and international research rankings (cf. LCEDN, POLKU).

The functions served by knowledge brokers were mediated in the AMR project through the engagement with industry and policymakers to develop policies based on the data obtained from the project. The research involved engagement with the Indian pharmaceutical industry through a process of co-production with project partners of the pathways to impact from their respective work packages. The principal investigator had intimate knowledge of the Indian context. The partners, specifically the biochemist from the World Bank, who were crucial in terms of their expertise, gave access to Indian policymakers and researchers, and to AMR sampling sites. The World Bank worked closely with the UK-based social scientist in developing the public health aspects of the study. In one of the LCEDN programmes, a session explored the suitability of 'participatory impact pathways analysis' for the kinds of multisectoral and transdisciplinary projects being developed in individual sub-projects. Other sessions focussed on how to engage key stakeholders successfully in planning for longer-term partnership development.

The EPPIC project's four work packages were designed to produce a strong evidence base to inform policy, and the team maintained good working relations with practitioners and policy users. The FFP project team had embedded its existing links with NGOs and government departments in the advisory group and continued to engage with them at various stages of the research, and after the completion of the project, despite this aspect not being a specific requirement of ERC award holders.

The BIAS project coordinators were responsible for generating theoretical, empirical, applied, and policy-related contributions, and for providing evidence to support the re-conceptualisation and review of policy and service development. The TROPICO project was predicated on the team's expertise in analysing and comparing the conditions and practices of innovative collaboration in policy design for e-governance. Their work involved public, private, and civil society actors, to ascertain how user knowledge is integrated in the process and to identify critical success factors in the practices employed.

CLICCS leaders produced knowledge transfer tools for the international scientific community and the wider public, as well as formulating guidance for decision-makers in politics and policy processes. The provision of a toolbox was central to the PRO-RES project's objectives to enable policymakers to monitor the ethical use of research results. Experts from the research institutions, chosen for their experience of the policy advice 'chain', were responsible for liaising with national policymakers and local authorities. The B–SET consortium was charged with creating low-cost portable innovative diagnostic tools and technologies. Through its many programmes and projects, LCEDN constantly engaged with government agencies and the World Bank in developing and delivering practical low carbon energy solutions in response to global challenges.

Dissemination Strategies

The organisation of dissemination strategies has become an important part of project planning and management. Project funders require information about dissemination plans to demonstrate accountability and value for money. In funnelling public funds to projects, research councils require that findings from the research that they support are made available as widely, rapidly and effectively as practicable to other researchers and potential users in business, charitable and public sectors, and the general public (NERC, 2022) (cf. AMR, LCEDN).

All the case studies provide web links to their projects with full details of the arrangements for workshops and other dissemination events, including interactive platforms, electronic newsletters, and public access to conferences, webinars and publications. A wide range of dissemination activities were implemented, including blogs, tweets and press releases, both during the lifetime of the projects and after they end (cf. EPPIC, FFP), to achieve the highest possible visibility and impact, for years to come in the case of completed projects.

The ongoing large-scale CLICCS project, funded by the German research council (DFG) in the context of the government's excellence clusters, includes knowledge transfer, accomplished jointly with the German Climate Service

Centre (GERICS). A press outreach office facilitates and coordinates interviews and comments on (social) media, and provides research profiles for publications by the press, for example in local leading newspapers. The dissemination tools employed include the consortium's regular climate quarterly, and an annual news magazine, *Hamburg Climate Futures Outlook*. In addition to contributing to UN climate reports, the consortium produces regular academic publications in well-established leading peer-reviewed journals. The LCEDN dissemination strategy grew as the network expanded, resulting in a member of the core research team being appointed as communications officer for one of their large programmes. The network's strategy did not focus on a specific publication. Over the years, the consortium produced briefing notes and numerous multi-authored articles in specialised journals, as well as conference proceedings and working papers.

The European Commission is committed to providing open access to publications, including books, produced from the research that it funds, albeit without necessarily allocating dedicated budgets. This requirement can be a constraining factor, given the associated costs to authors or their institutions, as reported in the TROPICO case study. ERC specified only a monograph (FFP), although a second academic book based on the comparative aspects of the research was published after completion of the award without dedicated funds from the European Commission.

Academic publishing has become ever more difficult to manage with the shift towards online-only open access journal articles and books. European and government funders are usually less concerned about dissemination in academic outlets, whereas these forms of publication are more highly valued by university institutions and research councils, which creates dilemmas for project managers. Knowing how to navigate the publishing process is a central concern for mid-career researchers in building their academic credentials (Clark et al., 2016). In a context where the members of research teams are drawn from very different disciplines and are at different stages in their careers, the need to publish in the most appropriate peer-reviewed journals raises questions about whether to publish in a high-impact single-discipline journal or in what may be a lower-impact journal that accommodates multidisciplinary articles.

When individual team members are left to decide where and with whom to publish academic outputs, their preferences are often dictated by previous experience and their knowledge of institutional expectations. The widespread application of bibliometrics in the assessment of scientific outputs across disciplines creates problems for multidisciplinary teams when planning publication strategies due to the preference, especially in the natural sciences, for articles in the highest-rated monodisciplinary journals in national and institutional research assessments and international rankings, in addition to the relative lack of highly-rated multidisciplinary journals (AMR).

Notwithstanding the creation of cross-disciplinary journals and multidisciplinary assessment panels, researchers who cannot match the criteria for publication in prestigious monodisciplinary journals may see their careers impeded. Social and human scientists participating in multidisciplinary collaborations are at a particular disadvantage due to their traditional practice of publishing lengthy monographs, whereas the natural sciences, but also disciplines such as economics, depend on bibliographic measures to assess peer-reviewed multi-authored articles in specialist journals (Hantrais, 2006).

The drive towards large-scale international multidisciplinary research collaborations and the need to publish findings in highly-rated journals have resulted in the widespread adoption of the norms of the natural sciences concerning the number of authors and authorship order, which may vary from one publisher to another (Daunt & McDermott, 2018; Wordvice KH, 2021). Most of the case study authors raise the issue of authorship. Early in the life of the EPPIC project, for example, team members, who had considerable experience of working together on similar European-funded projects with colleagues in cognate disciplines, discussed publication outlets as well as authorship. They agreed on the exchange of draft papers, and that authorship should be attributed to one or two people from the team leading on the paper and one person from each collaborating team. These discussions were largely uncontentious, and agreement was easily reached regarding the choice of outlet and quality of papers.

The AMR team had discussed and agreed their publishing strategy when drafting the project proposal and had reached the understanding that the authorship of papers would be managed so as to benefit the interests of the early career researchers associated with the project. Since the AMR study cuts across a wide span of disciplines, the team based its choice of journal on what it considered to be the most appropriate readership and likely to attract the greatest visibility in terms of audience and reach, with due regard to journal metrics and impact factors.

The TROPICO team was working with funders who were interested in the technical topic of e-governance, but where team members had relatively little publishing experience in ICT journals. Their publication plans gave rise to issues about the specific focus of articles, type of journal to aim for, number of authors, author order and language. The team members found that the articles they wrote on e-governance were more likely to be accepted for publication in public administration than in ICT journals due to the persistence of disciplinary silos and institutional requirements for research assessment, which varied from one country to another. Individual team members were left to decide where and with whom they published academic outputs, while being given an opportunity to contribute chapters to an edited book covering 15 EU member states.

Attention was accorded in the dissemination plans of the FFP project to managing the demands of publishing academic outputs and engaging with audiences outside academia in the context of the pervasive contemporary interest in food poverty, the topic of the research. Each partner was given access to the data and developed their own publication strategy. Although the Finnish prime minister's office assisted in public dissemination of the POLKU project progress reports and briefs for policy audiences, no funding was allocated specifically to support academic dissemination. The academic leads had taken the initiative to include theoretical aspects of their work in their proposal with the intention of publishing their findings in high-ranking (international) journals in the field of social policy in their own time once they had satisfied the funder's requirements.

Research assessment exercises, such as the UK's research excellence framework (REF, 2021), and institutional assessments of individual research outputs, irrespective of the number or order of authors in published work, increasingly require information about the extent of each named contribution. In agreeing the team's publication strategy, in line with its egalitarian structure, the BIAS project leads committed to cite the names of all team members who had participated in published outputs, and to provide information about their relative contributions. As illustrated by the BIAS case study, they used an author order combining the magnitude of the contribution for the first three authors, followed by an alphabetical list for the remaining nine. The POLKU and LCEDN teams adopted similar practices.

LESSONS LEARNT

All the projects reported valuable lessons that they had drawn from the experience of managing international multidisciplinary research programmes and projects, summarised in Box 3.1, to reflect the different stages in the research process.

BOX 3.1 LESSONS LEARNT (ABOUT PROJECT MANAGEMENT)

Project Coordination, Funding and Funders

The funding context needs be thoroughly researched in advance of preparing a project proposal. Project coordinators should:

- Be completely familiar with funders' expectations in terms of application procedures, administrative structures, and the scheduling of research deliverables
- Secure sufficient financial support for the research from the funder and adequate administrative support from their own institutions
- Consider employing a professional administrator to support the principal investigator
- Be prepared to negotiate with bureaucracies that are often slow to respond to requests, for example to move funding between budget heads
- Ensure the proposal is feasible and operational and refrain from being overly ambitious in promising what cannot be delivered within the resources and timeframe of the project

Project Team Management

Effective leadership is critical in the management of international and multidisciplinary projects. Managers should:

- Have appropriate administrative and people skills
- Be able to negotiate the coordinators' time allocation and management within their institutions
- Create flexible and egalitarian management structures alongside centralised project coordination
- Be prepared to delegate tasks by enabling team members with the necessary expertise to take responsibility for sub-projects and work packages
- Be creative in managing teams, for example by identifying team members capable of fulfilling 'bridging' roles
- Build in training sessions and provide feedback and encouragement, especially for less experienced researchers
- Provide mentoring and in-project training for less experienced researchers and create opportunities for the development of their academic profiles through publications
- Ensure that opportunities are provided for team members to learn new skills, and that time is allocated at the start of the project for the team members to learn from each other's disciplinary backgrounds and research interests to avoid future potential misunderstandings
- Create mechanisms for intra-disciplinary communication within small teams, as well as cross-disciplinary communication in large teams
- Be prepared to spend more time than is covered by the funding to produce outputs
- Be adaptable and able to deal with changing circumstances, including those of team members

- Be realistic in the demands made on team members

Building International Multidisciplinary Research Teams

In international multidisciplinary research projects, care must be taken in selecting team members and partners with appropriate complementary skills and competencies. Project coordinators should:

- Select a mix of senior and less senior researchers who have multiple, complementary and compatible skills, including experience in working across cultures and disciplines
- Include members who have engaged in successful past collaborations
- Seek colleagues with a strong commitment to collaboration and who are open and flexible to a variety of research approaches
- Select a disciplinary mix appropriate to the research questions
- While remaining aware that cognate disciplines often work better together than disciplines with little in common, ensure that barriers to cross-disciplinary collaborations are addressed at the outset

Developing International Research Designs and Methods

Since the research questions addressed by international multidisciplinary projects are complex, and given that mixed and multi-method research designs are increasingly employed, project coordinators and team members should:

- Stay open to accepting disciplinary differences in international research, while seeking to achieve multi- or interdisciplinarity, and recognising how they play out in research design, methods and interpretation
- Create mechanisms to avoid 'methodological nationalism' by ensuring that cultural assumptions and concepts are scrutinised and accepted by the whole international team
- Given the variable use of terminology across countries and disciplines, take time to make concepts sufficiently 'capacious' to apply to different social contexts and to embed them in the research
- Be sensitive to the risk of imperialism when using the English language as the dominant language of discourse
- Select countries or other units of comparison on the basis of theory and not only practicality
- Be aware that national sub-samples, even when carefully chosen, are likely to vary because country populations differ

- Bear in mind that research instruments may not 'travel' and that they should be developed and tested in each context
- Aim to visit the main study sites, although this may not be possible or adequate to absorb policy and cultural aspects
- Draw upon and conduct analyses of existing international datasets and other material to contextualise primary data
- Build time into project schedules for delays in accessing datasets or completing fieldwork
- Consider the usefulness of simulation methods in the analysis of the effects of policy solutions adopted in different countries

Communication Strategies in Team Working

Given issues of distance, size and duration of projects, effective communication is vital in international multidisciplinary research. Project coordinators and team members should:

- Use a mix of modes for project communication including in-person meetings, synchronous online meetings and email discussion forums
- Schedule regular meetings of the whole team and of sub-groups and allow for non-scheduled communication, for example for 'translating' disciplinary terminology
- Produce actionable minutes and allow for extensive offline discussions to resolve disagreements
- Use visual tools in meetings to communicate ideas in a more 'research universal' and accessible way
- Bear in mind the informal effort that is necessary to make team working successful, for example by allocating time for sociability, especially at international team meetings

Engagement and Dissemination

Given that publicly-funded research needs to be accountable to society and policy relevant, in an online multi-media world, different modes of engagement and dissemination are required in international multidisciplinary collaborations. Project coordinators and team members should:

- Set up national and international advisory groups as a valuable source of expertise, experience and contacts with stakeholders
- Discuss disciplinary preferences and institutional requirements for particular research outputs at an early stage in a project

- Agree dissemination strategies at both national and international levels, and a timetable for implementing them
- Select a wide range of methods of dissemination, including an interactive web platform, internet and social media presence, electronic newsletters, blogs, press releases and participation in scientific conferences and other events
- Avoid spending undue time on single-country/discipline reports, and allow sufficient time for outputs that foreground the international comparative and multidisciplinary results of the research
- Agree publication strategies at the outset, decide whether journal outputs will be targeted at monodisciplinary journals or at multidisciplinary audiences, and resolve issues of authorship and author order on published work
- Bear in mind that publishing international multidisciplinary research in high-profile journals requires considerable time investment
- Ensure that the content of publication is aligned with the needs of target readers, and that dissemination strategies for policy audiences are tailored to particular national policy contexts.

PART II

CASE STUDIES

HOW TO READ ACROSS THE CASE STUDIES

Each of the ten contributions in Part II is structured according to the same broad subsections as in Chapters Two and Three to enable users of the guide to track information about the different stages in the process by reading the case studies both horizontally and vertically, and by referring to the tables in the chapters.

Project Descriptors

The [project acronym] Case Study

- Aims and Objectives
- Themes and Research Questions

The Research Process

- Meeting Funders' Requirements
- Building the Project Team
- Research Design and Methods
- Engagement and Dissemination

Lessons Learnt

4. Antimicrobial resistance in the real world (AMR)

John Connolly, Fiona Henriquez and Andrew Hursthouse

BOX 4.1 PROJECT DESCRIPTORS (AMR)

Duration: 2020–2023 (3 years)

Web Link: https://www.uws.ac.uk/research/research-institutes-centres-groups/infection-and-microbiology-research-group/antimicrobial-resistance-amr-in-the-environment/

Principal Investigator: Fiona Henriquez, Institute for Biomedical and Environmental Health Research, University of the West of Scotland, UK (biochemical parasitology)

Co-Investigators: University of the West of Scotland – John Connolly (public health policy); Andrew Hursthouse (environmental geochemistry)

Partners: Indian Institute of Technology Bombay – Suparna Mukherji (environmental science and engineering); Soumyo Mukherji (biomedical engineering)
   World Bank Water Resource Group – Anjali Suneel Parasnis, (biochemistry)

Funding Organisations: UKRI Natural Environment Research Council (NERC), award number NE/T012986/1, amount £793,290.46 for the UK and India; World Bank contribution in-kind.

THE AMR CASE STUDY

Antimicrobial resistance (AMR) has been recognised as a global public health challenge, posing one of the most serious health threats. The role of effluent from antimicrobial manufacturing is particularly pertinent in India, since it has been a major producer of antimicrobials in the global supply chain of the pharmaceutical industry, and is a scientifically appropriate place to study this global issue. This case study on 'Antimicrobial resistance in the real world' describes the different stages in a project funded under the Natural Environment Research Council's (NERC) programme on 'India–UK tackling AMR in the environment from antimicrobial manufacturing'. The case study tracks the research process from the application for funding and formation of the project team through the first two years of funding, concluding with the lessons learnt from working across disciplines and remotely during the COVID-19 pandemic.

The project was led by the University of the West of Scotland. NERC established a programme coordination team composed of principal investigators (PIs) from the projects that were part of the wider programme. The coordination team was set up to ensure that funded projects complement each other by enabling a partnership-based approach to knowledge exchange and by dovetailing impact activities. The Indian partners reported on their progress to their national authorities via the Department of Biotechnology at the Indian Ministry of Science and Technology.

Aims and Objectives

The overarching aims of the AMR project were to understand the impact of antibiotic pollution on environmental microbiology within representative wastewater treatment plants in the Mumbai region serving communities with a number of small pharmaceutical production facilities; to design effective measures for monitoring antibiotic levels; and to remove them from the waste if they are present. These aims were mediated through engagement with industry and policymakers to develop policies based on the data obtained from the project.

The project was divided into four work packages, each addressing specific objectives:

WP1: Comprehensive mapping for AMR

- To create an AMR map through geochemical and metagenomic analysis
- To determine the influence of anthropogenic factors on microbial communities through their characterisation

WP2: Novel, optical and electrochemical sensing

- To develop and validate sensors that can detect a variety of antibiotics in effluent at different concentrations to limit environmental exposure

WP3: Fate of antibiotics in common effluent treatment plants (CETPs) and novel photocatalytic technology

- To track the fate of antibiotics in CETPs and novel photocatalytic technology
- To develop and validate photocatalytic technologies for a variety of antibiotics and at different concentrations in the effluent of CETPs

WP4: Policy and regulatory cycles

- To consolidate industry and government relationships and create and develop effective strategies to regulate antibiotic waste in the environment

Themes and Research Questions

The project concentrated on AMR sensor technologies, water treatment and remediation, drawing on the Indian expertise in environmental microbiology, metagenomics and geochemistry, and on policy and industrial regulatory processes, using UK expertise to engage with the issue of AMR proliferation in the environment. The specific focus of the project described here was on the potential for increased AMR due to aggravation by pharmaceutical waste entering waterways.

Communication with CETP owners and pollution boards had identified a need for these enterprises to deal with wastewater antimicrobial contamination. Research had been sparse on the wider effects of AMR on other micro-organisms and on complex microbial communities. For these reasons, the central research question was how to inform the development of strategies to limit environmental contamination by antimicrobial waste from effluent treatment plants in pharmaceutical manufacturing/formulation units and CETPs.

THE RESEARCH PROCESS

The project's key objectives, the composition of the project team and the research methodology were determined essentially by the funder's requirements as laid down in the formal call for proposals. This section of the case study examines how the amount of funding awarded and the prior experience of the coordinating team shaped the ways in which the international dimension and the multidisciplinary elements were integrated into the project.

Meeting the Funder's Requirements

Like other UK research councils, a primary requirement for all NERC-funded programmes is that the projects selected will deliver ambitious research while demonstrating value for money. Ensuring adequate costing for the time of the principal and co-investigators and research fellows was a primary concern. A key requirement of the funder was that applicants should justify the costs of the infrastructures underpinning the scientific testing, which was an integral part of the research. The laboratory costs needed to cover complex microbial community analysis, including isolation and culture of micro-organisms, verification, determination of AMR genes and susceptibility testing. Metagenomics analysis was needed to sequence microbial communities. Geochemistry costs were associated with the preparation of samples and the purchase of preservation kits and general laboratory consumables. The funder allowed for the costs of network building, knowledge transfer events and stakeholder meetings.

UK research councils provide detailed guidance for applicants, and host institutions are experienced in advising and supporting project leaders throughout the process (NERC, 2021a; NERC, 2021b). Since the principal investigator (PI) had previously worked with NERC, the team did not have difficulty in justifying the costs; they found that the funding was adequate to enable the delivery of the project's goals. A strong degree of cushion in the budget resulted from savings on travel during the COVID-19 pandemic, and NERC was flexible in allowing virement between budget heads.

Building the Project Team

The project PI, Fiona Henriquez, was the natural lead for the study given her microbiology research connections with India, her experience with multidisciplinary research council-funded projects, and the fact that the science in the project takes its lead from microbiology. NERC had funded previous international AMR work at the University of the West of Scotland (UWS), involving collaboration between Fiona Henriquez and Andrew Hursthouse on projects with organisations in China, India, the United States and across Europe. John Connolly and Fiona Henriquez had also worked together previously. Cross-university research forum meetings had brought the team members together to identify common interests, which reinforced the relevance of their disciplinary backgrounds and their suitability to apply to NERC for the specific funding call to address AMR in the environment.

The problem of AMR is significant in many parts of the world. The selection of India as the partner country was determined by the severity of risks resulting from environmental waste in that country. The composition and dynamics of industry waste excretion to waterways from pharmaceutical industry sites in India is recognised internationally as a major problem, which has implications for public health, agriculture and aquatic species, among others. In addition, the regulatory regime for governing AMR in the environment within India is not evidence based, and the public are not aware and do not understand how they can contribute to decreasing the risk of the emergence of AMR in the environment.

The principal and co-investigators for the study raised the mix of disciplinary insights and expertise to an international level. In terms of disciplinary backgrounds, the Indian partners contributed their environmental and biomedical engineering expertise on sensor technologies, water treatment and remediation, while the UK coordinating team provided complementary knowledge and skills in environmental microbiology, metagenomics and geochemistry, as well as public policy and industrial regulatory processes. The partners, especially the biochemist from the World Bank, who were crucial in terms of their expertise, gave access to Indian policymakers and researchers at the Indian Institute of Technology Bombay, and to AMR sampling sites.

In some senses, the project was conceptually light, though problem driven. The team member with expertise in the social sciences was able to contribute to the project by introducing a major conceptual focus to frame the study from a 'One Health' perspective (Connolly, 2017). The World Health Organisation (WHO, 2017) defines One Health as 'an approach to designing and implementing programmes, policies, legislation and research in which multiple sectors communicate and work together to achieve better public health outcomes'. One Health has become synonymous with the need to tackle health threats on multidisciplinary, intersectoral and integrated bases by seeking to understand the 'causes of the causes' of health threats. One Health, as an approach to governance, relies on developing strong connections between human and animal health, the environment and public policy to propose a set of scientific and social solutions, which was the role assigned to the public health specialist.

The project team members respected each other's disciplinary contributions while acknowledging the need for constant nurturing of different disciplinary perspectives within a diverse team. The risk was that concepts such as One Health could be open to interpretation, and the potential existed for one discipline to overshadow others. For example, within One Health research, the social sciences have often been regarded as an 'add on' or treated in a tokenistic way (Lapinski et al., 2015). By embedding social sciences into the study from the outset, a positive trajectory was set for the project, ensuring that all team members understood the value of the social sciences in translating evidence to multiple audiences, including policy stakeholders.

The skill sets of research fellows in the project were carefully planned. Three fellows were appointed. As postdoctoral researchers, they brought expertise in public health, microbiology and environmental science, together with prior knowledge and experience of working across disciplinary boundaries. They were supported through training and knowledge exchange events within the project organised by the investigators in the form of face-to-face meetings and video calls. Mentoring processes formed part of the work on an ongoing basis to ensure effective dialogue across the work packages. Learning a new academic language, in terms of scientific and social scientific terminology shared between research fellows who came from different disciplinary backgrounds, supported their career development.

Understanding the social, cultural and political context of India was crucial not only for accessing those in authority within government and industry but also for ensuring that researchers working at UWS and at the Indian Institute of Technology in Bombay were on the 'same page' when it came to implementing sampling requirements, project deliverables and timelines. Although English was the second language of the Indian project partners, team members were able to communicate effectively in English, both orally and in writing.

Agreement was reached on the research questions due to the respective knowledge associated with the partners' different disciplinary lenses on the problem of AMR in the environment. Since antimicrobial resistance (AMR) represents a major global health threat, as well as a major hazard to sustainable economic development and national security, it was vital to align to current policy development and implementation to alleviate a potential crisis (Cameron et al., 2022). The research team considered, for example, whether drivers of antibiotic resistance have already accumulated in the past, and whether they can be controlled in the future.

By bringing together their different areas of expertise and knowledge, team members were also able to address questions about the commercial determinants of health relating to the prevalence of environmental AMR that had not previously received sufficient attention within global regulatory frameworks in investigations of commercial (pharmaceutical) determinants of health, or the ways in which regulatory policy needed to be adapted in the context of AMR (Rodgers et al., 2019). Regular bilateral communication, both face-to-face and remotely, and scheduled project meetings provided opportunities to discuss conceptual and technical issues, and kept team members aware of the importance of the policy implications of their work packages. The core team members went to great efforts to ensure that partners were working to the same schedule for delivering their research, and that the work packages were phased in such a way as to deliver maximum impact.

Team members were made aware that the study would, by its very nature, be rather broad in scope when addressing such a massive area as the risks posed by AMR. Their varied experience meant they had confidence, in this inter-disciplinary study, that 'knowing a lot about a little' was more desirable than 'knowing a little about a lot'. This approach allowed them to have a degree of intellectual and practical flexibility and resilience when dealing with AMR as a multifaceted problem, as opposed to being too focussed or too 'academically set in their ways'.

Research Design and Methods

The multidisciplinary research teams from the UK and India were tasked with assessing the life cycle of pharmaceutical wastewater through analysis of chemical and AMR profiling surrounding small to medium pharmaceutical plants that discharge waste into CETPs. The research design and methods emerged from experiential learning across both teams. Discussion of potential sampling areas centred on local geography in Mumbai. Wastewater treatment plants were considered as natural resources given their receipt of waste from pharmaceuticals and drainage into the local environment. In short, the team deployed a targeted sampling campaign to provide samples likely to be of value rather than conducting a systematic spatial survey. The feasibility of the approach and research design was determined largely by the funder's requirements.

Because the coordinating team had already collaborated with colleagues at the Indian Institute of Technology Bombay (IITB), who had themselves worked in research institutes within the UK, team members shared an under-standing of ethical issues, a primary concern of UK research councils. Ethical approval was sought jointly between the UWS and IITB ethics committees. Applications were scrutinised by internal reviewers at both institutions. No problems arose in the process of seeking ethical approval. The combination of research expertise allowed the project team to navigate the Indian regulatory system efficiently.

As the lead institution, the UWS dealt with data protection, permissions, intellectual property, procurement and confidentiality, avoiding the need to negotiate within different legislatures. In this project, the biological material consisted of water containing micro-organisms from the sampling sites. UWS had import licences in place to enable the receipt of samples in the UK. Due to the sensitive nature of the work and the need to achieve 'buy-in' from industry, permissions to sample had to be sought through the facilitation of pollution control boards and the World Bank's Water Resource Group.

Low-cost sensors were deployed to detect what residues are present in the waste and to identify affordable photocatalytic technology allowing the residues to be removed before the effluent is discharged into the environment. Validation of these technologies was conducted under laboratory conditions using site samples and maintaining the chemical and microbial profile obtained from the mapping work.

UWS managed all the work packages (WPs) and collaborated with the Indian partners throughout the process. The WPs were not standalone; they were conducted simultaneously except for WP4. Because they were linked with each other, when the scientific evidence emerged from WPs 1–3, providing understanding of what needed to be fed into the science communication and policy activities, the researchers involved in WP4 responded by drawing out the policy implications and by conducting research involving partners from the World Bank's Water Resource Group. This process required clear communication and consistent engagement by the project lead and coordinators to ensure that the WPs fed into each other, consistency was maintained and 'stop and starts' were minimised within the study. This task involved constant review of the aims and re-enforcement of the message linking the WPs.

Engagement and Dissemination

By involving multiple academics in looking at problems from different perspectives, the research team undertook internal validation of the project throughout the process to ensure a shared understanding and ongoing enhancement of the contribution that it was making to the NERC programme. The opportunity to address many development goals, including aspects of the UN Sustainable Development Goals, was intrinsically motivating and made researchers feel that they were doing their moral duty to improve planetary health and society. The combination of research expertise and mutual understanding stimulated creativity and innovation, for example in finding ways of transferring samples during the pandemic.

External validation was also undertaken by sharing the findings with other grant holders through the NERC India–UK AMR programme coordination team. The establishment of the team was proposed by the funder and consisted of the PIs of the projects selected. A series of meetings took place between the five PIs to identify and explore how the projects could manage and coalesce the data produced by the networks to create real impact in a particular field. Funding was made available by NERC for this work, and a project coordinator was recruited in addition to extra support to standardise methods and promote knowledge exchange. Funds were ringfenced to create an early career researcher network to encourage collaboration between them and across disciplines when individual projects have been completed.

The research involved engagement with the Indian pharmaceutical industry to study the AMR production 'metabolism' within a complex interplay of environmental geochemical and microbiological processes, to refine policy and improve regulatory control in pharmaceutical waste management. Due to the sensitive issues surrounding the project, engagement with regulatory bodies and industry was critical. The data and technology were utilised by the project team alongside the work with the World Bank to influence the creation of policies that work for all stakeholders, including local communities and the environment, in reducing the impact of antimicrobial waste in the environment. The World Bank, particularly through its 2030 Water Resource Group, worked closely with the UK social scientist in developing the public health aspects of the study. The Indian project partners also had longstanding relationships with the group and were alerted to their needs through invitations to project discussions and engagement in team meetings.

Reporting and dissemination of findings was a co-production process. Since the core UWS team members had considerable experience of working cross-culturally and internationally, they were mindful of the legacy of UK imperialism. This challenge was overcome by working closely with a locally engaged research team, World Bank colleagues and members of local pollution boards. The core team members sought to ensure that Indian stakeholders were fully integrated in the research process, for example by avoiding being top down and exhibiting behaviours that could be perceived as UK researchers displaying any sense of superiority. They made sure that Indian partners led project meetings on a regular basis and were able to drive aspects of the research agenda. The Indian partners were well networked with policy and pharmaceutical companies, and they acted as facilitators in terms of language and access to stakeholders.

The project funders, as well as the institutional award holders at UWS and IITB, were required to publish their findings in international high-impact journals. The team agreed from the outset that the authorship of papers would generally be managed, as far as appropriate, to benefit the interests of the research fellows, who were early career researchers recruited specifically to work on the project. The challenge was agreeing which journals to target. The study cut across health security and regulatory policy, environmental science and health, public health, microbiology and biomedical engineering. The selection of journals led to discussions and, at times, to a degree of indecision in the early stages of the project as to which interdisciplinary and/or single-discipline journals to aim for on the basis of the most appropriate readership and journal visibility in terms of audience and reach.

The matter of journal metrics and impact factors exercised researchers in both the UK and India. Collective agreement had been reached between the team members, following discussions when applying for NERC funding. The agreement emerged through a process of co-production of the pathways to impact with project partners to ensure that each impact stream resulted from the respective work packages. The team had decided that the key principle would be to focus on the most appropriate journal for reaching academic audiences. Impact factors were a secondary concern, although team members acknowledged that the most appropriate journal and impact factors can often go hand in hand. Here, as in other areas, the fact that the Indian partners were familiar with the UK research context was an advantage in working collaboratively to achieve impact.

BOX 4.2 LESSONS LEARNT (AMR)

The AMR case studies afford a valuable illustration of how researchers from natural and social science disciplines can collaborate successfully across different cultures in response to global challenges in managing a project funded by a national research council.

- Managing international multidisciplinary research projects requires strong leadership and administrative skills, as well as academic credibility and support from the host institutions.
- Project leaders need to be familiar with the procedures of funders and able to meet their aims, objectives and requirements in terms of budget and time frames, content, process and outputs.
- If managed effectively, the process of addressing problems from different disciplinary and cultural perspectives can engender a sense of achievement by enabling the research team to get to the root of the problems and provide evidence-based solutions.
- The power of learning comes to the fore when listening and engaging with researchers to address topics through different disciplinary lenses, which can be exciting and enriching for academic life.
- In a context where multidisciplinary research is heavily promoted by research funders, and team members are committed to an interdisciplinary approach, academics need to put in place strategies for navigating issues around identity crises, external disruptions, potential academic credibility issues and disciplinary boundaries.
- The challenges of working with researchers in different disciplines and cultures can be eased if research coordinators have prior acquaintance with project partners and are able to communicate and work effectively with them.
- Team members need to be sensitive to different cultural codes and avoid any sense of research imperialism, especially when working with governmental actors and with industry in particular countries.

- As not all members of the team are at the same career stage or have the same amount of experience of multidisciplinary international research, it is important for the project lead to motivate everyone to make adequate contributions, while dealing with any crises of confidence that may arise.
- Involving early career researchers in international multidisciplinary research projects is an excellent way to train them through practical experience.
- Project managers must find ways of ensuring that the research fellows work as a team and understand the importance of communication with one another, with the study leads/coordinators, and with partners from different disciplines and cultures.
- Project managers must deal with the operational problems of working to the same schedule for delivering their research, especially when a study relies on analyses being conducted at particular phases, and they have competing demands on their time.
- Project administrators must remain alert to the issues of scheduling meetings across time zones, accommodating holidays, festivals and climate issues, for example by avoiding research trips to India at extremely hot times in the year.
- When travel restrictions are in place, alternative arrangements need to be made for partners to foster social contacts across research teams, to embed researchers in the main sites for the study, and to remain committed to policy and cultural dimensions in the project.
- Efforts must be made to agree collectively on dissemination strategies, the type of journals to which research papers should be submitted and the requirements of the researchers' own institutions.

REFERENCES

Cameron, A., Esiovwa, R., Connolly, J., Hursthouse, A., & Henriquez, F. (2022). Antimicrobial resistance as a global health threat: The need to learn lessons from the COVID-19 pandemic, *Global Policy, 13.* DOI: 10.1111/1758-5899.13049

Connolly, J. (2017). Governing towards 'One Health': Establishing knowledge integration in global health security governance. *Global policy, 8*(4), 483–494. DOI: 10.1111/1758-5899.12505

Lapinski, M. K., Funk, J. A., & Moccia, L. T. (2015). Recommendations for the role of social science research in One Health. *Social Science & Medicine, 129,* 51–60. DOI: 10.1016/j.socscimed.2014.09.048 [Epub 2014 Sep 28. PMID: 25311785]

Natural Environment Research Council (NERC). (2021a). *Funding for international collaborations.* https://www.ukri.org/councils/nerc/guidance-for-applicants/types -of-funding-we-offer/

Natural Environment Research Council (NERC). (2021b). *Handbooks, guidance and forms*. https://www.ukri.org/councils/nerc/guidance-for-applicants/handbooks -guidance-and-forms/

Rodgers, K., McLellan, I., Peshkur, T., Williams, R., Tonner, R., Hursthouse, A. S., ... & Henriquez, F. L. (2019). Can the legacy of industrial pollution influence antimicrobial resistance in estuarine sediments? *Environmental Chemistry Letters*, *17*(2), 595–607. DOI:10.1007/s10311-018-0791-y

World Health Organisation (WHO). (2017, 21 September). *One Health. Q&A*. https:// www.who.int/news-room/q-a-detail/one-health

5. Responsible AI for labour market equality (BIAS)

Alla Konnikov, Irina Rets, Karen D. Hughes, Jabir Alshehabi Al-Ani, Nicole Denier, Lei Ding, Shenggang Hu, Yang Hu, Bei Jiang, Linglong Kong, Monideepa Tarafdar and Dengdeng Yu

---

BOX 5.1 PROJECT DESCRIPTORS (BIAS)

Duration: 1 February 2020–30 July 2023 (3.5 years)

Web Link: https://www.lancaster.ac.uk/lums/research/areas-of-expertise/centre-for-technological-futures/responsible-ai-for-labour-market-equality/

Principal Investigators: Linglong Kong, University of Alberta, Canada (mathematical & statistical sciences); Monideepa Tarafdar, University of Massachusetts Amherst/Lancaster University, UK (management science)

Co-Investigators: University of Alberta, Canada – Nicole Denier (sociology); Karen D. Hughes (sociology & business); Bei Jiang (mathematical & statistical sciences)
   University of Essex, UK – Hongsheng Dai (mathematical sciences); Berthold Lausen (mathematical sciences)
   Lancaster University, UK – Yang Hu (sociology); Bran Knowles (computing & communications)

Postdoctoral Fellows and Graduate Students: University of Alberta, Canada – Lei Ding (mathematical & statistical sciences); Wenxing Guo (mathematical & statistical sciences); Alla Konnikov (sociology); Meichen Liu (mathematical & statistical sciences); Jinhan Xie (mathematical & statistical sciences)
   University of Essex, UK – Jabir Alshehabi Al-Ani (mathematical scienc-

es); Shenggang Hu, (mathematical sciences)
  Lancaster University, UK – Irina Rets (management science)
  University of Texas at Artlington, US – Dengdeng Yu (mathematics)

Funding Organisations: Economic and Social Research Council (ESRC) and Social Sciences and Humanities Research Council of Canada (SSHRC), funding programme Canada-UK Artificial Intelligence Initiative: Building competitive and resilient economies through responsible AI; award number ES/T012382/1, amount £508,000 and $460,000 (CDN).

THE BIAS CASE STUDY

The BIAS case study describes the aims and objectives of the 'BIAS: Responsible AI for labour market equality' project, the research process, and the lessons learned at the mid-way point of the project. It draws on two main sources of information: interviews conducted internally with six founding members of the project in August 2021, and a survey of the full team that was conducted in September 2021 to gather information on the backgrounds, perspectives, and experiences of all team members who were currently active in the project. Konnikov, Rets and Hughes led the study conceptualisation, instrument design, data analysis and writing-up activities. Konnikov and Rets led on the data collection and administration of the internal interviews and the survey with the other project team members. The remaining authors (in alphabetical order) contributed to the case study as it developed; they read, edited and approved the final text of the case study.

Aims and Objectives

An overarching aim of the BIAS project was to ensure a genuinely interdisciplinary approach. BIAS had two primary aims:

- To refine existing understandings of AI-driven bias, using an interdisciplinary, cross-national, multi-stakeholder approach
- To develop 'responsible AI' that can potentially mitigate gender and ethnic biases in algorithmic labour markets, using Canada and the UK as test sites

Themes and Research Questions

BIAS is an international interdisciplinary project that seeks to understand the role of artificial intelligence (AI) in reproducing gender and ethnic biases in labour market processes, such as job postings and hiring, that are increasingly digitalised. The project was motivated by the 'digital turn' in contemporary labour markets and growing concerns over the role of AI in reproducing and exacerbating market inequalities. The BIAS project speaks directly to several themes and national priority agendas in Canada and the UK, including the rise of AI and gender and racial disparities in hiring, pay gaps and innovative practices, since both countries embrace digital transformations as part of their economic and industrial strategies.

The project was designed to generate theoretical, empirical, applied and policy-related contributions by examining four research questions:

1. What are the sources and dimensions of gender and ethnic bias in labour market processes?
2. How do different parties in the labour market perceive and respond to bias, and how do biases lead to labour market inequalities?
3. How are biases currently reproduced in AI algorithms and through AI human interactions?
4. What approaches and techniques can be used to minimise and mitigate such biases?

THE RESEARCH PROCESS

The project's key objectives, research design and team composition were shaped by the funders' requirements in the formal call for proposals, and by the expertise and interests of the founding team members. This case study examines the decisions that were taken and the range of factors that came into play as the project evolved, focussing on the international and disciplinary dimensions of the study.

Meeting Funders' Requirements

The call for proposals from the Canada-UK Artificial Intelligence Initiative played an important role in shaping the aims and objectives of the project. A central goal of the initiative was to spark more interdisciplinary research on AI to aid the development of more inclusive and responsible AI technologies. Three requirements in the call determined the project design and objectives from the outset, including: the involvement of at least two distinct research domains; the participation of researchers from Canada and the UK; and an explicit focus on the development of 'responsible AI'.

Equally important for shaping the project were the expertise and interests of the founding project team. While topics such as smart cities, healthcare, and democratic governance were highlighted in the call for proposals, the issue of labour markets received only a brief mention. Yet, the social science team members had strong interests in labour markets and human resource management, and the growing role of AI in reproducing gender and ethnic bias. The team members in the mathematical and computational sciences were seeking new 'areas of application' for their research, and the issue of gender and racial bias seemed interesting and challenging.

The grant proposal was well received, and was one of ten projects funded under the initiative (8.8% success rate). Funding came from the two national councils, in roughly equivalent amounts, with sufficient funds to cover project costs, including postdoctoral and student funding, data and software. Institutions in both countries also provided basic support through technology infrastructure, office space and some administrative assistance.

Building the Project Team

While the funding call shaped the team composition, with respect to disciplinary and national location, equally important were pre-existing professional relationships developed through conferences and events, and from working at the same institution. Some connections went back many years, to graduate school colleagues. Others were more recent: for example, colleagues meeting at an event organised by their university to spark interdisciplinary research.

In the initial stage of the project, the team was assembled at two UK universities where faculty members had prior connections (Lancaster and Essex). While they shared their interests in AI, they were working in distinct, albeit inter-related, disciplines, including management science and information systems, sociology, computing and communications, mathematical sciences and computational statistics. One of the UK team members then contacted a colleague in Canada (Alberta) to gauge interest in a collaboration. A Canadian team was assembled quickly across three disciplines: mathematical sciences and computational statistics, sociology, and organisational studies. While some prior connections existed within each disciplinary field, the recruitment process required actively seeking out individuals with the requisite mix of disciplinary knowledge, experience and interests.

The final founding team included nine researchers representing two countries, three universities, and five different disciplines. Together they had educational and work experiences spanning six countries: Canada, China, Germany, India, the UK and the United States. Once funding was awarded, the project team expanded further with the hiring of postdoctoral research fellows and graduate students as research assistants.

Project leadership was provided by two principal investigators, one in each country: Monideepa Tarafdar in the UK and Linglong Kong in Canada. The team did not employ a professional project manager, but a small amount of administrative support was provided through Lancaster University. Much of the academic and collaborative work was accomplished through a 'self-managing team' approach with several team members fulfilling an important 'bridging' role. The project consisted of 18 researchers at its inception, though several graduate researchers ceased to be involved when they completed their formal programmes. It also included an advisory board of ten experts from industry and academia who provided advice and support as needed, and attended an annual meeting with all team members.

Beyond the requisite mix of disciplinary skills and backgrounds, one additional characteristic that proved to be important was an 'interdisciplinary mindset', together with interdisciplinary experience from past projects, or an active interest in related disciplines. Confirming the importance of this characteristic, the internal survey of team members found that 30.7% had 'significant' interdisciplinary experience and 46.1% had 'some' experience; 23.1% had no interdisciplinary experience. Research shows that an interdisciplinary background supports an increased appreciation of how different approaches, concepts and methods can produce novel insights. It also helps in understanding the challenges that arise when working across disciplinary boundaries, and how to resolve them productively (Fiore et al., 2008).

Research Design and Methods

The BIAS project utilises a new model of international interdisciplinary AI research that involves mixed/multi-method, co-produced AI research. The project was deliberately comparative and interdisciplinary. It used two interconnected work packages (WPs) to bring together different disciplines to pool national data and analytic techniques, using labour force and job platform data; to undertake qualitative interviews with platform participants at the organisational and individual level; to model, simulate and refine understandings of bias; and to develop and test AI designed to mitigate the biases detected. WP1 involved an algorithmic-oriented examination of bias, including data mining to detect bias, and to test new AI algorithms for bias mitigation. WP2 adopted a multi-stakeholder perspective (employer, employee, industry) and qualitative investigations to understand AI use in processes of job advertising, screening and hiring.

Qualitative research studies with recruitment companies and employers were undertaken firstly in the UK and then in Canada in 2022, using a complementary research design. Data collection and engagement with jobseekers were planned for the final year of the project, as were knowledge exchange activities with policy researchers, developers and computer scientists, and organisations involved in regulating the use of AI.

From the outset, work tasks were divided across smaller intra-disciplinary units, enabling collaboration to take place both within and between these smaller units, and then with the larger team. Results from the internal survey confirmed the effectiveness of this strategy, with the highest level of satisfaction for team members being associated with intra-disciplinary communication within the small teams. One of the investigators described working in these teams as particularly important for maintaining conceptual and methodological rigour in all disciplines: '... we meet in the bigger group for the bigger picture, but we also need to meet in the smaller groups, because each discipline has to have their own excellence there as well.'

The aim of ensuring that the project would have a genuinely interdisciplinary approach had a number of implications for the research processes and for the professional development of the scholars involved. A commonly held view in the project team was that the absence of any one of the project's constituent disciplines would constrain the whole process. Although in part a requirement of the grant, the project's interdisciplinary design enabled a more comprehensive and refined account of a complex problem such as bias, which can be understood at different levels (individual, cultural, personal, organisational, or structural), and as action or outcome. The involvement of diverse disciplines ensured the necessary theorisation and contextualisation for the research problem, supported by the knowledge exchange and interdependence between the intra-disciplinary teams.

Reaching agreement in interdisciplinary work can often pose challenges, a point that was highlighted in the interviews with team members. A particular example concerned the definition and operationalisation of the central concept of the project: 'bias'. In early meetings, it became evident that different disciplines defined, understood, and operationalised bias in different ways. One investigator illustrated the challenge involved: '... at the beginning, we actually struggled a lot. We asked the sociology and the management team to define bias. And for our AI team, we asked the same question. And we couldn't match each other, even in the same team, each definition was different.' To reach agreement on the conceptual definition of bias, the team conducted an exercise where each investigator wrote down their own definition of bias and then shared it with the rest of the team. This exercise enabled the whole team to gain a better understanding of different definitions and provided a starting point for future discussions.

In team meetings, the aim was not to achieve 'sameness' by coming up with one overarching understanding of bias, but rather to gain a better understanding of the ways in which bias was conceptualised and studied in each discipline (Fiore et al., 2008). This approach highlighted the dynamic nature of interdisciplinary knowledge exchange. The initial understanding of the main concepts in the research underwent transformations resulting from the contributions of each discipline. Remaining open to the incorporation of different views about the conceptual understanding of the phenomena of interest helped to bridge, rather than resolve, the conceptual interdisciplinary differences.

The meetings offered a platform for dialogue; they helped team members get to know one another, and to learn about the concepts, meanings and methodologies in different disciplines. To facilitate the process of reaching agreement on conceptual and methodological issues, team members developed the following strategies: learning about conceptual differences; embracing conceptual differences; and enabling conceptual and methodological understandings to evolve and change over time. The small intra-disciplinary meetings facilitated in-depth, rigorous discussion of concepts, while the small interdisciplinary meetings created conceptual bridges between the teams.

The interdisciplinarity of the research design also had implications for the innovative use of research methodologies. Since each project discipline was grounded in particular epistemologies, the mix of disciplines allowed for the integration of the methods associated with each discipline by drawing on their individual strengths (Fiore et al., 2008). Several team members felt that their research inquiries were expanded by the multidisciplinary methodologies embraced in the project. As one team member noted, instead of 'waiting for the next five–ten years' to import the methods from other fields into their analysis, the interdisciplinary collaboration meant that, together, the team was 'innovating for the next round of methods, in a fast-breaking way'.

The need to prevent potential misunderstandings increased interdependence between the different intra-disciplinary teams. They used visual tools, such as pictures, graphs and figures, offering a universal language that scholars from the different disciplines could all understand, to summarise ideas and concepts, and translate disciplinary terminology in a more 'research universal' and accessible way. Interdependence was developed between the different intra-disciplinary teams by creating shared tasks and fostering adaptivity to change, as the project's conceptualisations and methodologies evolved over time.

Some team members explained how what they initially envisioned as the primarily independent work of intra-disciplinary teams, with occasional collaboration, turned out differently as the project progressed. The complexity involved in conceptualising and operationalising bias sparked more frequent exchange. For example, the computational team found that, by collaborating closely with the sociology team, they were able to solidify concepts and methods, and make their analysis more meaningful. This process informed work on a paper where the sociology team took the lead in developing a list of gender-related words in job advertisements, which the computing team then used to refine their approach to gender bias mitigation (Ding et al., 2021; Hu et al., 2022). As explained by a computing team member: 'Although we could, probably, rely on common sense, we don't have to in this project. We can actually use input from the experts from other disciplines that can help us do a better job with finding the gender words, which will allow us to define gender bias more precisely.'

The team members highlighted two major approaches to interdisciplinary collaboration that were embraced as a part of the team culture in designing the research: openness towards various intellectual and methodological traditions; and 'flat', egalitarian divisions of labour within the team. Several strategies to support cross-disciplinary communication also emerged.

Team members described openness as an approach that facilitated greater flexibility, acceptance and dialogue between participants trained in different disciplines, explained by one team member as a constant 'willingness to be out of one's comfort zone'. Pairing an openness to diverse intellectual interests and goals with a degree of compromise was an essential strategy in a complex interdisciplinary and international project. As observed by another team member: 'We all had to carve out and include and exclude bits of our interests to make this collaboration work.'

This culture of flexibility and openness shaped the division of labour within the team, revealing a particularly egalitarian approach. Despite including academics of various ranks and with diverse specialties, the team's organisational and communication structures remained flat. Close attention was paid to members' unique interests and capabilities in assigning tasks and responsibilities. The internal survey with team members highlighted how a flexible division of labour had helped them to engage in activities that they felt most passionate about and most capable of pursuing. Team members also stressed the evolving nature of their roles over time, as some initial roles were revised and adjusted. One example of this adjustment was the evolving 'bridging' role played by team members who attended meetings of multiple intra-disciplinary teams and helped to facilitate the connections between them.

Over time, team members developed a combination of formal and informal communication strategies to promote understanding of specific issues and facilitate the process of reaching agreement. Ongoing internal communication practices included monthly interdisciplinary meetings with all team members present, and weekly and bi-weekly intra- and inter-disciplinary meetings of smaller teams working on similar tasks (Tarafdar & Davison, 2018). Larger team meetings offered a valuable platform for resolving ambiguities and misunderstandings, and for reaching consensus on work packages and processes. Virtual meeting technologies were especially helpful not only during the pandemic, but also for building connections within the team in the early stages, given the physical distance between the institutions involved in the project.

Within a large, interdisciplinary and international team, where collaboration unfolds remotely and involves a significant portion of email correspondence, the potential for misunderstanding is high, and the risks of accumulating problems are considerable. The team members consistently emphasised how the meetings could be used to resolve issues in a timely manner and improve the understanding of each other's perspectives. Smaller group meetings, typically intra-disciplinary, were rated in the survey as particularly effective for knowledge exchange and for clarifying the concepts and operationalisations practised in each discipline. Team members ranked the small group meetings as a top communication strategy and referred to them as the main facilitators of the working process. Flexible on-demand meetings were the second most highly-rated communication strategy. In the words of one team member, they 'expedited the work rhythm and cut the long chain of formalities'.

In addition to the positive roles of openness and the intra- and interdisciplinary meetings, team members also used other strategies to minimise misunderstanding and the mistranslation of concepts across disciplines. Each discipline used a different 'language' (terminology) that had to be 'translated' across the teams (Monteiro & Keating, 2009). According to one team member: 'We had to explain things, not using our own language. We had to explain things to make sure that a layperson can understand it.' Some team members took on responsibility for bridging the communication gap between the small inter- and intra-disciplinary group meetings by actively translating the concepts. These roles were naturally taken by the members of the team who 'fall in between the gaps that cover slightly different areas' and have a solid understanding of the concepts and methods used in different disciplines.

With respect to the professional development of the scholars involved in the project, interdisciplinarity encouraged each researcher to perceive the familiar research methods that they commonly used in a new light. In the internal survey, team members ranked the development of new skills and new ways of intellectual thinking through interdisciplinary work as highly impactful for their career advancement. As one team member explained: 'I'm a quantitative sociologist. It's [the approach used in another discipline] not something entirely new to me, but I started thinking more broadly about using, for instance, text as the data, rather than people. So, expanding horizons.'

For early career researchers, interdisciplinary approaches may have positive and negative implications. Since they first need to gain sufficient expertise in their own disciplines, being part of an interdisciplinary project may pose a career risk. Outcomes and publication in larger projects may also take more time to achieve. More positively, involvement in an interdisciplinary project teaches researchers to be aware that big research problems cannot be solved within one discipline. It can also help them to develop skills in communicating with different people and to respect other disciplines, while sparking new ideas that may contribute to future collaborations. As noted by one team member: 'I learned a lot from others in the project. ... that reflects two things: firstly, we have made considerable intellectual headway in our thinking about the area, we're already breaking into new ground, thinking about new projects; and secondly, we work so well together.'

Engagement and Dissemination

The BIAS project aims to engage with a number of stakeholders through ongoing discussion, exchange, and knowledge sharing. Key stakeholders include public and private sector employers using AI for human resource management; jobseekers and employees' encountering AI in their working lives; developers, computer scientists and technicians involved in the design, testing and maintenance of algorithms and job platforms; organisations regulating the use of AI; academic and policy researchers working on related issues; and the general public who are interested in and experiencing digital transformations in society.

In the initial stages of the project, stakeholder engagement was intentionally limited to allow for a strong internal focus while team members laid the necessary conceptual and methodological groundwork for the project. In 2020, soon after the project was launched, all working relationships moved to a remote format. The team communicated entirely via digital tools (email, Zoom, Google docs) both internally and with the organisations that they were studying. Valuable engagement took place with the advisory board, both on an individual basis with team members reaching out for advice or suggestions, and through a first annual meeting in 2020, which was held online. During the event, the team members presented preliminary results and work-in-progress, and received helpful feedback from the advisory board. A similar event was planned for June 2022.

Engagement with other stakeholders involved working with recruitment companies and employers in both countries. Data collection and engagement with jobseekers were scheduled for the final year of the project, together with conference presentations, publications, and other knowledge dissemination activities to enable active engagement with academic and policy researchers, developers and computer scientists, and organisations involved in regulating the use of AI.

Decisions about publications and other intellectual outputs from the project also reflected the team's philosophy, involving discussion of what would be of most benefit to individual team members. In the internal survey, all team members rated the anticipated publication outcomes highly, suggesting a positive evaluation of the team's egalitarian approach. In some specialist fields, publications in monodisciplinary journals are the primary outlets recognised by institutions, and interdisciplinary journals are considered to be less prestigious. While there are exceptions, such as the journal *Nature*, such outlets are not an obvious choice for management, sociology or computer science scholars. The team accepted that targeting such 'higher risk, higher return' journals would require prolonged investment, but could also result in a more significant intellectual contribution to interdisciplinarity.

BOX 5.2 LESSONS LEARNT (BIAS)

By reflecting upon the objectives of the BIAS project, the strategies developed for overcoming challenges, and the emerging implications at an early stage in the research process, the project team identified some concrete 'lessons learnt' that could be applied more widely to the management of international multidisciplinary research projects.

- Interdisciplinary project teams are more easily formed when there are pre-existing professional relationships developed through conferences, professional events, and working at the same institution.
- Research institutions and funders can enhance the capacity for interdisciplinary research through structural supports that connect researchers across different disciplines, faculties and across countries: for example, by including joint multidisciplinary training events within or between universities, or through the formation of research centres and research theme groups involving academics who are working on similar (broad) issues but in different disciplines and cultural settings.
- Effective teams require a diverse mixture of skills, disciplinary orientations and training, as well as an 'interdisciplinary mindset' and an openness to learning.
- Specific tasks should be distributed among team members with appropriate skill sets to ensure that their contributions fit into the big picture and match the original grant proposal.
- Reaching agreement in interdisciplinary projects poses challenges that can be resolved by dividing work tasks across smaller intra-disciplinary units, and allowing collaboration with and between smaller units and the larger team.
- Intellectual and administrative coordination through a 'super bridger' can help to ensure the integration of results, to enable small intra-disciplinary teams to stay informed about each other's findings, to generate pathways for additional collaborations and provide valuable project management support for the principal investigators.
- Interdisciplinary research can bolster methodological development through rigour and the innovative use of research methodologies, and visual tools can help to 'translate' across disciplinary vocabularies and avoid potential misunderstandings.

- An egalitarian 'flat' approach to the division of labour can be a successful collaboration strategy, provided that an equitable balance is struck between empowering the project members to improve and innovate at their own pace and ensure the process remains manageable.
- Openness and flexibility are important in establishing acceptance and dialogue between researchers belonging to different disciplines, particularly when deciding on intellectual outputs from the project.
- In international projects that involve researchers based in different countries, remote meetings with synchronous communication (Teams, Zoom, Skype) offer an effective means of maintaining 'visibility' and a high level of engagement among the team members, while also preventing research-related misunderstandings and roadblocks.
- Regular communication within and across sub-projects or work packages can include monthly whole-team multidisciplinary meetings, as well as bi-weekly intra- and inter-disciplinary meetings of smaller teams working on similar tasks.
- Both planned and unplanned communication are important in keeping immediate tasks and broader project goals on track, and in responding to unforeseen issues that are common in interdisciplinary work that is focussed on evolving concepts and methods.
- Frank and open discussions need to take place at an early stage about what different team members want to get out of the project, including the negotiation of preferences associated with project disciplines for different research outputs.
- Project managers need to remain attentive to the training needs of early career researchers associated with the project, and to assist them in building a publication portfolio.

REFERENCES

Ding, L., Yu, D., Xie, J., Guo, W., Hu, S., Liu, M., Kong, L., Dai, H., Bao, Y. & Jiang, B. (2021). Word embeddings via causal inference: Gender bias reducing and semantic information preserving. arXiv preprint arXiv:2112.05194.

Fiore, S. M., Hoffman, R. R., & Salas, E. (2008). Learning and performance across disciplines: An epilogue for moving multidisciplinary research toward an interdisciplinary science of expertise. *Military Psychology, 20*(sup1), S155-S170. DOI: 10.1080/08995600701804939

Hu, S., Alshehabi Al-Ani, J., Hughes, K. D., Denier, N., Konnikov, A., Ding, L., Xie, J., Hu, Y., Tarafdar, M., Jiang, B., Kong, L., & Dai, H. (2022). Balancing gender bias in job advertisements with text-level bias mitigation. *Frontiers in Big Data.* DOI: 10.3389/fdata.2022.805713

Monteiro, M. & Keating, E. (2009). Managing misunderstandings: The role of language in interdisciplinary scientific collaboration. *Science Communication, 31*(1), 6-28. DOI: 10.1177/1075547008330922

Tarafdar, M. & Davison, R. M. (2018). Research in information systems: Intra-disciplinary and inter-disciplinary approaches. *Journal of the Association for Information Systems, 19*(6), 523-551. Available at: https://aisel.aisnet.org/jais/vol19/iss6/2

6. The Bloomsbury SET: science, economics, technology (B–SET)

Aygen Kurt-Dickson

BOX 6.1 PROJECT DESCRIPTORS (B–SET)

Duration: 1 April 2018–31 March 2021 (3 years, plus 3 months no-cost extension)

Web link: https://bloomsburyset.org.uk/

Principal Investigator: Ray Kent (programme PI), the Royal Veterinary College (RVC), UK (geology, research and knowledge exchange management)

Steering Group Members: The Bloomsbury SET – Adelia de Paula (knowledge exchange manager) (chemistry, knowledge exchange management)
   London International Development Centre (LIDC, and RVC), UK – Claire Heffernan (academic lead) (global development, interdisciplinary studies)
   London School of Economics and Political Science (LSE), UK – Aygen Kurt-Dickson (political science, research development, science and technology studies)
   London School of Hygiene and Tropical Medicine (LSHTM), UK – Alex Anderson (medical sciences, research and knowledge exchange management), Hannah Whiteman, UK (medical sciences, research and knowledge exchange management)
   The Royal Veterinary College – Emma Tomlinson (steering group chair) (biological sciences, research and knowledge exchange management)
   School of Oriental and African Studies (SOAS), UK – Ying Chen (biology, research and knowledge exchange management); Jess Pavlos (psychology, research and knowledge exchange management)

Funding Organisation: Research England, Connecting Capability Fund (CCF), project number CCF17-7779, amount £4,960,000.

THE BLOOMSBURY SET CASE STUDY

'The Bloomsbury SET (Science, Economics, Technology)' programme owed its title to the decision by a group of research managers in institutions close to Bloomsbury Square in London to propose a collaborative research programme in 2017. They were responding to a call for funding from Research England's Connecting Capability Fund (CCF), set up by the UK government under its industrial strategy in 2017. Funding was granted for the first phase of the programme in 2018. Follow-on funding for a second phase from 2021–2022 was awarded in 2021. In the second phase new partners were added, and the London School of Economics and Political Science (LSE) discontinued its formal partnership to allow it to prioritise its involvement in another CCF programme that it was leading.

This case study concerns the experience of the author in the first phase of B–SET, during which she was a member of the programme's steering group. The case study is also based on a semi-structured Zoom interview conducted between the author and the programme's principal investigator (PI) in October 2021, and on the author's own reflections about the research process.

Aims and Objectives

The overarching aim of the B–SET consortium was to deliver a programme of knowledge exchange activities leading to tangible evidence and outputs that would enable major human health benefits, improvements in animal health, welfare and productivity, and enhancements in biosecurity and food safety.

A primary objective of the B–SET programme was to assess the risks posed by infectious diseases and antimicrobial resistance, and to find ways of addressing the lack of low-cost portable diagnostic tools, vaccines, valuable and accurate data. The consortium was also seeking to create greater certainty in mathematical modelling of disease transmission and spread. In connecting places, people, businesses, ideas and infrastructures, the programme was designed to generate innovative solutions that could contribute to safeguarding human health, while searching for paths leading to desired outputs and outcomes, and producing performance indicators for measuring success. In doing so, the team also planned to investigate the social, economic and political aspects of relevant public health interventions.

A secondary, but no less important objective, was to contribute to a cultural shift across partner institutions by attempting to break down the barriers in siloed research and encourage collaborative thinking.

Themes and Research Questions

The topic of the proposal was 'organically' defined to address a scientifically proven, robust research problem with real-life, economic, health policy and societal implications. The overarching theme of the B–SET programme focussed on connecting capability to combat the threat from infectious diseases and antimicrobial resistance. The programme was concerned with resolving the threat to human and animal health created by infectious diseases and the rise of AMR.

The core research themes identified in the funding calls issued within the programme addressed four topics:

1. Developing, testing and prototyping low-cost portable diagnostic tools and technologies
2. Developing and testing effective vaccines for endemic and emerging diseases of humans and animals
3. Modelling, including the application of machine learning, and artificial intelligence (AI) techniques to the understanding of disease transmission
4. Improving understanding of the social, economic and political acceptability of current and potential public health responses to disease emergence events

All the sub-projects in the proposal broadly addressed the key research question: How can the organisation of knowledge exchange based on robust research provide solutions to the risks posed by antimicrobial resistance and infectious diseases to humans and animals?

THE RESEARCH PROCESS

The B–SET collaboration differed from most traditional externally funded research programmes in that it was driven by a university research administration office as a strategic programme of activity that would benefit academic teams in partner institutions, thereby increasing their collaborative interdisciplinary project activity (Aldridge & Derrington, 2021). The programme was delivered through competitive project and fellowship funding calls that were open to B–SET institutions only. The B–SET case study describes how the programme was structured to meet the funder's requirements and how partners and team members were selected, before presenting the research design and methods, engagement and dissemination strategies, and lessons learnt from the process.

Meeting the Funder's Requirements

The funder needed to consider the expectations of the UK government's Department for Business, Energy and Industrial Strategy (BEIS) in the CCF programmes, by aiming 'to share good practice and capacity internally across the higher education sector, forge external technological, industrial and regional partnerships, and deliver the Government's Industrial Strategy priorities' (UKRI Research England, 2021). Proposals had to reflect the government's priorities by supporting the foundations of a productive, successful economy through its focus on people, skills, innovation, place and infrastructure (HM Government, 2017).

Since Research England's CCF scheme was an outcome of the UK government's industrial strategy, the B–SET's programme's aims and key performance indicators had to be directly linked to the government's ambitions to support the growth of UK life sciences clusters that would be capable of offering 'a single front door', and would attract applications of new technologies, including artificial intelligence (AI) in various areas.

Because the CCF scheme was the first of its kind, detailed guidance was not provided in the call about the funder's requirements. This omission meant that the proposers had more flexibility when writing the bid, but that more negotiations and discussions were needed with the funder once the bid was in the pipeline for an award. Given the uncertainty of the funder's expectations, the proposal was developed in anticipation of aspects in the government's industrial strategy that would need to be explored: it focussed on the 'big picture', while remaining truly innovative and original.

At the proposal planning stage, no decision was taken about who would run the programme if the bid was successful. When the proposal had been accepted, and since the scheme was being operated for the first time, the PI at the Royal Veterinary College (RVC) led a negotiation phase with the funder to identify the key performance indicators of interest to BEIS. Research England was looking for hard technology transfers and practical solutions as required by BEIS, which meant that social and economic aspects of the solutions provided by the programme had to be subordinated during the negotiation phase, despite the reference to 'economics' in the title of the B–SET proposal.

The CCF funding scheme required demonstration of the collaboration's capacity, existing research expertise across the partnerships and potential to take research into new avenues and end-users' practices, which determined the composition of the research consortium. The proposal described how basic research would be translated to meet the needs of consumers, patients, citizens, policymakers, industrialists, and others by creating a knowledge exchange platform for competitive and collaborative grant-funded activity across the partner institutions.

The programme's budget was agreed as submitted, and the funding was adequate to start implementing the aims and objectives. The budget covered staff and non-staff costs for core B–SET activities such as symposia, sandpits, travel and subsistence for meetings with industrial partners, training and professional development, patenting, legal costs, and consumables. Each partner institution was expected to provide in-kind contributions towards staff costs in addition to the award. For example, the workloads of each institution's research and knowledge exchange professionals and steering group members, as well as specific academic champions, were included in the programme's operational activities covered by their institutions.

Since the grant offer letter was issued one month after the project's start date, it took longer than anticipated to establish the project management team and the governance structure. The PI and the chair of the steering group spent the first six months setting up the programme's consortium agreement, developing partnerships, arranging the governance structure, and issuing the first call for project grants.

Building the Project Team

An unusual feature of the B–SET programme was that it was constructed by a group of 'blended professionals' in research, innovation and knowledge brokerage in the UK higher education sector who had moved from academic spaces into research administration (Whitchurch, 2008). The CCF call gave them an opportunity to develop their skills in designing and leading a major programme of translational research.

The programme PI had already set up an informal Bloomsbury research managers' group among peers from the Francis Crick Institute, Birkbeck University of London, London School of Hygiene and Tropical Medicine (LSHTM), RVC and School of Oriental and African Studies (SOAS) in 2016. The group established a multidisciplinary international consortium to deliver the B–SET programme. Many discussions had already taken place by the time the call was formally announced in 2017. Being physically close to the Bloomsbury Square in Central London meant that peers could easily meet to exchange ideas about the funding call and project design. The core team built mutual trust and understanding, which they knew would be key to successful collaboration, as a result of their experience of combining applied and basic research to produce higher impact.

As the head of research administration at the RVC, the programme PI had already built informal and formal ties with peers in research institutions in the Bloomsbury area of London. These key professionals and their academic colleagues were connected to strategically placed research projects that could be further developed for knowledge exchange. As research and innovation strategy manager at LSE, the author was chosen by the School's senior management to represent the institution on the steering group after the application had been accepted. The director of LSE's research division had engaged with the proposal in the final stages before submission and gave his consent for LSE to be a partner. Responsibility for delivering the programme was assigned to the author due to her expertise in research facilitation for collaborative projects and her ambition to raise the voice of social sciences research in multidisciplinary settings.

Each partner institution had a named academic champion with research interests that fell within the programme's remit, and who was tasked with raising awareness and attracting other academics to engage with B–SET. The application was driven by the programme PI, who had training and experience of complex collaborative multinational projects. Claire Heffernan, director of London International Development Centre (LIDC) and part-time faculty in RVC, agreed to be the academic lead and to endorse the scientific direction of the proposal together with the RVC senior management at pro-vice-chancellor research and innovation level.

The PI's connections to peers in partner institutions and his experience in preparing multi-partnered bids meant that the collaborative arrangements and partners' roles and expectations were agreed before the bid was submitted. The B–SET programme required additional human resources to help with delivery of activities, which provided opportunities for career development and promotion of existing staff, and the appointment of project and knowledge exchange managers.

The application was submitted with RVC as the lead coordinator and three other universities as partners. The project governance was established such that each partner institution was represented on the steering group by one or two key contact persons, rather than by an academic co-investigator from each institution. The steering group served as the programme's central decision-making body for delivery and implementation, drawing on existing contacts through the B–SET consortium.

The steering group met once every month. Meetings were used to guide the programme delivery, discuss calls for proposals, and identify gaps and issues in building further collaborations among academics across partner institutions. Members of the group agreed on new partnerships and discussed progress in programme delivery reported by the management team. They were involved in providing academic reviewer contacts beyond B–SET for funding calls, and to approve dissemination and impact plans. They were specifically tasked with promoting B–SET in their institutions, encouraging academics and ongoing research projects to connect with partner institutions, being the key named contact person for any queries, and liaising between B–SET partners and their respective institutions' senior management.

The original plans also included hiring technology transfer officers to help with taking innovations to the market. As the activities in the first half of the programme were not expected to result in technology transfer, the steering group prioritised hiring a project manager and a knowledge exchange manager. The project manager's role specification required candidates to have generic competencies and experience in multidisciplinary programme management, as well as an understanding of financial and commercial markets, and event organisation. The skill-set requirements were kept broad to attract people from a wider pool of applicants.

The knowledge exchange manager's role, which was originally intended to be filled by two individuals, targeted applicants with complementary skills to those of the project manager: good communications skills, understanding of the research field, and experience of working with industry. The first project manager recruited to the role was chosen for their experience in running an interdisciplinary unit, good understanding of different institutional cultures, and for being a good communicator. Although the skill sets sought referred specifically to international development experience, in selecting the project manager, preference was given to interdisciplinary experience, noting the importance of this element in the proposal.

Although the B–SET proposal was built on the UK's industrial strategy, its implications and contexts extended beyond the UK, especially to the Global South. The international networks and backgrounds of the steering group members and academic champions spanned the UK, Europe, Africa, Asia, Australia and Latin America. The existing connectivity between partnering institutions, especially the LSHTM and RVC, provided opportunities to access public health policy circles and key influencers through their networks in the UK, Africa, the Middle East and Asia. The disciplinary academic backgrounds and training of steering group members ranged from political science, biology, chemistry, geology, neuroscience, physical science, psychology and medical sciences to natural sciences. They were all interested in conceptualising the problem of antimicrobial resistance through an interdisciplinary lens drawing on their experience of working across such a wide range of disciplines.

The PI identified potential industry, public and third sector partners from the UK and the developing world, specifically Africa, for innovation and commercialisation purposes. The proposal team secured pledges from these partners for their involvement as potential matched-funders and/or users of research results from the programme. An advisory council with representatives from industry and government was set up to advise the project management team on the progress to date and governance matters.

Research Design and Methods

As a translational research and knowledge exchange platform, the B–SET programme was designed to commission research projects, technology transfer projects and innovation fellowships through an academically peer-reviewed and externally validated competitive process. The steering group and the programme's core team worked together to organise the competitions, funding calls, selection of assessors, organisation of peer-review processes, and management of the funded projects' delivery. The intention was to connect the capacity and capabilities of the research bases of the partnering institutions through the steering group members and funded projects, focussing on the development of innovative tools and vaccines to tackle infectious diseases and increasing resistance to antimicrobials.

The PI and the steering group led the governance of the process. During the first few months of the programme, the PI and RVC project team concentrated on setting the programme's activities and organising the first call for projects. The representatives from each partner institution agreed on the size of the projects that the programme would fund.

To raise awareness, promote funding calls, and steer academics for collaborative work across B–SET institutions, several networking events and two one-day-long sandpits were organised to bring together 'academics and industry professionals from different disciplines, institutions, and places ... with a view to creating new projects around a given theme' (Benneworth et al., 2018). This approach was designed to facilitate collaborative thinking and networking.

The competitive process required the project calls and innovation fellowships to be externally validated and peer-reviewed. For each funding call, the steering group and project manager created a pool of academic reviewers external to the B–SET partner institutions but did not participate in the evaluation. Over 100 expert evaluators contributed to the assessment of grant applications on a voluntary basis.

Since the CCF call for proposals had not issued clear directions, the funder's expectations were not sufficiently obvious in the initial stages of the award, which created an 'exciting but terrifying situation' from a programme management perspective, as recalled by the PI when interviewed in October 2021. In launching their own calls for projects, the B–SET programme team adopted a light touch and broad approach to allow applicants maximum flexibility in defining how they would address B–SET's key concerns. A condition of the grants specified by the consortium in the B–SET calls was that each project should involve a minimum of two B–SET partner institutions. External partners from outside the four universities were encouraged to work with B–SET academics but needed to bring their own funding.

No steer was provided for proposers apart from requiring that they tackle the main problem from an interdisciplinary perspective and had the potential to turn project outputs into new therapies, products, services or policies. The programme team relied on the academics leading each project to meet the overall programme objectives and the expected knowledge performance indicators.

Rather than being prescriptive, the PI and core team waited to see what cross-institutional applicants from among the B–SET partners would propose. This approach meant opportunities may have been missed by researchers in some areas due to the short (six-week) timescale of the first call for proposals (SQW 2021, p. iii).

Two project funding rounds, and an innovation fellowships call, led by the PI and steering group, were announced in 2018, allowing up to £300,000 for direct costs. In addition, a machine learning/mathematical modelling call for antimicrobial resistance was launched in 2019. In 2020, calls were announced for follow-on funding for technology transfer and for humanities and social sciences-led small grants. The competitive process required the project calls and innovation fellowships to be externally validated and peer-reviewed. For each funding call, the steering group and programme manager created a pool of academic reviewers external to the B–SET partner institutions but did not participate in the evaluations.

Project selection relied on academics submitting proposals of sufficiently high quality to be funded. The programme awarded grants to the most highly-rated innovative projects in line with the overall aim. Each proposal was assessed by up to five experts representing the range of disciplines covered, or with interdisciplinary backgrounds. Key assessment criteria were scientific excellence, novelty of the collaboration, added value for interdisciplinary working, and the feasibility of delivery. Each call was supported by an ad hoc grant assessment panel comprising four to six peer reviewers chaired by the PI. One of the funding calls focussed on awarding six social science and humanities-led projects. The assessment process, including management and chairing the panel, was coordinated by the author of this case study.

The projects allowed the B–SET programme to touch upon a range of areas, without specifying how many should be awarded funding in each call for proposals. Within the four broad research themes, the proposals varied in size and duration, and targeted different communities and objectives. Thirty projects were funded, with 72 individual investigators, from the four partner institutions and external partners. Certain disciplines and organisations attracted more interest and representation among the applicants (see project website). The steering group had hoped to see more social science and humanities-led, and mathematical modelling proposals among the submissions, but these did not materialise.

The social science projects, for which the author had coordinated the selection, included 20 investigators from across four B–SET partner institutions, most of whom had interdisciplinary backgrounds. The disciplines represented among the social science-led projects' investigators included: applied economics in food systems, animal health and agribusiness, microbiology, veterinary science, epidemiology, anthropology, international studies (specifically diplomacy), communication studies, visual arts in Africa, social psychology, political economy and public health.

Project-level evaluations were performed using a light-touch approach. The aim was to be as supportive as possible to allow the projects to progress with their research, knowledge exchange and innovation activities. The B–SET team requested only a list of publications and outputs, and a final report. The programme did not have the capacity to evaluate the success of individual projects in meeting their aims.

Two reports were commissioned on the programme, including an evaluation by an independent consultant of the B–SET funding and delivery process (SQW, 2021). The external consultants interviewed each steering group member, the programme management team at RVC, and selected academics from each partner institution. They shared their report with the steering group at its final meeting in July 2021. The consultants found that the programme had contributed to making collaborative thinking a norm in solving the societal challenges of infectious diseases and antimicrobial resistance.

The programme PI prepared a self-evaluation report on lessons learnt from the B–SET project. This self-reflection was shared with the steering group members in March 2021 and sent to the funder as part of the regular progress reporting on knowledge exchange indicators. The report provided a useful sense-check and was also potentially valuable for all members of the consortium.

Engagement and Dissemination

The steering group not only connected the capacities and capabilities of critical masses of researchers, but also the research and knowledge exchange professionals who formed the heart of the implementation and decision-making elements of the programme. B–SET contributed to opening-up to new areas of research creatively and encouraged multidisciplinary thinking. It brought together experienced researchers, experts, and teams to develop new knowledge and translational research opportunities.

The programme manager led the website development by subcontracting to website designers and setting up B–SET LinkedIn profile and Twitter accounts to enhance its visibility via social media. From a base at RVC, the knowledge exchange manager worked on project deliverables and dissemination activities in support of partner institutions.

The steering group approved the content and design of the programme's website, brochure and other channels. Its members identified academic, industry-facing and professional conferences at which to deliver B–SET related information and to promote the programme's activities. These conferences included disciplinary academic events covering natural and medical sciences, as well as knowledge exchange and technology transfer professions. In total the B–SET programme organised 11 events, including conferences, networking sessions and symposia. The last in-person symposium of the programme, which was on public health responses to infectious diseases and antimicrobial resistance, was held on 5 March 2020 in London. Due to the pandemic, all subsequent events, including a sandpit, two symposia and two conferences, were held online, and steering group meetings moved from in-person encounters hosted by different B–SET partners to virtual meetings.

Each funded project and fellowship award was supported by the B–SET programme delivery team based at RVC, including the knowledge exchange manager and their respective host B–SET partner institutions. Project leaders participated in engagement and dissemination activities, for example a B–SET stand at the LSE research festival in 2019, or news items, press releases and project promotions on the B–SET website.

All project grant holders were required to sign a contract between the hosting institution and the B–SET programme (with RVC named as lead partner), as well as a collaboration agreement with other partner institutions if applicable. These agreements and the original B–SET consortium agreement between RVC and the partner organisations stipulated the intellectual property rights, including innovation and patenting, data sharing and confidentiality matters, as well as co-authorship, communication and dissemination principles according to normal academic practice.

BOX 6.2 LESSONS LEARNT (B–SET)

At the end of the first phase of the B–SET programme, the consortium was able to take stock before embarking on the second phase. They drew valuable lessons from the perspective of research and knowledge exchange professionals applying their experience to international and multidisciplinary project management.

* Programmes designed and built by teams of research management professionals can provide an effective knowledge exchange platform

for scientific collaborations by creating a formal basis for developing capabilities and capacities.

- Time and effort must be committed at the planning stage to building relationships and establishing leadership roles.
- Particular attention needs to be devoted to building trust, consensus and new relationships, developing new skills, managing career progression, and connecting to new people.
- Provision needs to be made at the outset to deal with unforeseen events that might affect the ability to meet funders' requirements for the programme's delivery.
- The resources and infrastructures required for programme management need to be planned and agreed at the outset.
- Proposal leaders must be prepared, if necessary, to (re)negotiate budgets with funders and financial and logistic support within their institutions.
- Throughout programme delivery, it is essential to establish staff mobility opportunities, to understand cross-institutional pressures and standpoints, and to focus on the people in each institution who will be competent and ambitious in building such connections.
- By delegating powers and accountability to a steering group, programmes can be run more smoothly and efficiently.
- The design of multi-partner interdisciplinary programmes needs to be flexible and adaptive, while also being radically inclusive in terms of interdisciplinary engagement.
- The disciplinary mix brought to the programme needs to be determined in accordance with the programme's aims and objectives as identified in the proposal.
- By breaking down programmes into work packages or small sub-projects, more effective collaborations can be achieved, and opportunities can be provided for less experienced researchers to hone their skills.
- During and at the end of funded projects, it is important to carry out both external and internal evaluations of the research process to identify not only the achievements and impacts of the work but also areas for improvement.

REFERENCES

Aldridge, J. & Derrington, A. M. (2012). *The research funding toolkit.* Sage.

Benneworth, P., Maxwell, K. & Siefkes, M. (2018, 15 October). Sandpits can develop cross-disciplinary projects, but funders need to be as open-minded as researchers, *LSE impact blog.* https://blogs.lse.ac.uk/impactofsocialsciences/2018/10/15/sandpits-can-develop-cross-disciplinary-projects-but-funders-need-to-be-as-open-minded-as-researchers/

HM Government (2017). *Industrial strategy: Building a Britain fit for the future* [White paper]. https://www.gov.uk/government/publications/industrial-strategy-building-a-britain-fit-for-the-future

Kurt-Dickson, A. (2021, 25 May). Collaborating not competing, connecting higher education institutions (HEIs), *Bloomsbury SET: Connecting Capability in Knowledge Exchange* [Conference presentation]. London, UK. https://bloomsburyset.org.uk/resources/

SQW (2021, July) *Evaluation of the Bloomsbury SET: Executive summary.* London. https://bloomsburyset.org.uk/wp-content/uploads/2021/07/Evaluation-of-Bloomsbury-SET-Executive-Summary.pdf

UKRI Research England (2021). *Connecting Capability Fund (CCF).* https://re.ukri.org/knowledge-exchange/the-connecting-capability-fund-ccf/

Whitchurch, C. (2008). Shifting identities and blurring boundaries: The emergence of third space professionals in UK higher education. *Higher Education Quarterly, 62*(4), 377–396. DOI: 10.1111/j.1468-2273.2008.00387.x

7. Climate, climatic change and society (CLICCS)

Antje Wiener

BOX 7.1 PROJECT DESCRIPTORS (CLICCS)

Duration: 01.01.2019–2026 (7 years)

Web Links: https://www.uni-hamburg.de/en/forschung/forschungsprofil/exzellenzcluster/cliccs.html
https://gepris.dfg.de/gepris/projekt/390683824?language=en

Sprecher/Sprecherinnen (Principal Investigators): Universität Hamburg – Anita Engels (sociology, globalisation, sustainability); Detlef Stammer (oceanography, earth system research)
Max Planck Institute for Meteorology (MPI-M) – Jochem Marotzke (meteorology)

Partner Institutions: Deutsches Klimarechenzentrum GmbH Hamburg; HafenCity University; Universität Hamburg; Helmholtz-Zentrum Hereon; Institut für Friedensforschung und Sicherheitspolitik an der Universität Hamburg; Leibniz-Institut für Globale und Regionale Studien, Hamburg; Max-Planck-Institut für Meteorologie (MPI-M), Hamburg; Helmut-Schmidt-Universität; Technische Universität Hamburg; Zentrum für Marine und Atmosphärische Wissenschaften (ZMAW)

Co-Chairs (section B2): Universität Hamburg – Stefan C. Aykut (sociology); Grischa Perino (lead) (economics); Antje Wiener (political science)

Funding Organisation: Deutsche Forschungsgemeinschaft (DFG), German Government's Excellence Strategy. EXC 2037: Climate, climatic change, and society (CLICCS), award number 390683824, amount €46.56 million (c. €1.7 million for B2).

THE CLICCS CASE STUDY

The 'Climate, climatic change, and society' programme, which draws on a broader range of expertise than at any other centre in Germany or elsewhere in the world, was launched in 2019, with research council funding for an initial period of seven years. This large-scale programme, which is hosted at Universität Hamburg, has brought together researchers from a range of universities and affiliated leading science institutions within a single German city, where many of the contributors work at the same institution. The programme is led by three principal investigators ('spokespersons' in German scientific nomenclature) from different disciplines. About 230 researchers are grouped in three thematic research units, each composed of three or more subsections, five for Theme B, totalling 69 researchers.

This case study summarises the research aims, objectives and organisation of the overall CLICCS programme, focussing on the research accomplished during the first two years of funding. The author of the case study, who co-chairs section B2 and co-leads chapters of the cross-cutting 'Hamburg climate futures outlook' project, describes how her unit managed its contribution to the wider programme.

Aims and Objectives

The long-term aims of the CLICCS programme are to understand climate change, taking account of internal variability, extreme events, and unexpected side effects, while also addressing the natural and social spheres as well as their interactions. The consortium is investigating how the climate is changing and how society is changing with it. By understanding these changes, and how societies are adapting, the aim is to give researchers far greater confidence in assessing the range of conceivable climate futures. Based on extensive experience in multidisciplinary climate research, the CLICCS team seeks to identify plausible climate futures on all scales, from micro to macro, and to apply their knowledge and competence in providing the information needed by decision-makers in planning a sustainable future, including the capacity to cope with surprises, such as extreme events, in the climate system.

The broad aim in section B is to assess reasons for the effectiveness, or otherwise, of the key drivers of climate governance agreed in the 1992 United Nations (UN) Framework Convention on Climate Change (UNFCCC), focussing on the concepts of norms, contestation, and policies. The B2 project team is seeking to identify dynamics of climate governance that are consistent with understanding both climate and social change, as well as those aspects expected to unfold with appreciable probability as a necessary prerequisite for separating plausible from possible climate futures. Specific objectives apply to CLICCS over the lifetime of the programme:

- To boost the understanding of the crucial natural processes that either enhance or reduce anthropogenic climate change, allowing estimates of possible climate futures to be more tightly reined in
- To identify which social dynamics support or prevent the deep decarbonisation required to meet the targets of the Paris Climate Accords, enabling an assessment of which greenhouse-gas emissions pathways are more probable than others
- To characterise comprehensively the magnitude and mechanisms of chaotic variability in a warming climate, and to explore how the resulting irreducible (aleatoric) uncertainty could be accounted for in climate socio-economic interactions and in decision-making processes
- To establish an understanding of the competition between climate targets and other societal goals in concrete case studies of sustainable adaptation to climate change, by combining possibly unstable social dynamics with the impulses arriving from the physical system marked by unpredictable variability and extreme events

Themes and Research Questions

CLICCS began from the observation that, by accepting that the world is warming and humans are largely responsible, the Paris Climate Accords in December 2015 provided a powerful impetus not only for climate policy but also for climate research. UNFCCC drew attention to the importance of knowledge production, global climate governance, climate litigation and political protest, and their interplay across the scales of the global order. To address these new challenges, the CLICCS consortium established a long-term programme extending from basic research on climate change and climate-related social dynamics to the transdisciplinary exploration of human–environment interactions.

Within this wider context, three intertwined research themes are being addressed, as illustrated in Figure 7.1. The first theme (A) provides the natural basis for understanding climate system dynamics, including climate variability and extremes, the climate change already unfolding, and the climate change expected for the future. The leading research question for this theme asks: Which climate futures are possible, and which are plausible?

The second theme (B) is investigating the climate-related dynamics of social systems and provides the social science foundation for the construction of plausible climate scenarios, with a specific emphasis on deep decarbonisation, by asking: Which climate futures are plausible?

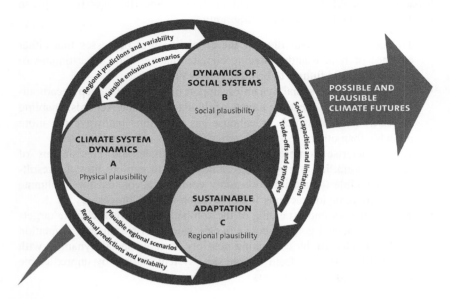

Figure 7.1   CLCSS research themes and units

Source: Universität Hamburg, CEN/CLICCS.

The third theme (C) focusses on coupled human–environment dynamics at a regional level where climate change becomes visible, asking: Where can sustainable adaptation be realised by local actors?

THE RESEARCH PROCESS

The consortium's key objectives were developed against the background of their prior experience of large-scale collaborative research funding that drew mainly on evidence-based natural science methods and technical knowledge. An interdisciplinary group was constituted within CLICCS to address the programme's overarching questions. This section of the case study examines how the amount of funding awarded and the prior experience of the coordinating team members shaped the ways in which the international dimension and the multidisciplinary elements were fully integrated into the programme.

Meeting the Funder's Requirements

The CLICCS consortium is funded by the Deutsche Forschungsgemeinschaft (DFG), the national research council, which acts as the channel for federal and state research funding. DFG funding extends to all academic and science-related activities of nationwide relevance that are conducted by universities and their cooperation partners. The CLICCS programme was proposed in response to DFG's call for applications under its excellence strategy, which consists of two funding lines: clusters of excellence and universities of excellence. The clusters of excellence line supports project-based funding in internationally competitive research fields at a university or university consortium (DFG, 2016). The DFG's strategy, which was launched initially in 2005, fosters the advancement of German universities by 'supporting research of the highest standard, enhancing research profiles and facilitating cooperation in the research system' (DFG, 2016). The intention in the excellence strategy since 2019 is to maintain and build on the new dynamism generated by the 2007–2017 excellence initiative within the German research system, and to ensure longer-term prospects for successful projects.

DFG (2021) provides detailed information about the process in its 'How to…' guides for applicants. The DFG's application procedure is highly competitive, and the preparatory period usually takes two to three years. The CLICCS cluster was successful in a process that began with 195 short applications, of which 88 were shortlisted for full applications, and 57 of these received awards. The research described in this case study was part of a large-scale programme, initially involving around 230 collaborators from 15 disciplines, including oceanography, meteorology, biology, sociology, economics, political science and the humanities. The host institution, Universität Hamburg, had considerable knowledge about DFG's funding schemes, and experience of responding to calls for proposals, negotiating the application process, and meeting the funder's terms and conditions.

The project's large-scale structural design and the multidisciplinary composition of the project team were favourably rated by the funders even though they were not essential requirements in the formal call for proposals. The prior knowledge and experience of the senior researchers and research managers in the consortium meant that no problems were encountered in responding to the requirements in the call, and in negotiating a budget that matched DFG's specifications.

The budget funded the establishment of a 'cross-disciplinary lab' for High-Performance Computing and Data-Intensive Science, where three CLICCS computer and data scientists could collaborate with climate scientists and model developers. The laboratory was designed to support the whole programme in bringing about conceptual improvements, development and application-oriented evaluation of innovative methods across the programme in areas of climate model software engineering, including high-volume data visualisation and data management for simulations and observations.

The DFG award covers expenses for conference, workshop activities and resources for the dissemination of results, as well as the cost of employing undergraduate and postgraduate students as research assistants, and postdocs as research fellows. The general guidelines included an allocation of one month's time towards CLICCS research on behalf of extant chairs. In practice it turned out that a few chairs dedicated considerably more time, and others considerably less than this.

Teaching buy-out of one hour per week was provided for the author as co-chair of section B2 for work package two (WP2), allowing for one ninth of teaching obligations for full professors and one sixth for junior professors, for the duration of the project. The time that the author and the other co-chairs spent on the project reached proportions that went significantly beyond the anticipated work hours allocated to CLICCS research activities, although the budget enabled work on CLICCS's guiding research question to proceed according to expectations by meeting the costs of employing research assistants. The author's additional time was required mainly during the writing stage of the grant proposal and for her contribution to the cross-cutting project for the programme's first *Hamburg Climate Futures Outlook* (hereafter *Outlook*) (Stammer et al., 2021). The host institution was also made aware of the unanticipated shortfall in funding for this budget head, enabling it to adjust the budget in a follow-up research proposal.

DFG requires all the research that it funds to be made publicly available and expects project leaders to engage actively with interested stakeholders at local and national levels. The research consortium committed to meeting these requirements at the proposal stage and was supported throughout the period of the award by an international advisory board.

Building the Project Team

The author and co-chair for sub-project B2 is a political scientist with expertise in global governance and international relations. She has had experience of living and working abroad for more than two decades, including positions in Canada, Italy, Mexico, the UK and the United States. She brought to the project extensive work on practice-based norms research, with a special interest in norm contestation in processes of building global governance from below, driven by the central question of 'Whose practices count?' when generating norms of global governance (Wiener, 2018, p. 1). Her input was key during the first two years of the programme in conceiving a framework for analysing the role of societal agency and in addressing the leading CLICCS research question. Given her background of expertise, she was invited to co-chair and shape the interdisciplinary B2 section of the CLICCS programme together with colleagues from economics, sociology and geography.

As co-chair, and in accordance with the approach chosen by the CLICCS employment strategy, the author selected the members of her team based on public calls for applications (in English). Short-listed applicants were invited for interview to identify whether and, if so, to what extent they met the required skills and competences: conceptional, empirical and methodological approaches, open-mindedness towards interdisciplinary research, and the ability to draw on different fields of study and disciplines of relevance to the research theme. The B2 project recruited researchers and assistants not only from cognate disciplines. In line with the focus on 'contested climate justice in sensitive regions', such as the Arctic, western Asia and northern Africa (WANA) region, co-researchers were also recruited with other disciplinary backgrounds, for example economics, sociology, human geography and Islamic studies.

Research Design and Methods

The mix of disciplinary backgrounds of team members enabled the coordinators to implement an interdisciplinary approach to the research. The programme was designed to use observations and models from the natural and social science environments, and social systems to understand the processes governing these systems, and to formulate adaptation and mitigation strategies. A carefully orchestrated structure was established consisting of themes (A, B, C), co-chaired subgroups and work packages (WPs), with B2 composed of WP1 to WP4.

Working with researchers from different disciplines meant engaging frequently in exchanges about approaches, concepts, methodologies, methods and research techniques. The multidisciplinary B2 unit needed to return to the drawing board not only to clarify, update and refine key concepts such as 'global governance', 'scales', 'levels', 'institutions' or 'norms', but also to justify the choice of terminology and the most appropriate approaches. The coordinators had to decide, for example, whether to adopt a model-based universalistic or a qualitative inductive comparative methodology.

While this process of iterated interaction was more time-consuming than originally anticipated, it facilitated the production of unexpected and innovatory research results. The frequent meetings also generated a growing familiarity with different epistemologies, in turn stimulating respect for, and knowledge about, working methods in other disciplines. These interactions led to a number of spin-off projects where newly formed research groups worked on shared research topics, for example the development of a new approach to decolonising global climate governance, led by a postdoctoral and a doctoral researcher from WP2 in B2 (Wilkens & Datchoua-Tirvaudey, 2022).

Drawing on their own and recent international findings, the B2 interdisciplinary group developed a genuinely novel research tool – the Social Plausibility Assessment Framework (SPAF) – specifically to assess the social drivers qualifying the plausibility of achieving deep decarbonisation. The SPAF was designed to address the leading research questions raised by themes A and B, and provided feedback between the larger organisational units. It relied on the expertise of the two lead authors and co-chairs of B2, Aykut and Wiener (Aykut et al., 2021). They encouraged a bottom-up process to frame the leading research questions and undertake empirical research based on the respective research objectives and appropriate themes. The empirical research, which involved a comparative spatio-temporal methodology, was designed to identify, retrace, evaluate and compare a selection of ten social drivers of climate action over a period of more than two years. The team-based research processes involved the organisation of regular meetings of the entire group to generate feedback in interdisciplinary exchanges through the four steps in the process:

1. Defining the scenario and describing its key characteristics
2. Identifying a selection of key social drivers that represent relevant ongoing and emergent dynamics toward that scenario
3. Assessing past and emergent driver dynamics, their trajectories, enabling or constraining conditions, prospects for change, and the visibility and accessibility of the global resources they provide
4. Synthesising the individual driver dynamics to provide an overall evaluation of the scenario's plausibility, and describing the emerging global opportunity structure as a potential repertoire of resources generated by the different drivers and their interaction

Given the intrinsic complexity of social reality, the list of drivers is potentially endless and their identification is, at least partly, an analytical choice (Aykut et al., 2021). To identify the social drivers, the researchers applied 'Occam's razor' based on the two choices: first, choosing as few drivers as possible and as many as necessary; second, choosing drivers that are as aggregated as possible and as detailed as necessary. They argued that, while existing definitions tend to relate drivers to techno-economic variables, societal macro-indicators, individual action or policymaking drivers should be understood more broadly as overarching social processes that generate change toward or away from a given scenario and its characteristics. As social processes, drivers mediate between societal agency and social structure.

The team's interdisciplinary approach enabled them to show how drivers represent (emergent) social processes that are identified in relation to a given scenario – deep decarbonisation by 2050 – because they are considered key to its realisation. Not only did the research consider social dynamics that span different sectors, including the state, business and civil society, it also involved multiple sites that span micro-, meso- and macro-scales of order, including global, inter- and subnational processes, and that generate 'climatising' effects by diffusing climate concerns in new governance arenas and societal domains. Each of the ten drivers selected was characterised by a historic trajectory and specific contextual conditions which enable or constrain societal agency for change. The explicit consideration of constraining conditions breaks with the optimism bias that pervades much of existing decarbonisation research. The in-depth study of these ten social drivers enabled the research team to establish 'that limiting global surface warming below about 1.7°C by 2100 is currently not plausible' (Stammer et al., 2021, p. 4).

By identifying a set of overarching social processes that constitute 'social drivers' for deep decarbonisation, and by examining the institutional enablers and constraints for these processes, the research unit accomplished a first systematic step towards framing the variety of global societal agency in climate change using social science concepts. The SPAF foregrounds societal factors as both the main barriers and the main drivers of low carbon climate futures. Drivers were thereby shown to reflect 'societal multiplicity and the agency of a plurality of stakeholders', as well as dynamics in markets and socio-technical regimes, and in social movements and conflicts.

This work was not conducted in isolation from the other research themes. The SPAF was closely integrated in the cross-cutting project synthesis of ongoing findings. These project summaries, *Outlooks*, were designed to forge specific pathways for interdisciplinary research collaboration. The first *Outlook* used the SPAF as 'a framework that enables the analysis of the social drivers of decarbonization, their enabling and constraining conditions, and emerging resources and structures that could influence plausible future developments of these drivers' (Stammer et al., 2021, p. 4).

Engagement and Dissemination

Having committed in the proposal to engage with stakeholders and to make the research findings publicly available, the research consortium was already actively promoting its work during the early years of the programme covered in this case study, mainly through responses to the media and other societal agents.

The CLICCS cluster addresses knowledge transfer using several strategic tools, including the annual *Outlook* publication of cross-cutting research results, while also publishing ongoing research in the *Climate Quarterly* reports. A press outreach office facilitates and coordinates interviews and comments on (social) media, and research profiles for publication with the press, for example in leading local newspapers. The CLICCS cluster communicates information beyond academia based on advisory positions on councils and committees at all levels of governance, including learned academic organisations and academies of science. For example, several researchers have been invited to become members of advisory boards and/or committees at local, regional, national, and international levels of political and legal climate regulation; and one of the B2 programme chairs, Grischa Perino, advises the EU Commission (DG CLIMA), as well as the German Federal Government.

Knowledge transfer also takes place at regularly scheduled meetings with the external advisory board, and climate knowledge from the cluster is being promulgated in the form of assessment reports in national or international contexts to raise awareness and exert pressure on governments. For example, members of the consortium participated as authors in the 2021 report of the Intergovernmental Panel on Climate Change (IPCC). The United Nations provides meeting and networking opportunities for transnational governance actors, and CLICCS team members are observing the ongoing process of the conference of the parties (COP).

These activities are cross-cutting not only in generating new knowledge within the framework of CLICCS, but also in bringing this knowledge to bear in drafting global climate policy. For example, the analysis carried out using the SPAF identified a series of 'resources' produced by the selected social drivers, which could be used to engage with other societal actors. In their annual reports, the programme coordinators highlight these social drivers and present their analyses of pressures and sources of resistance.

Together, these knowledge transfer tools address both the international scientific community and the wider public, as well as decision-makers in politics and policy processes. A press conference was held when the first *Outlook* was published. Following press briefings, interviews were arranged with all leading newspapers and media outlets, including television, radio and social media in Germany, as well as leading international media such as *The Washington Post* in the US and the BBC in the UK.

In addition to the reports and regular academic publication outlets in leading peer-reviewed journals and with academic publishers, a central synthesis project regularly distils and publishes CLICCS research results addressing key cross-cutting questions on an annual basis. Knowledge transfer is accomplished jointly with the German Climate Service Centre (GERICS), located at Helmholtz-Zentrum Hereon in Hamburg. The Centre collaborates in the production and dissemination of the regular CLICCS' *Climate Quarterly*, which operate as the news magazine of the excellence cluster, and the annual *Hamburg Climate Futures Outlook,* which presents cross-disciplinary cutting-edge research results.

In each theme and sub-project, researchers agree on their types of publication and choices of publication outlets. When, as a result of numerous and ultimately successful exchanges about the SPAF, a publication strategy was being proposed, the question of co-authorship and appropriate publishing outlets arose. Decisions were taken within each unit about authorship and whether to opt for a mono- or multidisciplinary journal.

Senior researchers supervising postgraduate research students and postdocs advise them on their publication strategies at regular meetings with supervisory assessment panels. Jointly authored publications that cut across themes and/or disciplines have been initiated through the different types of CLICCS activities including workshops and annual retreats. In support of less experienced colleagues, the B2 research team takes particular care to encourage early career researchers to co-author and target high-ranking disciplinary journals with high impact factors such as *International Affairs* (Wilkens & Datchoua-Tirveaudey, 2022).

BOX 7.2 LESSONS LEARNT (CLICCS)

In the first two years of the CLICCS programme, attention was devoted primarily to implementing the design and management structures of this large-scale multidisciplinary project. The lessons drawn concern aspects that arose in responding to the call for proposals, setting up the multidisciplinary collaboration and planning its long-term sustainability.

• In a large-scale long-term programme, strategic planning is critical at the proposal stage if the research consortium is to deal effectively with the considerable challenges involved in the process.

• Agreement needs to be reached about the distribution of tasks between professional research administrators and academic leaders, and managers of sub-projects and work packages, extending to postdoctoral researchers, enabling them to take over management roles in addition to their academic research.

• Programme administrators need to know how funding organisations are equipped (and be prepared) to address issues of delay or reductions in budgets, due to external events and crises such as natural disasters and the pandemic.

• Forward planning is essential when budgets are being negotiated to deal with potential disruptions to the progress of the research due to internal

- problems such as illness or accidents among team members, or the loss of core team members if they are head-hunted by another organisation.
- Systems and funds need to be in place to enable the recruitment and integration of new researchers with appropriate knowledge, skills and competences, if research assistants move on to permanent positions elsewhere.
- When budgets are being negotiated with funders of interdisciplinary collaborations, account must be taken of the requirements for distinct methods or research tools (lab work, field work, desk studies and experiments).
- Appropriate conditions need to be negotiated in multidisciplinary research processes to provide adequate time and resources for regular meetings and other forms of communication between team members, and to allow for the time needed to hear out the expert opinions of all contributing scholars.
- Project managers need to make realistic assessments of their own time commitment to the research, and to work with their institutional administrators to ensure that they are allowed adequate remission from teaching and other administrative tasks.
- Project managers need to be ready to take advantage of opportunities afforded by large-scale funding to identify and develop a specific focus, such as 'diverse ways of knowing', exemplified in the CLICCS project by building it into the project design as a cross-cutting interdisciplinary theme.
- In a multidisciplinary research setting, especially in projects involving both the natural and the social and human sciences, and applying a deliberately interdisciplinary approach, attention must be paid to the selection of team members with complementary skills and experience of working across disciplinary boundaries.
- Project managers need to ensure that research assistants associated with the project receive appropriate training and are fully integrated in the research process.
- The process of selecting publication outlets and authorship requires careful consideration at the proposal stage to ensure the funders' requirements are met as well as the best interests of all the contributors to the research.

ACKNOWLEDGEMENT

Research funding has been granted by the Deutsche Forschungsgemeinschaft (DFG, German Research Foundation) under Germany's Excellence Strategy,

EXC 2037 'CLICCS – Climate, Climatic Change, and Society', Project Number: 390683824. For comments on earlier versions of the case study, I would like to thank Martina Bachmann and Grischa Perino.

REFERENCES

Aykut, S.C., Wiener, A., Engels, A., Gresse, E., Hedemann, C., & Petzold, J. (2021). The social plausibility assessment framework. In D. Stammer, A. Engels, J. Marotzke, E. Gresse, C. Hedemann, & J. Petzold (Eds), *Hamburg Climate Futures Outlook, 1*(1), 31–37. DOI: 10.25592/uhhfdm.9104

Deutsche Forschungsgemeinschaft (DFG). (2016). *Germany's excellence strategy: Call for proposals in the clusters of excellence funding.* https://www.dfg.de/en/ research_funding/announcements_proposals/2016/info_wissenschaft_16_59/index .html

Deutsche Forschungsgemeinschaft (DFG) (2021). *Individual grants programmes – A how-to guide.* https://www.dfg.de/en/research_funding/individual_grants _programmes/index.html

Stammer, D., Engels, A., Marotzke. J., Gresse, E., Hedemann, C., & Petzold, J. (Eds.). (2021). Assessing the plausibility of deep decarbonization by 2050. *Hamburg Climate Futures Outlook, 1*(1). https://www.cliccs.uni-hamburg.de/results/hamburg -climate-futures-outlook/download.html

Wiener, A. (2018). *Contestation and constitution of norms in global international relations.* Cambridge University Press.

Wilkens, J. & Datchoua-Tirvaudey, A. R. C. (2022) Researching climate justice: A decolonial approach to global climate governance. *International Affairs, 98*(1), 125–143. DOI: 10.1093/ia/iiab209

8. Exchanging prevention practices on polydrug use among youth in criminal justice systems (EPPIC)

Betsy Thom and Karen Duke

BOX 8.1 PROJECT DESCRIPTORS (EPPIC)

Duration: 1 January 2017–31 December 2019 (3 years, plus 2 months no-cost extension)

Web Links: http://eppic-project.co.uk
http://drugandalcoholresearchcentre.org/eppic-portal/

Principal Investigators/Coordinators: Betsy Thom (health policy); Karen Duke (criminology), Middlesex University, UK

Partners: Austria, European Centre for Social Welfare Policy and Research – Cees Goos, Rahel Kahlert, Willem Stamatiou, Günter Stummvoll (criminology and social policy)

Belgium, Ghent University – Florien Meulewaeter, Lore Van Damme, Wouter Vanderplasschen (special needs education, external evaluators)

Denmark, Aarhus University – Vibeke Asmussen Frank, Maria Dich Herold (anthropology and psychology)

Germany, Frankfurt University of Applied Sciences – Niels Graf, Babak Moazen, Heino Stöver (criminology)

Italy, Eclectica – Franca Beccaria, Sara Rolando (sociology)

Poland, Institute of Psychiatry and Neurology – Katarzyna Dabrowska, Jacek Moskalewicz, Agnieszka Pisarska (sociology)

UK, Middlesex University – Helen Gleeson, Rachel Herring (psychology, sociology); Change, Grow, Live (CGL) – Raj Ubhi, (young people's services, service provider)

Funding Organisation: European Commission Health Programme, Consumers, Health, Agriculture and Food Executive Agency (CHAFEA), grant number 738162, amount €599,512.

THE EPPIC CASE STUDY

The EPPIC case study describes an international multidisciplinary research project, 'Exchanging prevention practices on polydrug use among youth in criminal justice systems', funded within the European Commission's Health Programme (2014–2020) by the Consumers, Health, Agriculture and Food Executive Agency (CHAFEA), which worked in close cooperation with the Directorate-General for Health and Food Safety (DG SANTE), and the Directorate-General for Justice and Consumers (DG JUST). The research, which was carried out between January 2017 and December 2019, was hosted by Middlesex University, UK, and included partners from six EU member states.

Aims and Objectives

The EPPIC project aimed to identify principles of good practice on interventions to prevent illicit drug use among young people (aged 14–25) in touch with the criminal justice system in European countries; to elaborate guidelines; and to initiate a European exchange network of relevant stakeholders.

Specific objectives were associated with the different work packages (WPs):

* To collect and disseminate existing knowledge and new data on evidence for effective approaches and interventions to address illicit drug use (WP4)
* To analyse the potential for interventions and different innovative approaches to influence drug-using trajectories among young people in touch with the criminal justice system (WP5)
* To examine the appropriateness of the existing European drug prevention quality standards to the criminal justice context and develop a set of guidelines adapted to initiatives aimed at drug-using young people in touch with criminal justice agencies (WP6)
* To assess the extent to which intervention models are transferable across countries and cultures (WP7)
* To set up dissemination mechanisms for knowledge exchange and collaboration between relevant stakeholders at local, national and international levels (WP2)
* To conduct process, outcome and impact evaluations of the project to establish whether project objectives were being met (WP3)

Themes and Research Questions

The project focussed on illicit drug use, the development of polydrug use and use of new psychoactive drugs among vulnerable and at 'risk' young people in touch with the criminal justice systems in partner countries. The research addressed a complex interaction of multiple problems, including physical and mental health needs, criminal activity, family and social difficulties, educational problems, and deprivation. A major theme in the project was prevention responses encompassing multi-agency interventions to delay the onset of drug use and to prevent escalation and harmful use.

The research questions were designed to identify transferable innovations and principles of good practice among interventions to prevent illicit drug use:

- What can be learned from the exchange of knowledge and best practice in the countries included in the project?
- What practices, innovations and principles of good practice in interventions to prevent illicit drug use are transferable to other countries?
- How can quality standards based on the European Drug Prevention Quality Standards (EDPQS) be adapted to initiatives aimed at the target group?
- How could a European knowledge exchange network for practitioners and stakeholders be established to work with young people in the criminal justice system?

THE RESEARCH PROCESS

The EPPIC case study describes and analyses all the stages in managing the research process of a completed EU-funded project in six EU member states, with partners from four cognate disciplines, within a period of 36 months. It examines the issues that arose in organising the funding, building the research team, and designing and conducting research through to the dissemination of findings.

Meeting the Funder's Requirements

EPPIC was one of the projects funded within the European Commission's third health programme, under the auspices of the Consumers, Health, Agriculture and Food Executive Agency (CHAFEA). Unlike many other projects funded under the EU's framework programmes, the budget was based on a joint funding approach. Allowable costs covered staff, travel and meetings, external evaluation and any subcontracting, as well as dissemination events for the UK coordinating team. The funding provided by the EU represented 60% of the full costs. This level of joint funding was known from the start, and partners were aware that they had to cover 40% either from internal resources or by raising the money elsewhere.

Joint funding did not deter any of the partners approached from collaborating in the research, possibly because they had all worked together on former EU projects and were familiar with the joint funding model. In one case, this arrangement caused problems for the researchers in covering costs for meetings, but it did not affect the conduct of the project.

The total amount of the grant was not negotiable, but the funders were quite flexible in allowing changes between the categories originally allocated and were willing to take changing circumstances into account. For example, some WPs had to be rescheduled to allow extra time for unanticipated problems with recruitment, and a no-cost two-month extension was granted for the preparation of the final conference.

Time allocated to coordination and to the research tasks was set as part of the study design at the outset and was agreed by the partners. In retrospect, the research coordinators may have promised too much in the application. Problems encountered in data collection and keeping to schedule meant that partners spent more time on the work than was allocated in the budget. Since team members recognised that this issue frequently arises in research collaborations, it was not a cause of particular concern.

Building the Project Team

The project was coordinated by Middlesex University, supported by their European research office team. The decision by the principal investigator (PI) to apply for funding was based on her previous experience of coordinating large European projects in the drug and alcohol field, and the co-investigator's background in drugs research in criminal justice contexts, which meant that they had an existing network of potential European partners, with whom they knew they could cooperate. The project application drew on their previous research on 'risk' and 'risk and young people', and on involvement in other large-scale European projects, such as 'Addiction lifestyles in contemporary Europe: Reframing addictions project (ALICE-RAP)', which explored the role of stakeholders in the drug and alcohol field in different countries.

Since the project was designed to have a European comparative dimension, partners were selected by the project coordinators from networks established during other European collaborations, including countries in Scandinavia, eastern, central and southern Europe with different criminal justice contexts and drug service provision frameworks. All the partners were known to have relevant expertise and networks in their own countries across health, social care and criminal justice boundaries, and to use interdisciplinary perspectives in their research.

Early in the process, the coordinators discussed bringing in service provider partners in each country, but they were able to make the necessary arrangements to include only a UK service provider from the charity Change, Grow, Live (CGL) when the funding application was submitted. After the proposal had been accepted, all academic partners except Germany were able to identify and work with service providers, thereby balancing the expertise and exchange of knowledge between countries and services.

A project advisory group was set up to include representatives from the European Monitoring Centre on Drugs and Drug Addiction (EMCDDA), United Nations Interregional Crime and Justice Research Institute (UNICRI), and the funding body, CHAFEA. They were selected for their expertise and knowledge of the subject and for their positions in relevant high-level organisations rather than their disciplinary backgrounds. The group's members proved to be a valuable source of expertise in relation to the drug prevention quality standards and interventions within the criminal justice system, and provided useful links to wider networks. In addition, each country set up its own national advisory group to provide feedback on interim findings to the research partners and to assist with dissemination of the learning from the project through their networks.

Research Design and Methods

The research application specified the key research questions and, in broad terms, the methodological approach to be adopted. Each work package (WP) specified aims, objectives and details of the methods to be used, expected outputs and outcomes, which were agreed by partners and provided the basic framework for conducting the research. Many potential problems were avoided at this early stage because of the partners' history of joint working, because they were from cognate disciplines, and because the research coordinators were conscious of the need to identify areas of concern that might affect the research or the collaboration.

When the EPPIC project was launched, very high-quality evidence was not available about 'what works' in preventing drug use and related harms among young people in criminal justice systems. Four of the WPs were designed to produce a strong evidence base to inform policy. The sensitive nature of the material being collected meant that the project team had to conform with a harmonised data protection framework across the EU (European Commission, 2018).

At the outset, Middlesex University's legal department drew up a simple consortium agreement, which was circulated to partners for discussion and amendment before signature. The agreement covered, for example, the roles and responsibilities of the coordinator and partners, joint working procedures, provisions for changes in the partnership, financial obligations, and ownership of results. Securing ethical approval from Middlesex University's Health and Social Care Ethics Committee entailed producing information sheets for distribution to practitioners and young people explaining the informed consent requirements.

Since the proposal involved fieldwork, care had to be taken where informants were aged under 18 to ensure compliance with local safety regulations and proper conduct towards these young people. All participation was voluntary and all participants were guaranteed confidentiality and anonymity. Codes were assigned to each young person's interview. The focus groups occasionally used the names of participants, but they were not cited in any of the reports.

All partners were familiar with the constructivist/interpretivist theoretical approach that was proposed by the coordinators, since it was suited to exploring the perceptions and experiences of young people and the practitioners working with them. Mixed qualitative methods were used: interviews, focus groups, an open-ended scoping survey, and consultative and discussion groups. A template of interview and focus group schedules was constructed jointly, as were coding systems and the structure of the database. These instruments were drafted and revised multiple times and finally agreed by all project partners. Care was taken by the project partners to ensure, as far as possible, equivalence of research procedures and tools, and in the use of concepts and language, which were discussed and debated at length, both through comments on written drafts and during in-person meetings.

In the different countries, the research was conducted in the partner's own language. English was used as the common language to communicate across the research teams. Partners agreed that all outputs would be in English. Key concepts, spanning prevention, intervention and harm reduction, young people in different age ranges, vulnerability, 'at risk', youth and criminal justice, were identified early on and checked for common understanding and definition.

The research team aimed to use non-stigmatising, non-labelling terminology throughout the project. Following discussion at a partner meeting in the first year of the project, team members agreed to use 'people first' language, for example: young people who use drugs, young people involved in crime, and the expression 'young people in contact with the criminal justice system'. They also agreed to avoid the terms 'addict', 'addicted', 'prisoners', 'juvenile delinquents', 'young offenders' and 'vulnerable', except if used in policy and practice documents. Given the variable use of terminology in different social contexts, even within the social sciences, and because, in some countries and disciplines, the tendency was to prefer more traditional terms such as 'delinquency', it took some time to embed this language into the WP reports and other outputs. In addition, agreement on the use of language evolved over the course of the research as the partners became sensitised to different terminology and reflected more on their own work.

Following discussions with the project teams, the coordinators had chosen the lead partners according to their specific areas of knowledge and relevant contacts. Research tools and research processes were elaborated by the WP leads, circulated to all the partners and discussed with them before use. Extensive commenting on research instruments and findings as well as regular discussion in online and face-to-face meetings were used to address any issues that arose.

WP1 to WP3 covered management (UK), dissemination (Austria) and evaluation (external, Ghent). The dissemination and communication strategy was laid out in the original proposal as a dedicated WP with all partners involved in its design and development. It was developed further during the first months of the project, and the amended version was agreed by CHAFEA.

WP4, led by the Polish team, used a scoping survey of service providers to map existing interventions and projects for the target group (young people aged 14–25), a literature review and interviews with practitioners to provide in-depth contextual information regarding current evidence on the issues and interventions available in each partner country.

WP5 consisted of two parts, interviews with young people and further interviews with practitioners. A common schedule was used to interview 198 young people in the six partner countries regarding their drug use and offending trajectories, experiences and access to services. This part of WP5 was led by the Italian team. The Danish team led the interviews with 68 practitioners working with young people and, in each country, further discussions took place in country advisory groups.

The young people and practitioners were selected from a broad range of interventions, covering prevention, treatment and harm reduction approaches, which aimed to prevent the onset or escalation of drug use for young people in contact with the criminal justice system. The interviews were conducted in different contexts, such as youth detention centres, therapeutic communities and community settings for those under alternative measures, depending on access to specific institutions in the different countries. Practitioners working in these contexts acted as intermediaries for the recruitment of potential interviewees. As a result, the national sub-samples differed in terms of their characteristics, including the proportion of prisons versus community settings, males versus females and adolescents (up to age 18) versus young adults. Since young participants were selected by 'gatekeepers', some bias may have been introduced, especially when comments were made regarding their experience of services currently attended.

The interview data were collected across more than one agency in each country. To protect anonymity, the agency names were not used. In the published reports and papers, any identifying features of the young people and practitioners were removed. Despite the precautions taken regarding ethical approval, one partner collected data before approval had been obtained. The data could not therefore be used for the project, and new interviews had to be conducted, resulting in some delays with this part of the research. No other ethical issues arose in interviewing young people and practitioners.

WP6, led by the German team, used findings from WP4 and WP5, and focus group discussions with practitioners in each country to develop the set of ten quality standards.

WP7, led by the UK team, used key informant workshops, individual interviews and email surveys to examine perceptions on the transferability of interventions and approaches identified from prior work.

For each of the WPs, analyses were firstly undertaken separately by each partner. A country report was produced in English and sent to the WP lead, who produced a report drawing on all country reports to address the research questions and themes. In total, 24 country reports and five cross-national reports were submitted to the funders. These reports were stipulated by the applicants in the project proposal to comply with the funder's reporting requirements. Each report was read and commented on by the other research teams, WP lead partners and national level advisory groups. The project advisory group and all partners assessed the cross-national reports and their feedback fed into revised versions.

Occasionally, issues arose regarding the timeliness of the research, participation of some of the partner team leads in joint meetings, and delays in completing the required six-monthly reports for the funder. At times, the coordinators had to provide additional support to ensure the work was successfully completed. These practical administrative problems were more difficult to deal with than the conceptual issues, since the solutions involved balancing maintenance of personal relationships within the network with getting the work done on time and to a high standard.

When it had been agreed that the project would contain a comparative dimension, concerns had been raised among partners regarding the kind of comparisons that would be possible and credible due to differences in country sampling procedures, data collection methods and the study samples achieved. This concern, together with an emerging emphasis on the similarities between the countries, despite differences in culture, context and systems, meant that the outputs had a stronger focus on commonly experienced issues, such as restrictions related to working in a criminal justice context. Some of the nuances of country variability were lost in the wider project reports, although, as far as possible, similarities and differences were commented on in the cross-national reports, and differences in policies, structures and services were clearly described in publicly available country reports.

Engagement and Dissemination

Internal and external engagement was ensured throughout the research process. The project began, as usual for European Commission research, with a kick-off meeting of all partners and the advisory group in Luxembourg, where CHAFEA had its headquarters. Four subsequent face-to face partner meetings took place in Aarhus, Lisbon, Warsaw and London, and nine tele-conference meetings were held over the project period. Regular email correspondence was maintained, and other virtual contact took place as needed between relevant partners. Virtual meetings, less common at the time, were used to save resources and to facilitate a flexible schedule, while also allowing a larger number of meetings than would have been possible face-to-face.

The interviews and workshops with practitioners, and their participation in meetings with national advisory groups, were important vehicles for engaging them as collaborators in the research. Their input added significantly to the multidisciplinary nature of the work and the dissemination of findings. EPPIC's report on the development of guidelines and best practice on 'engagement' resulted in some changes in how practitioners develop relationships and engage with young people and influenced subsequent work within at least one of the partner organisations.

Advisory group members were invited to all face-to-face partner meetings. They received final reports from WPs and all outputs from the research team and were consulted (by email) as needed on specific topics. They distributed information about the project through their own networks, provided opportunities to give presentations, and attended as guests at project meetings and at knowledge exchange events. The main project advisory group was also helpful in linking the partners to wider international networks.

All partners provided six-monthly reports of WP activities and commented on the coordinators' six-monthly reports before submission to CHAFEA. The cross-national reports and the publications 'compared' the countries to some extent and were most effective in identifying a series of themes where considerable similarity was found despite different policy and service structures, and cultural contexts.

The requirement on the coordinators to return comprehensive reports every six months to the funder was experienced by the coordinator and partners as onerous, and it was not always easy to obtain the information needed from all partners to produce the reports on time. The coordinators were required to explain to the funder (via liaison with the CHAFEA project manager) why objectives were not achieved, and how the team was going to catch up.

The external evaluators conducted a survey among the partners and held interviews with all the researchers and a sample of advisory group members both for the interim evaluation at 18 months and for the final evaluation.

Partners met to discuss the interim evaluation report, and the feedback was taken into consideration, resulting in minor adaptations to work practices.

External evaluators were kept informed about project actions. They attended one partner meeting and the final EPPIC conference in February 2020 at Middlesex University in London, as did the CHAFEA project manager. The conference was organised by the coordinators, attended by 90 participants from the UK and Europe (academics, practitioners, policymakers) and live-streamed to 269 people.

The funder did not write a formal assessment. They seemed to be pleased with the project. All final reports were accepted without amendments. In addition, the CHAFEA project manager provided helpful suggestions for funding the translation and production of a set of quality standards, which was a key part of the work and was made available in four languages – English, German, Italian and Polish – on the website of the European Monitoring Centre for Drugs and Drug Addiction (Graf et al., 2019).

Countries were able to raise additional funds from local and regional health authorities for the translation and production of the standards since the coordinators had not allowed for this work in the budget. Production of these quality standards informed workforce learning, training and development of 'best practice' among practitioners working in criminal justice systems and substance use services, and, more marginally, youth services. In the UK, it initiated further development of the quality standards for service delivery.

In line with the dissemination strategy in the funding proposal, a project website was set up, and all information and project reports were placed on the website throughout the project. As no funds or support were available to sustain the website after the project ended, the coordinators took it over and extended the domain name for another three years. Some dissemination was undertaken in the partners' own languages for presentations and short reports relating to the findings at national level. A twitter account was set up and used throughout the project. The project website and twitter feed used English, although some links and uploaded documents were in different languages.

The research generated a number of papers in English language peer-reviewed journals. Presentations were given at national and international levels, some in the languages of the countries concerned. Early in the life of the project, team members discussed publication and authorship. The planned output from WP5 was a set of papers for a special issue of a journal (Frank et al., 2021). Initially, it was agreed that each team would prepare the first draft of a paper, using country reports, and circulate it to the other teams for additions and comments. It was decided that authorship should be attributed to one or two people from the team leading on the paper and to one person from each collaborating team. This approach was adopted as a general guideline for all publications by partners from different country teams. Other papers were authored by country teams alone (Duke et al., 2020; Graf & Stöver, 2019). Papers were published in drugs, youth work and youth justice journals considered to be the key journals for reaching relevant target groups.

The authorship arrangements worked effectively, except when author allocation seemed unfair to people whose contribution was central to the paper. In these cases, it was agreed to add further authors. While overall agreement was reached on most occasions regarding the quality of papers, a problem arose concerning the suitability of one paper for submission to a peer-reviewed journal. When the situation was difficult for team members to resolve, final arbitration was left to the review process of the journals where the article was submitted.

BOX 8.2 LESSONS LEARNT (EPPIC)

Although the coordinators of EPPIC had been part of other EU-funded projects and had led work packages, this was their first experience of coordinating an international multidisciplinary research project, and they were able to draw useful lessons for mid-career and more established research managers.

- When preparing a research proposal, the project manager needs to ensure that the funder's requirements are feasible and tractable within the time frame and budget allowed.
- If the funding organisation requires applicants to cover a proportion of the costs, project managers need to ascertain that partners are prepared to accept these terms and conditions, are able to raise matching funds, and know that institutional and logistic support will be available.
- Project managers need to make provision for unforeseen developments such as the production and translation of policy documents, the organisation of dissemination events, or the creation and maintenance of a web page that were not costed in the original proposal.
- When building a project team for international multidisciplinary research, it is important to be able to call on partners with the necessary skill sets, knowledge and experience of multidisciplinary collaborative work across national borders, and who share the project leader's commitment and approach to comparative project design and working methods.
- Project coordinators need to remain alert to the issues of managing the day-to-day relationships with partners who have different time commitments and work schedules over a period of several years, to ensure that project deliverables are produced on time and to the expected standard.

- Project coordinators should consider employing a dedicated research administrator (even part-time) to alleviate the administrative burden, while being mindful that the need to conduct all the administrative tasks themselves means they are made fully aware of issues and problems as they arise, and are able to keep abreast with the progress of the work packages.

REFERENCES

Duke, K., Thom, B., & Gleeson, H. (2020). Framing 'drug prevention' for young people in contact with the criminal justice system in England: Views from practitioners in the field. *Journal of Youth Studies, 23*(4), 511–529. DOI: 10.1080/13676261.2019.1632818

European Commission (2018). *Data protection: Rules for the protection of personal data inside and outside the EU.* http://ec.europa.eu/justice/data-protection/reform/index_en.htm

Frank, V. A., Rolando, S., Thom B., Beccaria, F., Duke, K., & Herold, M. D. (2021). Editorial DEPP: Drug experienced young people in contact with the criminal justice system. Understanding the challenges and working towards solutions. *Drugs: Education, Prevention and Policy, 28*(1), 1–6. DOI: 10.1080/09687637.2020.1825627

Graf, N., Moazen, B., & Stöver, H. (2019). *Handbook on quality standards for interventions aimed at drug experienced young people in contact with criminal justice systems (EPPIC).* EMCDDA Document library. https://www.emcdda.europa.eu/drugs-library/handbook-quality-standards-interventions-aimed-drug-experienced-young-people-contact-criminal-justice-systems-eppic_en

Graf, N. & Stöver, H. (2019). Critical reflections on quality standards with drug demand reduction. *Drugs and Alcohol Today, 19*(3), 172–181. DOI: 10.1108/DAT-12-2018-0070

9. Families and food in hard times (FFP)

Rebecca O'Connell and Julia Brannen

BOX 9.1 PROJECT DESCRIPTORS (FFP)

Duration: 1 May 2014–30 April 2019 (5 years)

Web Links: https://cordis.europa.eu/project/id/337977
https://foodinhardtimes.org/

Principal Investigator: Rebecca O'Connell, Thomas Coram Research Unit, University College London, UK (social anthropology, sociology of food and families)

Core Team: Thomas Coram Research Unit, UCL Institute of Education, UK – Julia Brannen (senior researcher) (sociology, social science methodology); Laura Hamilton (multidisciplinary social science); Abigail Knight (history, social policy, social work, sociology); Charlie Owen (social research methods); Antonia Simon (social policy); Cécile Brémont, Penny Mellor (project administrators)

Partners: National Institute of Consumer Research, Norway – Silje Skuland (sociology); Anine Frisland (sociology)
Instituto de Ciências Sociais da Universidade de Lisboa, Portugal – Manuel Abrantes (sociology); Fábio Augusto (sociology); Sónia Cardoso (social psychology); Vasco Ramos (sociology); Mónica Truninger (sociology); Karin Wall (sociology)

Funding Organisation: European Research Council, Starting Grant FP7/2007–2013 ERC award number 337977, amount €1,370,937.

THE FFP CASE STUDY

The official name of the study in the proposal to European Research Council (ERC) was 'Families and Food Poverty' (FFP), which provided the acronym used in the case study. Given the potentially shaming nature of being unable to feed one's children, and the differential 'visibility' of (food) poverty in the three countries, the international team and the advisory group had a detailed discussion about the public-facing name of the project. After much deliberation, the idea of 'hard times' was settled upon as a way not only of alluding to the work of that title by Charles Dickens, but also as a means of reframing and depersonalising the problem of poverty.

The case study presented here describes the different stages in the FFP project, from the decision to apply for ERC funding and the formation of the research team, through to the completion of the project. The grant was hosted in the UK by the Thomas Coram Research Unit at University College London, which provided administrative and logistic support.

Aims and Objectives

The research aimed to understand the causes and consequences of food poverty and their relationship to social structures and public policies by applying a mixed-methods international comparative case study design.

The specific objectives of the study were:

- To examine and compare the extent of food insecurity in three European countries, the UK, Portugal and Norway, by conducting secondary analysis of international quantitative data
- To explore and compare the experiences, perspectives and understandings of children and young people (aged 11–15 years) and parents in low-income families in rural and urban areas in these countries, by applying a range of in-depth qualitative methods
- To develop the methodology in this area through the use of a multi-method comparative research approach
- To inform the intervention and advocacy work of not-for-profit organisations, policymakers and practitioners by engaging with them at various stages of the research

Themes and Research Questions

The project examined the extent of food insecurity for low-income families with children in three European countries impacted by high (UK), medium (Portugal) and low (Norway) levels of austerity policies. The research set out to identify which children and types of households were at greatest risk of food insecurity, and which public, charitable and other types of initiatives and provisions aimed to address household food insecurity. The project also sought to examine how food insecurity was framed discursively as a 'public issue'.

In formulating the study's research questions, living on a low income and experiencing food insecurity were considered not only to be variable but also to be specific to the social conditions in which families find themselves in terms of the resources available to them and the ways in which they manage poverty. The investigation included: the ways in which households procured food, covering the effects of local (un)availability of food; the effects of parents' paid employment, and how far school meals mitigated food poverty for children; the effects of food poverty on the social participation of both parents and children, and the emotional consequences for children of social exclusion from their peer groups, for example by generating feelings of stigma and shame (O'Connell & Brannen, 2021, pp. 33–34).

A number of the research questions required detailed qualitative study of families:

1.   How does food figure in children's and families' everyday routines and social relations?
2.   How do families manage food in the context of poverty and the types of help they access?
3.   Do families rely on public and charitable sources of support?
4.   Who takes responsibility for food work, including children's contributions?
5.   How far do families draw on informal sources of help, including extended families and social networks?

THE RESEARCH PROCESS

Since European Research Council (ERC) grants are awarded on the basis of research excellence to support investigator-driven research across all fields, the European Commission (2007) is less prescriptive about the topics and approaches selected and the way the funds are dispersed than in projects funded under other programmes. This case study examines how the type and amount of funding awarded and the prior experience of the team shaped the ways in which the international dimension and the disciplinary elements were integrated into the project as it developed.

Meeting the Funder's Requirements

The ERC Starting Grant provided generous funding and required the principal investigator (PI) to be employed on the grant at a minimum of 60% full-time equivalent. Adequate time was built into the project for its management, including dedicated administrative support and regular face-to-face meetings within the team and with the project advisory group.

A challenge to the project's success in the early stages was a major change in the administrative support that was available to the project at the institutional level. The host institution (Institute of Education, IOE) 'merged' with (was taken over by) a much larger institution, University College London (UCL), very soon after the project started. The project changed from being the only ERC-funded study in the IOE to being one of more than a hundred at UCL with its well-established – but less personal and more thinly spread – structures for managing European awards. These changes brought both advantages and disadvantages.

In particular, the timing and process of the change from one system of 'support' to another caused delays in the negotiations when it was necessary to replace the Portuguese partners. Ultimately, it took around 18 months for the new partners in Portugal to be instated. ERC funding proved to be adequate to support the work described in the proposal, although one item was disallowed at the contract stage, since ERC deemed that not enough justification had been provided for the line of the budget that included costs for transcription and translation. Consequently, insufficient funding was available for translation of the Portuguese and Norwegian interviews, meaning only the interview case summaries and field notes were translated into English. In some ways, this reduction in the data was helpful because it meant that the team had to find other less onerous ways to 'handle' the raw data. But it also meant that the PI and senior researcher could not analyse more deeply topics and assumptions that were not foregrounded in the summaries, and, occasionally, had to ask the partners to provide further details.

Unlike many other EU funding schemes, ERC is interested, above all, in scientific excellence. It does not require applicants to demonstrate policy relevance or to include societal 'impacts' among its aims. Although ERC was not the most obvious choice of funders for the FFP as conceived by the award holder, the PI was able to make the case at interview that this aspect of the project was vital given the empirical context in which it was situated.

Building the Project Team

ERC starting grants are intended to support excellent principal investigators at the stage in their careers when they are starting their own independent research team or programme. The FFP PI was (self-)selected to apply for an award because she fitted the criteria for the scheme by having fewer than seven years' postdoctoral research experience. She had gained an ESRC funded MRes and PhD in social anthropology before training as a postdoctoral researcher at TCRU.

The idea for the project topic and the rationale for the selection of the (core) research team were generated in the aftermath of the global financial crisis that occurred in 2008. At that time, the detrimental effects of this event on those who were already among the most disadvantaged in society were becoming increasingly evident across Europe. The evidence, often based on international media reports, was alarming: increasing numbers of children were arriving at school hungry, and the number of food banks handing out food parcels to families forced to choose between 'heating and eating' was rising dramatically. Little evidence existed about the types of families to which the growing numbers of children who lack enough decent food to eat belonged, or about the particular ways in which food poverty manifests and is managed and experienced in different places. Hardly any first-hand accounts were available presenting the experiences of children and young people, an omission that members of TCRU, which since 1973 had specialised in research on children and families, were keen to address.

The PI had not previously managed an international team, although she had led research teams including members with a mix of seniority and backgrounds. She was guided in the methodological strategy and supported in the management of the process by senior members of the core team, who were highly experienced in international comparative approaches.

In selecting the core team members and partners, the study aimed to bring together and build on insights from, and contribute to, three subfields of cognate disciplines: sociology of the family; food studies, which straddles sociology and anthropology, primarily, but also geography; and social policy. The international team brought a range of methodological expertise in quantitative, qualitative and mixed-methods approaches. The inclusion of researchers from cognate disciplines, though some of them identified first and foremost as social researchers, was important to the project's successful implementation. But perhaps more important was the cooperative relationships that were achieved within the national and international teams. The core team members at TCRU had worked together on previous projects and were involved in developing the idea and the proposal.

Three European countries, Norway, Portugal and the UK, were selected to provide contrasting contexts for an analysis of the conditions surrounding 'austerity'. They also differed in terms of the type of welfare state, levels of poverty and inequality. Background data were readily available for secondary analysis in the first phase of the project for all three countries. An additional reason for selecting Norway was that the TCRU team members were keen to work with Silje Skuland at the Norwegian National Institute of Consumer Research.

Most of the participants were recruited on the basis of earlier professional contacts with one exception: the recruitment of a public health nutritionist in Portugal. An initial aim in selecting the wider international team was to include a mix of disciplinary expertise. Early in the project, it became clear that this collaboration was not going to work. Having sought advice from the senior researcher, Julia Brannen, and the chair of the project's advisory group, Elizabeth Dowler, an expert on the social and policy dimensions of food and human nutrition, the PI applied to ERC for an amendment to terminate the Portuguese contract and set up a new contract. The new partners were a group of sociologists in a policy-focussed research unit similar to that of the core team who had already collaborated with its members.

Among the problems that resulted in the termination of the contract with the first Portuguese partner were differences in expectations about preparation for meetings and time keeping. These problems were compounded by differences in 'attitudes to authority'. As the PI of a starting grant, the award holder was younger and had fewer years of research experience than the head of Portuguese team. The rapidity with which the newly contracted research team in Portugal was able to get to grips with the methodology and methods, recruit a sample and make up for lost time caused by the protracted amendment process was partly attributable to their familiarity with the underlying concepts and research approaches geared at understanding children and families' everyday (food) practices. In addition, the concentration of resources and relatively low cost of labour in Portugal meant that more staff and time could be devoted to fieldwork than anticipated. Recruitment was also aided by relatively higher rates of poverty in Portugal and existing connections of the research unit (Instituto de Ciências Sociais) and team members with third sector organisations and schools.

Research Design and Methods

A primary concern in selecting the core team members was to ensure that they had the expertise and skills required to implement an international mixed-methods research design. The study used both quantitative and qualitative methods to address differently framed research questions. This design was well suited to the nature of the award received and the project's aims and objectives. The design required a methodology involving secondary analysis of several large-scale datasets, in combination with micro-level qualitative studies requiring a case-based approach.

A documentary analysis was first carried out to examine the discourses and policies concerning food insecurity in each country and how they changed over time. National policies and programmes were analysed, alongside relevant official statistics and newspaper reports on families, poverty and food (Knight et al., 2018). This part of the research contextualised food poverty by taking into account the different histories of the three countries and their welfare states (O'Connell & Brannen, 2021).

To examine the research question about how many and which types of families and children were at risk of food insecurity in each country, the quantitative researchers in the UK team carried out secondary analysis of the EU Statistics on Income and Living Conditions (EU-SILC) and the Health Behaviour in School-aged Children study (HBSC). They recognised that although the questions asked in the surveys on which these datasets were based had undergone testing and employed widely used indicators, for example of deprivation, they had the potential to be interpreted differently in different contexts. For example, EU-SILC includes in its material deprivation module an item that has been used as a proxy for household food insecurity: the inability to afford a meal containing meat, chicken, fish or a vegetarian equivalent as a source of protein every second day, an amount generally recommended in dietary guidelines across European countries. As revealed in the ethnographic literature and discussions with the Portuguese team, a 'meal' in some countries by definition includes meat or fish. Interpretations of data in international surveys therefore need to be carefully scrutinised.

Central to the subsequent case-based qualitative methodology was its power to make comparisons between families. Comparing and contrasting cases, selected on the basis of the apparently similar characteristics in different countries and places, was an important part of the comparative research. But the FFP team sought to avoid the risk of 'methodological nationalism' by overemphasising aspects of cultural context in interpreting data within a single societal context. They were interested not only in contextual differences but also in similarities.

A second danger that they wanted to avoid in comparing the same phenomenon was the failure to realise that questions, assumptions and concepts that seem self-evident may have entirely different meanings in other contexts, in the knowledge that concepts cannot be separated from contexts since 'each national context has its own demography, cultural expectations and social welfare regime, based in political, cultural and ideological traditions' (O'Connell & Brannen, 2021, p. 47).

Because it is not legal in Portugal to collect data about ethnicity, the recruitment of a diverse sample of low-income families in the qualitative phase of the study could not be carried out with ethnicity as a variable. In practice, this issue was not a problem since the recruitment of families focussed on self-defined financial need. A major aim of much of the qualitative analysis was to compare household food insecurity across family types – lone parents and couples – as discovered in the analysis of the EU-SILC. Because the EU-SILC data on the risk of poverty and food insecurity were collected at the household level, it was not possible to investigate their differential impact on multiple families living within the same household. This limitation meant that it was potentially misleading to assign a lone-parent family the poverty status associated with another family or person living within the same household when resources may not be shared. For this reason, it was decided not to include multi-family households in the analysis of the EU-SILC.

The EU-SILC finding that less difference existed in household food insecurity by family type in Portugal, compared to the other two countries, could be partly explained by methodological reasons, since the analysis excluded lone parents living in multi-family households, which represent a significant share of families in that country. These multigenerational families defied conventional definitions of lone parenthood and were possibly miscoded in large-scale international datasets. In other words, it was possible that those most likely to experience food insecurity lived in multi-family households and were not included in this aspect of the macro-level analysis. The Portuguese team was able to supply another explanation based on their intimate knowledge of the Portuguese policy environment, namely that the families with the lowest incomes in Portugal are likely to be those least able to provide and rely on familial support. In contrast, the qualitative research alerted the team to the phenomenon of multi-family households and their experiences of food poverty.

The qualitative research provided the means to conceptualise the food poverty of families in the context of their own societies by drawing on budget standards data to examine how the food expenditure of families compares with the cost of diets that meet health and social participation needs determined nationally (O'Connell & Brannen, 2021). The team in Portugal found it difficult to translate some terms from the UK team's list of 'strategies' for coping with food poverty that were based on previous research and formed part of the interview; for example, one strategy termed 'cooking from scratch' in English had no synonym in common Portuguese parlance.

The qualitative 'case summaries' were written up from the transcripts and researchers' field notes in accordance with a standardised template of format and content, which was agreed by the research teams in each country. Examples of this 'thick description' were subsequently collectively analysed in team meetings that involved the discussion and comparison of case summaries. In these annual international meetings, online discussions and monthly national meetings, researchers sought to elicit aspects of cultural, local and national features of context which impinged upon the families' lives and might otherwise have remained unspoken or invisible, both in the material collected in their own country and in the material collected elsewhere. This discussion and the exchange of case summaries across the team at earlier stages of the analysis were especially important because the Portuguese and Norwegian interviews were not translated in full.

Engagement and Dissemination

The advisory group, which was composed of representatives of academia and charities in the UK, was closely involved throughout the project. The PI reported regularly to ERC. Draft dissemination strategies were prepared by the PI and shared with the team and advisory group for comment.

Given the growing relevance and high profile of the problems addressed in the project − household food insecurity − especially in the UK, and the aim to achieve social as well as scientific impact, attention was accorded in the dissemination plans to managing the demands of publishing academic outputs and engaging with audiences outside academia. Although the project completion date was 2019, the outbreak of the COVID-19 pandemic added to the interest shown by policymakers and other stakeholders in the findings and recommendations produced by the project after the end of the award.

A blog written for the Child Poverty Action Group (O'Connell et al., 2019a) compared a free school meal in Portugal and the UK and was published on international school meals day. It complemented a book, published in 2019 with CPAG (O'Connell et al., 2019b), that focussed on the findings regarding children's experiences of food, and lack of food, in the context of low income in the UK. The launch of the book at the House of Commons was widely covered in the print and online news media, and the authors spoke about the research on the television news and BBC Radio 4's Woman's Hour. Although this work led to some important publicity and societal impacts, it encroached on the time available for working on academic outputs within the timespan of the funded project.

The ERC proposal included a commitment to produce a monograph on the comparative research. An academic book focussing on the international comparative research was written by the PI and senior researcher and published open access by UCL Press after the end of the award (O'Connell & Brannen, 2021).

It was agreed that, in general, the relationship of the findings to public policies and priorities was best pursued at country level to allow recommendations to be tailored toward national contexts. Each team took control of disseminating the findings to different audiences within their own countries. In the UK, it was useful to draw on comparisons with Portugal in engaging with debates about the provision of free school meals. The approach adopted in the outputs by the partners was to attribute first and second authorship to those who carried out the analysis for the publication, followed by other contributing authors in alphabetical order.

BOX 9.2 LESSONS LEARNT (FFP)

As the holder of a five-year fully funded ERC award that provided experience of managing an international team, the principal investigator of the FFP project drew a number of lessons that are relevant to other mid-career researchers.

- ERC awards are extremely competitive, but once obtained offer conditions – generous funding over a long period of time with minimal reporting requirements – that are conducive to developing a career and experience in international research.
- Funding proposals need to budget for local administrative and academic support to ensure that ERC award holders can take full advantage of the opportunities afforded by the grant.
- Recipients of ERC grants need to be able to rely on their host institution to support their project and to assist them in overcoming financial, legal and practical issues that arise in the course of the research.
- Awards holders can gain valuable experience of how to build and manage an international interdisciplinary research team by being involved in research programmes led by senior colleagues, or by leading research programmes that involve senior colleagues as advisers.
- The success of international multidisciplinary collaborations depends to a large extent on pre-existing relationships with researchers trained in cognate disciplines who have experience of working across cultural and disciplinary boundaries using a combination of methods, are proficient in English, and are highly motivated to engage in constructive and productive working relationships.
- In teams composed of established and less experienced international researchers, it is important for senior researchers to train and mentor junior colleagues, who may be completing their own linked projects.
- Provision needs to be made for research training to be conducted on the job, for example, by carrying out the fieldwork interviews in pairs, or by following the guidance given by core team members to researchers undertaking secondary analyses of quantitative and qualitative data.
- Effective communication should be maintained throughout the project by organising regular international and UK team meetings, keeping all team members updated with minutes of meetings, listing actions agreed, and factoring in time for socialising when planning collaborative events.
- Throughout the process of managing an international interdisciplinary project, principal investigators need to ensure that they meet the funder's requirements for engagement with a variety of stakeholders, including policy audiences.

• It is necessary to develop a publishing strategy and to learn how to manage relationships with publishers and the media.

REFERENCES

Knight, A., Brannen, J., O'Connell, R., & Hamilton, L. (2018). How do children and their families experience food poverty according to UK newspaper media 2006-15? *Journal of Poverty and Social Justice 26*(2), 207–223. DOI: 10.1332/175982718X 15200701225223

O'Connell, R. & Brannen, J. (2021). *Families and food in hard times: European comparative research*. UCL Press. https://discovery.ucl.ac.uk/id/eprint/10127576/1/ Families-and-Food-in-Hard-Times.pdf

O'Connell, R., Brannen, J., & Knight, A. (2019a, 14 March). 'A proper meal'? Free school meals in Portugal and England. *CPAG blog*. Online: https://cpag.org.uk/ news-blogs/news-listings/proper-meal%E2%80%99-free-school-meals-portugal -and-england

O'Connell, R., Knight, A., & Brannen, J. (2019b). *Living hand to mouth: Children and food in low-income families*. Child Poverty Action Group. https://cpag.org.uk/news -blogs/news-listings/living-hand-mouth-now-free-access

10. Low carbon energy for development network (LCEDN)

Ed Brown, Ben Campbell, Jon Cloke, Joni Cook, Simon Batchelor and Long Seng To

---

BOX 10.1 PROJECT DESCRIPTORS (LCEDN)

Duration: January 2012–2022 (10 years)

Web Links: https://www.lcedn.com/
https://www.lcedn.com/uses-network
https://www.lcedn.com/initiatives/category/TEA
https://mecs.org.uk/

Lead Coordinators: Durham University – Ben Campbell (co-chair) (social anthropology)

Loughborough University, UK – Ed Brown (co-chair) (energy and human geography); Jon Cloke (national network manager) (human geography, political economy)

Co-Investigators: Loughborough University – Simon Batchelor (director Gamos, USES programmes lead, MECS research coordinator) (global energy challenges, international development); Joni Cook (TEA project research administrator, MECS communications officer) (plant ecology); Long Seng To (TEA project research associate, research fellow) (engineering for development)

Founding Partners: Durham Energy Institute (DEI); Energy Futures Lab, Imperial College London; Midlands Energy Consortium (MEC); Science Policy Research Unit (SPRU), University of Sussex; UK Energy Research Centre (UKERC)

Funding Organisations: Department for Energy and Climate Change (DECC); Department for International Development (DfID); UK Energy

Research Centre (UKERC); Engineering and Physical Sciences Research Council (EPSRC); World Bank's Energy Sector Management; amount £100,000 initially, reaching £40 million in 2022.

THE LCEDN CASE STUDY

The 'Low carbon energy for development network' (LCEDN) was founded in 2012 with initial funding of £100,000 from the UK's Department for Energy and Climate Change (DECC). The LCEDN was built around hubs in Durham and Loughborough and drew together five academic research centres. Over a period of ten years, the LCEDN evolved into a wide-ranging network of individuals and organisations working together in the UK to promote low carbon energy for development research, in collaboration with researchers, research institutions and stakeholders drawn from academia, industry, government and civil society across the Global South.

The LCEDN case study focusses on three major programmes representing the main externally funded activities and interests pursued by the network across its first ten years: from the Understanding Sustainable Energy Solutions (USES) programme (2013–2018), via the Transforming Energy Access (TEA) initiative (2016–2018), and the ongoing Modern Energy Cooking Services (MECS) programme (2018–2023, with an award of £40 million), through to the relaunch of the network in 2022.

Aims and Objectives

The overall aim of the LCEDN at its foundation in 2012 was to serve as a multi-disciplinary intersectoral platform for academics, practitioners, policymakers and private sector organisations from across the UK working in partnership with global stakeholders on low carbon energy and international development.

The USES research programme aimed to contribute to the longer-term goal of increased clean energy access, resilience and wealth creation for low-income households and communities in developing countries, by undertaking high-quality research that improves the understanding and evidence base of opportunities and challenges associated with scaling up clean energy for development.

The USES programme pursued three specific objectives:

- To improve understanding of clean energy options and opportunities for developing countries, including the social, market and political economy aspects of scaling up sustainable energy access for poor people
- To strengthen developing country research capacity on clean energy

- To improve access to practical and policy-relevant knowledge on the challenges and opportunities for sustainable energy solutions in developing countries

The objectives targeted by the LCEDN's involvement within the TEA initiative included:

- To champion efforts considering the context within which innovation takes place, and promote comparative interdisciplinary analysis of developments in markets from systemic and more actor-focussed intersectoral perspectives
- To focus on governance issues in understanding how new forms of energy access will affect the lives of poor people across the Global South, and in recognising unintended social consequences of technological and financial interventions
- To build capacity, focussed particularly on equity, empowerment, governance, justice and longer-term developmental impact rather than only finance and technology

The MECS programme champions a new approach to tackling the global challenge of clean cooking by rapidly accelerating a transition from biomass to genuinely clean cooking with electricity or gas.

Important objectives of the programme include:

- To examine the socio-political contexts, availability and distribution of cooking solution supply chains
- To help integrate modern energy cooking services into planning for electricity access, quality, reliability and sustainability
- To analyse how the social factors, cultural preferences, affordability and availability of purchase plans for consumers are influencing the suitability and choice of the clean cooking technology adopted within specific communities

Themes and Research Questions

The LCEDN programme focusses on policy and practice in international development and low carbon energy transitions through interdisciplinary science and technology research, capacity building and collaborative project delivery. A central theme running through the LCEDN programme is the need to complement work on the development of new technologies and/or a search for methodologies that could take new technological developments 'to scale' with more nuanced contextual understandings.

The USES programme brought together 13 projects to deal with topics as diverse as political decentralisation and energy policy, community energy initiatives, city-level energy planning, energy efficiency drives across cities and within building design, and barriers to the adoption of clean cooking. The TEA work, in contrast, focussed on consolidating the LCEDN knowledge base, by reviewing the state of the UK research community, and expanding a variety of capacity building partnerships with academic and non-academic researchers in the UK, and with partners from the Global South. MECS concentrated on ways of integrating modern energy cooking services into government plans to meet cooking needs of households through investment and action on access to affordable, reliable, sustainable modern energy for all.

The network's various programmes and projects raised four fundamental questions, which were addressed across a wide variety of specific initiatives, country contexts and sectors. The MECS programme added a fifth more specific question:

1. How can interdisciplinary research contribute to the knowledge base on low carbon energy solutions and development?
2. How can better, more effective projects be engendered through the collaboration of different disciplines that also consider the unintended and often uneven social consequences of technological interventions, the roots of energy poverty and its complex social dynamics?
3. How are interventions embedded within different contexts and how do user decisions, cultural norms and practices affect the adoption of specific technologies?
4. How can governments, industry and civil society use scientific evidence to sustain low carbon energy solutions to mitigate climate change?
5. How can governments and other agencies use research findings to accelerate the transition to modern energy cooking services?

THE RESEARCH PROCESS

This LCEDN case study describes how the network was originally established and grew from its humble academic beginnings to a large-scale multisectoral enterprise. Given the diversity of the funding that it received, and the ways in which the network was structured, the case study focusses on the transversal issues that arose across the USES, TEA and MECS programmes, representing the range of activities and interests of the different funders and teams as they recruited partners, built research teams, developed and sustained projects in international multidisciplinary environments.

Meeting Funders' Requirements

The idea for the network was developed following discussions between the organisers of an international workshop held in Loughborough in 2010, which was funded as part of the second phase (2009–2014) of an initiative in the UK Energy Research Centre's (UKERC) meeting place scheme, originally launched in 2004 by three UK research councils: Engineering and Physical Sciences Research Council (EPSRC), Economic and Social Research Council (ESRC), and Natural Environment Research Council (NERC). The workshop highlighted the need for flexible, critical and proactive responses from the research community to build bridges between existing pools of expertise in the energy and development fields, supported by existing and new funding mechanisms.

Meetings between DECC, the Department for International Development (DfID), Research Councils UK (RCUK), and the research communities resulted in an initiative being developed in 2012 with a small amount of funding provided by the Midlands Energy Consortium and the Durham Energy Institute. This pump-priming activity enabled the core team to prepare an initial bid to DECC for the formation of the LCEDN, which was awarded later that year.

With funding support from RCUK, DfID and DECC, during its first 15 months LCEDN organised three major international conferences and quickly established a significant presence within the energy and international development arena. The LCEDN was influential in scoping and developing a major research programme (USES) financed by the same three funders. At the end of 2016, the LCEDN was contracted by DfID to lead an 18-month £1.3 million programme of work on partnerships for skills development under the TEA programme.

Government funders worked in conjunction with a variety of academia and policymaking bodies, each with their own funding mechanisms, requirements, expectations and priorities, as presented in calls for proposals or more directly funded collaborations. Although government departments and research councils were working in tandem, the research councils were more interested in academic outputs, whereas government departments demanded policy relevance, value for money, external visibility and impact, a requirement amply fulfilled by the MECS research programme, launched in 2018 with funding from DfID.

The £40 million MECS programme is being led by Loughborough University in close partnership with the UK development consultancy Gamos, the World Bank's energy sector management assistance programme, and a range of UK and international partners. The funders required that the programme should produce evidence of how governments and other agencies can accelerate the transition to modern energy cooking services. By the end of 2021, the programme had already been instrumental in initiating a major change in narrative and approach to the provision of low carbon energy for cooking and has been working directly with governments, businesses and other stakeholders in implementing that new narrative.

In line with what has become a key requirement of research funders that draw, directly or indirectly, on public finances, research councils and UK universities are expected to demonstrate societal and/or economic impact from funded research. The 13 individual sub-projects within the USES programme were evaluated formally via research council reporting procedures, while TEA and MECS were monitored by DfID, with its strong emphasis on measuring impact. The Foreign, Commonwealth and Development Office (FCDO), so-named following the merger of the Foreign and Commonwealth Office (FCO) and DfID in 2020, has maintained this interest in the evidence generated, its dissemination and policy uptake. FCDO assessments of impact are part of the annual reporting process alongside detailed evaluation of a range of much more specific milestones and deliverables and longer-term assessments of impact and outcomes.

The different cycles of funding were found to be having an impact on the capacity to nurture the longer-term international partnerships on which the LCEDN is so reliant. A frequent comment to funding bodies was that the cycles of funding were themselves disruptive and that a new, more prolonged, approach to more promising projects was required, supported by a review framework operated by funding bodies.

Several working relationships outside the UK established during the USES programme were strengthened and built upon during subsequent phases. For example, relationships with the African Centre for Technology Studies in Kenya were present in all three programmes. The major funding cuts to DfID's budgets in 2020 therefore presented the network with difficult decisions resulting in some of the long-established relationships having to be ended. Another issue that the LCEDN core team had to address arose from the success of the MECS programme, which had the effect of drawing several of the key actors within the LCEDN away from work on the management and growth of the LCEDN itself. Alongside the loss of any organisational funding for the LCEDN, this shift in activity meant that the network remained virtually inactive for almost two years. In December 2021, some of the key LCEDN actors came together to discuss how, reflecting on ten years of experience, to seek follow-on funding to reinitiate LCEDN activity.

Building the Project Team

When the network was established, the community of low carbon energy for development research in the UK was nascent and fragile, and professional links between technical and social specialists were virtually non-existent. The heterogeneous assortment of fragmented research was reflected in the difficulties of pulling together insights from the existing research portfolio, and encouraging connectivity and the emergence of stronger, more transdisciplinary research trajectories. Part of the problem was due to the 'siloised' arrangement whereby research funnels in the UK did not foster cross-thematic blending through collaborative initiatives. The systematic review by DfID (Watson et al., 2012) into the extent of energy research projects in the UK specifically mentioned the need for transdisciplinarity within universities in energy research, but also the frequent failure to satisfy this need. Government support for the LCEDN provided the incentive and opportunity to enhance the systemic complexity of this research field by cross-fertilisation with the innovations taking place in the private sector at a time when the research councils were actively promoting cross-council research initiatives.

The LCEDN core team argued that the hitherto limited understanding of 'solutions' needed to be broken open, and that the dominant focus on technology should be re-directed towards a strengthening of socio-technical knowledge of social energy systems (Campbell et al., 2016). In developing the network, the team sought partners from different disciplinary backgrounds capable of persuading project designers, funders and the private sector to think in a transcalar interdisciplinary way, for example through understanding the different use values accorded to technology from across rural Africa to the Global North.

One of the key features of the LCEDN is that most of its core team members came into energy research from backgrounds in wider studies of international development, rather than being energy or climate researchers who became interested in development. Several of the key actors who initiated the negotiations between Durham and Loughborough in the establishment of the network were geographers.

As a human geographer, LCEDN co-coordinator Ed Brown brought research interests in the fields of governance and international development issues focussing on questions of transparency and corruption; financial globalisation and the financial needs of the poor; and energy access and low carbon energy transitions. Jon Cloke, who became the national network manager, was a human geographer and political economist. He had worked with various NGOs including the UK-based Practical Action. He had cooperated closely with Brown at Loughborough for many years on questions of financial justice, corruption and transparency.

Ben Campbell, as co-coordinator, brought expertise and experience of anthropological research on low carbon energy in development contexts, having championed this agenda with the newly formed Durham Energy Institute. His research in social anthropology had focussed on poverty, livelihoods and resources in Nepal and on the impacts of environmental conservation measures on local institutions of common property management.

Joni Cook, with a background in plant ecology, worked with the LCEDN founder members as a project manager during the first phase of the research, and operates as a communications specialist on the MECS programme. Simon Batchelor became involved in the network when Gamos participated in several of the USES projects. Deepening the collaboration with key figures in the LCEDN, he became a visiting researcher at Loughborough and went on to co-lead the MECS programme. He brought many years of practical experience of bridging research and project implementation, initially in agriculture and water, and then on wind and solar energy, in Africa and Asia. His contribution is to the role of social factors in technology adoption (Batchelor, 2012). Long Seng To, with her background in engineering and development, was initially recruited as a project research associate with the TEA programme. She went on to secure a prestigious RAEng Engineering for Development Research Fellowship and is joint director, with Ed Brown and Mark Howells, of the Loughborough Centre for Sustainable Transitions: Energy, Environment and Resilience (STEER), launched in 2021.

The intention has always been to encourage longer-term partnerships between researchers from different academic backgrounds, geographies and cultures, as well as between a variety of researchers and stakeholders be they academics, policymakers, businesses or individual communities. The network has been progressively extended to other UK universities and stakeholders, and a host of international partners across the Global South. In 2021, the LCEDN database of expertise, which largely focusses on the UK community, contained over 300 researchers' profiles.

Research Design and Methods

From its inception, the LCEDN was structured around a management committee, originally chaired by John Loughhead, who later became chief scientific adviser to DECC. The committee comprised representatives from the two founding universities and from a range of other stakeholders including DECC, DfID, RCUK, and other interested parties such as the Ashden Awards, Practical Action, the Royal Academy of Engineering, and the UK Collaborative on Development Research (UKCDR). The LCEDN was designed initially as a large-scale international multidisciplinary network, although quite how large it was to become was difficult to predict in a rapidly changing political, economic and environmental context, where funding and other support could be withheld at short notice.

The activities of the network were largely delivered via a secretariat based at Loughborough and Durham involving Brown, Campbell and Cloke (and initially the late Paul Johnson), who recruited other colleagues to support them on specific tasks or, when funding allowed, for the appointment of dedicated staff. Each of the LCEDN initiatives drew on a range of methodologies and research approaches, including landscape mapping, participant observation, focus groups, qualitative interviews, practical project development, practical actions and workshops, to deliver its objectives.

The first phase in building the LCEDN focussed on the creation of a membership database, which was compiled by Jon Cloke in a trawl of all energy and development/low carbon transition researchers from every university in the UK. The membership grew thereafter through self-application. This scoping and mapping exercise prepared the ground for the development of the USES programme before its launch in 2013.

One of the network's guiding principles implemented in the USES programme was the insistence that all funded project teams should be multidisciplinary, multi-country and multisectoral. As the kinds of alliances proposed by the LCEDN increased, it also became obvious that there was a need for a wider involvement with NGOs, as well as the private and government sectors.

The second phase of developing the LCEDN focussed on:

- Building the multidisciplinary academic community
- Distillation visualisation of research data and the engagement of research users across sectors
- Building the international presence

Numerous LCEDN activities were designed to identify the meanings of impact in the low carbon energy and development context, and how it could be achieved. During the annual USES network meetings, different approaches towards impact planning were discussed. For example, one session explored the suitability of 'participatory impact pathways analysis' for the kinds of multisectoral and transdisciplinary projects being developed in the individual USES projects. Later sessions focussed on how to engage key stakeholders successfully in planning for longer-term partnership development.

The search for methodologies that could take new technological developments 'to scale' was made possible through the creation of new 'delivery models', built on approaches that considered the unintended and often uneven social consequences of technological interventions, the roots of energy poverty and its complex social dynamics. These new models, which were debated and developed in workshops and practical projects, examined how interventions are embedded in different contexts and the complex ways in which user decisions, cultural norms and practices affect technological fit.

LCEDN programmes and projects used participant observation, focus groups and qualitative interviews, alongside more quantitative approaches to modelling and technological development, to illustrate how, by linking disciplines and cross-fertilising systemic complexity, innovations take place across sectors. From the early formation of a mixed-discipline community of practice, particular members of the LCEDN were explicitly exploring others' perspectives on energy and development, building up 'thick' descriptions of contexts and histories of innovation, and cultivating methodological empathy for how others' ways of knowing can be practically brought into dialogue, for example by embedding researchers from one discipline within contrasting teams. Country-specific cooking diaries research was one of the methods used by MECS in collaboration with in-country partner organisations and communities.

As a taster for transdisciplinary collaboration, anthropologist Ben Campbell and engineer Jon Leary used the concept of 'ethno-engineering' workshops to experiment in different locations and institutional settings with ways of democratising technological innovations by recognising 'the engineer within everybody'. By shifting the expert focus from the engineer to the cultural practitioner, the challenge of co-producing a research design, for example to adapt highly valued local foods and meals for low carbon energy systems, privileged the expertise of the local culture bearer in the frame of socio-technical enquiry. This approach generated a positive sense of collaboration among those involved to bring about a very different relational dynamic to innovation processes than that normally associated with the phrase 'behaviour change'.

Other examples of the LCEDN's interdisciplinary work included workshops across the USES projects to explore gender and energy as a problematic that could be addressed from all their perspectives. Working in small groups, thinking about less dominant voices, and calling for recognition of the effects of energo-patriarchy helped elucidate deeper attention to unconscious bias and other factors that perpetuate gender blindness in energy research and practice. The integration of development and research innovation strategies mobilised capacities and expertise in the energy and development field across communities in north and south.

Several of the USES projects identified local levels of government as being particularly important and neglected within the energy access sector. Stakeholders in Kenya were, for example, engaged in the network in a context of political decentralisation, which was emerging in the longer term across many African countries. A number of the key partnerships worked together to build capacity in local energy planning culminating in the engagement of Loughborough University, the International Institute for Environment and

Development (IIED), Practical Action East Africa and the African Centre for Technology Studies within a major EU-funded capacity building initiative with the Kenyan Energy Ministry, led by the French consultancy Innovation Energie Développement (IED).

Engagement and Dissemination

Government and research council funders require that outputs from their programmes are made publicly available. LCEDN researchers were expected to engage with interested stakeholders at local, national and international levels. The network committed to meeting these requirements in their proposals and actively promoted their work through their websites and social media, in public events and in scholarly publications targeted at a range of stakeholders.

The LCEDN's engagement strategy has involved the planning, coordination and publicising of a diverse schedule of events to promote interdisciplinarity for scientists working in the fields of low carbon energy transitions and international development, while expanding its size and its global and multisectoral reach. The LCEDN's dissemination and influencing strategy also included the co-organisation of events targeted at specific sectors or stakeholders. For example, sessions were arranged at several events highlighting the UK's contribution to energy transformation through showcasing initiatives funded by DfID under Innovate UK's Energy Catalyst programme.

These sessions provided a timely opportunity for delegates from academic, public and private sectors to foster further multisectoral collaborations, and to exchange ideas of how barriers and bottlenecks to industry scale-up of low carbon technologies can be overcome. Events fostering interdisciplinarity were key in building effective partnerships and have led to subsequent positive shifts of policy objectives and priorities in accelerating low carbon energy transitions.

The LCEDN's ethos of building interdisciplinarity and multisectoral collaborations is being carried through and developed further in the activities of the MECS programme. These approaches are being used to promote key messages from MECS' outputs, for example through the planning of coordinated joint press releases by MECS and Energy 4 Impact for the launch of each report of the co-authored 'Financing clean cooking' series via websites and social media channels.

Given its diversified funding sources, multidisciplinary and multisectoral partners and stakeholders, the LCEDN has had to address the issue of where and how to publish its findings. The core team is aware that many of its targeted published outputs in the form of reports, reviews, technical briefs, blogs, working papers and conference proceedings, whilst of crucial importance to securing impact, are significantly undervalued in the research excellence framework (REF) that drives the prioritisation of academics' research time on a daily basis in the UK. The greater importance being attributed to impact in the last REF to some extent compensated for the lack of other forms of academic recognition, although severe doubts continue to be expressed about the future of impact assessment as an indicator of scientific excellence (Wilsdon, 2020).

BOX 10.2 LESSONS LEARNT (LCEDN)

The LCEDN case studies provide a valuable illustration of how, from modest beginnings and with like-minded colleagues, a group of mid-career researchers was able to initiate, develop and manage a large-scale international multidisciplinary, multiscalar, multisectoral research network supported by a combination of national government and research council awards.

- Opportunities should be seized to attend training and pump-priming events, seminars and conferences for researchers interested in acquiring the necessary skills and competences to work in international settings, and to manage multidisciplinary teams on a transdisciplinary basis.
- Time and effort need to be devoted to building and growing cross-disciplinary research teams and networks in preparation for applications for funding and to sustain them in the longer term.
- Multiple funding sources (government departments, research councils, other funding agencies) should be approached when a network is being developed, bearing in mind their priorities and the appropriateness of their programmes.
- Research coordinators of enlarging networks need to be realistic in negotiating funding support and meeting the requirements of funders, particularly in terms of the organisational and financial barriers for international partners.
- Interdisciplinary project management requires an openness to conceptual understandings and a willingness to accommodate different approaches and mindsets.
- In international settings, project managers should be prepared to perform bridging roles between researchers and stakeholders, and to ensure that proposals are adapted to contexts.
- Network leaders need to have an in-depth knowledge and understanding about how the projects can be realised in different cultures, societies, political and academic systems.

- Networks that last for several years need to develop strategic plans to deal with the loss of resources (funds and personnel), and they must be prepared to adapt their objectives and working methods accordingly.
- They need to be conversant with the institutional requirements of their team members in terms of research assessment and career progression.
- Programme managers need to ensure that early career researchers from diverse disciplinary and cultural backgrounds are fully integrated into a community of practice assembled around the core agenda of a network, and able to share in its sustainability to develop their potential.

REFERENCES

Batchelor, S. (2012). Changing the financial landscape of Africa: An unusual story of evidence-informed innovation, intentional policy influence and private sector engagement. *IDS Bulletin, 43*(5), 84–90. DOI: 10.1111/j.1759-5436.2012.00367.x

Brown, E., Campbell, B., Cloke, J., Seng To, L., Turner, B. & Wray, A. (2018). Low carbon energy and international development: From research impact to policymaking. *Contemporary Social Science, 13*(1), 112–127. DOI: 10.1080/21582041.2017.1417627

Campbell, B., Cloke, J. & Brown, E. (2016). Communities of energy, *Economic Anthropology, 3*, 133144. DOI:10.1002/sea2.12050

Watson, J., Byrne, R., Opazo, J., Tsang, F., Castle-Clarke, S., Fry, C., & Morgan Jones, M. (2012, 1 January). *What are the major barriers to increased use of modern energy services among the world's poorest people and are interventions to overcome these effective?* [CEE review 11-004]. https://www.gov.uk/research-for-development-outputs/what-are-the-major-barriers-to-increased-use-of-modern-energy-services-among-the-world-s-poorest-people-and-are-interventions-to-overcome-these-effective-systematic-review

Wilsdon, J. (2020, 27 January). A requiem for impact? *Wonkhe blog.* https://wonkhe.com/blogs/a-requiem-for-impact/

11. Different pathways to employment (POLKU)

Minna van Gerven, Tuuli Malava, Merita Mesiäislehto and Peppi Saikku

---

BOX 11.1 PROJECT DESCRIPTORS (POLKU)

Duration: November 2020–May 2022 (1.5 years)

Web Links: https://www2.helsinki.fi/en/projects/different-paths-to
-employment
   https://vnk.fi/-/1927382/eri-poluilla-tyollisyyteen-suomen-sosiaaliturvaja
rjestelman-erityispiirteet-ja-ongelmakohdat-kansainvalisessa-vertailussa

Principal Investigator/Coordinator: University of Helsinki, Finland – Minna van Gerven (social and public policy); Tuuli Malava (social and public policy)

Co-Investigators: Finnish Institute for Health and Welfare – Merita Mesiäislehto (social policy); Joonas Ollonqvist (economics); Peppi Saikku (social and public policy)
   Stockholm University, Sweden – Rense Nieuwenhuis (sociology); Kenneth Nelson (sociology)

Partners: University of Bath, UK – Jane Millar (social policy); Levana Magnus (sociology)
   University of Utrecht, Netherlands – Rik van Berkel (law, economics and governance)

Funding Organisation: VN TEAS (Valtioneuvoston selvitys ja tutkimus-toiminta), Finnish Prime Minister's Office, amount €149,919; Universities of Bath and Utrecht, own resources.

THE FINNISH CASE STUDY

This case study describes the different stages in the POLKU project, 'Eri poluilla työllisyyteen: Suomen sosiaaliturvajärjestelmän erityispiirteet ja ongelmakohdat kansainvälisessä vertailussa' ['Different pathways to employment: Special features of the Finnish social security system and problem areas in international comparison'], from the application for an award under the Finnish government's programme for analysis, assessment and research activities, through the formation of the project team to its final months.

Aims and Objectives

The POLKU project aimed to provide internationally comparable information on the problems of integrating social security benefits and services for the working-age unemployed population, and the possible solutions adopted in Finland, Sweden, Denmark, the Netherlands and the UK to dismantle barriers to employment. This small-scale project was designed to deliver evidence-based data to inform political decision-making.

Themes and Research Questions

The Finnish team set up five sub-projects focussing on the topics identified in the call for proposals: social security employment benefit systems; job-seeking processes; problem areas in integrating benefits and services; solutions adopted in other countries and their effectiveness; and the transferability of solutions.

In examining these topics, the sub-projects addressed four research questions:

1. What kinds of problems are most salient in Finland in coordinating income security benefits and services for the working-age population?
2. How common are the corresponding problem areas in the selected comparison countries?
3. How are other countries seeking to prevent and alleviate similar problems?
4. How effective are the solutions adopted in the selected countries?

THE RESEARCH PROCESS

The project's key objectives, the composition of the project team and the research methodology were determined essentially by the funder's requirements as laid down in the formal call for proposals. The case study examines how the amount of funding awarded and the prior experience of the coordinating team shaped the ways in which the international dimension of the project and the disciplinary elements were integrated into the project.

Meeting the Funder's Requirements

VN TEAS projects are supported by government funds provided for joint analysis, assessment and research activities coordinated by the Finnish prime minister's office. The aim of the funder is to create a basis for systematic and broad-based use of research data in decision-making in government and its ministries, and to strengthen the knowledge base for use in decision-making, knowledge-based policy and overall strategic foresight planning. The VN TEAS calls are frequent: several dozens a year on various topics. They are open to applications from organisations including universities for applied sciences, research institutes, companies and third sector organisations, and intersectoral and international organisations. The prime minister's office identifies the research topics, and the responsible government department – the Ministry of Social Affairs and Health in the case of POLKU – evaluates and selects the winning proposals. The evaluation process is transparent: the assessment criteria are publicised, and all evaluations are communicated to all applicants.

The VN TEAS call themes are directly linked to the requirements of the Finnish government. The research questions are announced in the call for proposals. Applications must include all the objectives and disciplines identified in the call. The VN POLKU proposal was designed to contribute to information needs for the reform of social security, which was being addressed by a parliamentary committee in 2020–2027. The research questions prescribed by the funder concerned basic social security, earnings-based benefits and social assistance, their financing and the connections between these forms of support, as well as the integration of services and benefits.

The steering group, led by the Ministry of Social Affairs and Health, and composed of members from the Finnish Ministry of Economic Affairs and Employment and prime minister's office, together with the project coordinators, was set up to oversee the research process.

The main obstacle facing the POLKU project was the limited funding, especially given the ambitious pre-set research agendas of VN TEAS projects. The Finnish budget for an 18-month project covered the employment costs of one Master's student for 11 months and very limited time for the principal investigator (PI) and other senior colleagues, and for fieldwork and dissemination of findings to a wider policy audience. No funding was allocated for academic dissemination. Nor did the total funding cover the reimbursement of expenses for all the national teams despite the funder's requirement for international comparisons to be made of the arrangements in various European countries. The Swedish partner was included in the budget for the work in Sweden and Denmark, but the contributions of the partners in the UK and the Netherlands were not covered.

Another administrative obstacle that the project coordinators faced in setting up the project was in arranging the consortium agreement between the funded partners. This issue required protracted discussions, and it took several months to resolve the problem of how to obtain exemptions from the VN TEAS general terms and conditions for the project from national legal departments, due to differences in the legal frameworks of the participating countries. Only after ten months, and following an intervention by the legal team at the prime minister's office (on request), could the legal departments settle and finalise the consortium agreement for the project. The start of the fieldwork was delayed in some of the countries, without ultimately jeopardising the integrity of the project.

Building the Project Team

Most partners knew each other from previous collaborations and/or conferences. The researchers in the Department of Public and Social Policy at Helsinki University and the Finnish Institute for Health and Welfare (THL), a Finnish research and development institute operating under the Ministry of Social Affairs and Health, decided to prepare a joint proposal in response to the call. The main applicants from the two institutes had a shared interest in comparative research in the area of social security, and the call was seen as a fruitful way to pool their expertise. Helsinki University took the lead since it was easier for them to recruit a Master's student to assist with the research. The Swedish partners were invited to participate in the project due to their expertise in quantitative research and their access to the Swedish and Danish cases.

Since the timeline was tight, opportunities to recruit new staff were limited, and most work had to done by team members 'in house'. Because the funder did not directly finance all partners, the consortium depended on unfunded assistance from the international partners to be able to carry out the fieldwork in two of the countries (the Netherlands and the UK) from the total of five being compared. The funding in the budget for the Swedish team enabled them to employ senior staff and research assistance for the fieldwork in Sweden and Denmark.

This VN TEAS call required an international comparison. The countries were not predetermined in the call. In principle, the project could have been conducted without international partners. Given the focus on policy learning, the proposal needed to cover systems in countries that would be relevant for Finnish policymaking. The coordinating team selected European comparators that were broadly similar to those in Finland but that varied in detail, namely Denmark and Sweden, together with countries that differed in several respects, namely the Netherlands and the UK. The country selection covered different types of welfare regime: the Nordic states and the Netherlands insofar as they shared characteristics of the 'continental/corporatist' systems, compared to the UK with its more 'liberal' system (Esping-Andersen, 1990).

The project team was seeking to compare and contrast different approaches to welfare provision and to draw lessons from them. Since VN TEAS funding does not allow direct support for a large number of countries, the selection of the Netherlands and the UK was partly determined by the project manager's professional and personal connections with those countries. The partners accepted that they would need to secure their own funding and/or devote their own time to the project.

The coordinating team opted for a consortium with experience of working on international comparisons, using mixed methods, and with expertise in both social security and public employment service delivery. The project manager had worked with most of the team members prior to this project, including THL staff, on government-funded projects and had been an adviser to the Finnish government. The VN TEAS call provided an opportunity for researchers with complementary methodological and thematic knowledge to collaborate. The project manager was experienced in qualitative case studies comparing social security systems, and THL colleagues had experience in quantitative cross-national projects, and had worked on integrating services in the health and social welfare sectors.

The Department of Public and Social Policy at Helsinki University led the project together with THL. Additional partners were selected to supplement the core teams' expertise, including a colleague at THL who was able to run microsimulations. Although project partners varied in their disciplinary backgrounds (from management to sociology), they were all experts in analysing passive and active social policies. Their complementary disciplinary expertise and approaches gave added depth to the analysis and enabled them to adopt a mixed-method research design.

VN TEAS funds relatively short-term high-intensity projects of a maximum duration of about two years. Since the POLKU project was premised on the collection of additional primary data, a very tight time management plan was drawn up. The need for easy access to data resulted in the prioritisation of existing data for the other sub-projects. The Swedish partner had the advantage of direct access to comparable datasets that the project team wanted to utilise. The other European partners provided access to respondents for the vignette survey. They assisted with the project design and implementation, and in locating relevant policy documents.

Finnish was the main language for the project, since the principal deliverable (research report) was to be submitted in Finnish. The national partners conducted the fieldwork in their own languages: Swedish, Danish, English and Dutch. They translated the vignette questions and instructions and supplementary documentation into the project languages.

Research Design and Methods

The POLKU project aimed to achieve a genuinely collaborative approach utilising a combination of established and innovative methods to compare and understand how welfare benefits and services can be most effectively integrated. The project needed to be firmly wedded to its aim of contributing to the decision-making process and providing evidence-based support for Finnish policymakers in the context of plans to reform the social security system.

The prescribed focus in the call guided the adoption of a broad theoretical framework. Because VN TEAS research proposals are expected to be very short (maximum ten pages), they leave little room for extensive theoretical development. From the outset, the VN POLKU consortium had made a firm commitment to contribute both to the theoretical discussion and to the empirical analysis of the topic. The funders accepted the proposal and later commented positively on the approach at a steering committee meeting, even though theoretical advancement had not been a priority.

The requirements in the call for information about Finland's policy needs were not always easy to reconcile with the comparative approach, and much of the discussion in the steering group meetings focussed on how this issue was being resolved. Comparative study of the integration of benefits and services, the focal point of the VN POLKU, was challenging due not only to variations in the understanding of intersecting concepts across countries, but also to differences between disciplines.

The research questions prescribed in the VN TEAS call led to discussion and clarification of conceptual issues within the coordinating team and with the foreign partners throughout the research process. For instance, the integration of welfare benefits and services lacks theoretical clarity, and various terms are used by scholars in different disciplines to describe concepts such as the governance of activation, as in 'integrated activation policy' (Heidenreich & Aurich-Beerheide, 2014), 'integrated services' (Minas, 2016), or 'integrated social and employment policies' (Heidenreich & Rice, 2016). In the POLKU project, the systematic literature review and a discussion at a social policy (ESPAnet) conference with a large number of European scholars in the field enabled the project team to reach a consensus in defining the terminology to be used within the research team.

Many of the questions in the call for proposals presupposed the application of a particular method. Although VN TEAS often looks for innovative methods, consortia are left to decide what to offer predicated on their skill sets. The project structure was based on five interrelated sub-projects designed to address the topics raised in the call for proposals using a combination of different research methods.

The first sub-project focussed on social security benefit systems for unemployment and social assistance, and publicly provided employment services, including social and employment-related training and upskilling, as well as rehabilitation and health-related services. Since the consortium wanted to produce publishable policy-relevant findings based on practically oriented research, they began by conducting a systematic literature review. The review involved analysis of national social security systems, using policy documents and evaluations of national 'best practice' programmes, to identify the challenges that arose and the solutions adopted when integrating welfare benefits and services in European countries between 2010 and 2021. This approach provided an overview of changes in the past decade. The impact of similarities and differences in national systems was later analysed in sub-project four by comparing the effects of social benefit systems with a set of harmonised quantitative indicators.

The second sub-project investigated the processes involved in jobseeking in the countries selected. The call mentioned a preference for vignette studies. The consortium considered it to be feasible and a unique selling point given that the THL already had this rare skill set available in-house. The vignette method was therefore included in the research proposal to address issues such as how to compare practices between countries, and to identify the consequences of case selection for the findings and dissemination plans. The method enabled the research team to achieve a more in-depth understanding of the practices of integrating benefits with the services used in different European countries. This choice had the advantage of raising the academic value of the project, but the disadvantage of requiring the collection and analysis of new data, which was challenging within the 18-month time frame.

The partners conducted vignette studies in Finland and the four comparator countries, supplemented by expert interviews. The selection of countries and number of vignettes had been decided by the core applicants. The vignettes focussed on four main hypothetical categories: unemployed young people, long-term unemployed with insurance benefit, long-term unemployed with social assistance benefit, and long-term unemployed with a refugee background. These categories were later refined with reference to the literature (Björklund et al., 2020; OECD, 2020), and in consultation with the steering committee.

Because some categories of jobseekers in Finland are quite specific (OECD, 2020), the vignettes were designed to reveal process-related issues, for example, when, by whom and how services are provided, and what major obstacles are faced by the claimants and jobseekers, as well as the administrators. It was necessary to broaden the focus of the Finnish jobseeker categories so that the vignette questions were meaningful for participants in other countries. Compromises, such as the extension of categories, were reached to ensure comparability, while maintaining a research design that would meet the funder's requirements.

At least three respondents were selected per country to ensure the validity and reliability of the findings. The respondents for the vignettes were experts in local social security and public employment services administration in small, medium and large cities. Local partners were left to contact people who they thought would be best able to answer the questions in the vignettes. The respondents were mostly managers working in municipal administration of welfare benefits and services. They were asked to reflect on typical benefit and service pathways for each of the unemployed categories. For instance, questions were posed about the rights and responsibilities relating to benefits and services, their service needs, and the determination of additional services in cases of prolonged benefit dependency.

The vignette questions were decided in virtual meetings and in correspondence with the foreign partners. Discussion about concepts within the core team and with the partners covered issues such as how to compare practices in different countries. Training sessions were organised for the fieldwork researchers (partners and their research assistants). Joint and bilateral online meetings were arranged to examine issues arising in the fieldwork. Many adaptations were made to the original template based on the feedback received to clarify questions that did not make sense in different policy contexts, and to identify opportunities for mutual learning.

The third sub-project was interested in the outcomes of the different social security systems and public employment programmes in the comparator countries. The Finnish system is often criticised for its complexity due to the large number of benefits for the unemployed and the low labour force participation rates of certain population groups, such as (female) migrants from countries outside the EU and persons with reduced work capacity, for example with a long-term chronic illness or conditions limiting their daily activities. The project team used a wide range of international comparative quantitative survey data statistics to gain an understanding of how other countries have succeeded in supporting and integrating the different population groups in the labour market: EU-SILC, MISSOC, OECD, and existing evaluation studies in the target countries, such as the Swedish social policy indicators (SPIN) database. The research team examined employment status and income sources – earnings from full-time or part-time work, social assistance benefit, unemployment benefit, disability benefit, pension or other provisions – for the different population groups and their reasons for being unemployed. In addition, evaluation studies of public employment programmes were reviewed to obtain information about their effectiveness.

The aim of the fourth sub-project was to identify and analyse solutions adopted in other countries that could be applied in Finland's social security reform. The POLKU proposal was especially ambitious in that it included a microsimulation approach, based on the EUROMOD microsimulation model, to compare the effectiveness of the solutions adopted in different countries. The aim was to evaluate the possible effects of some of the solutions identified on the level of benefits and financial incentives for work. The simulation method enabled the production of possible alternatives for achieving benefit reforms, although it could not be used to carry out a systematic analysis of differential practices within services and their roles in pathways to employment.

The fifth sub-project was designed to assess the potential for transferring effective solutions between countries. The results from the microsimulation were evaluated in relation to the solutions obtained from the vignettes to provide a better understanding of the compatibility of benefit systems. The combination of methods allowed the project team to answer the broad set of questions posed by the funders by providing both country (policy) specific knowledge and systematic comparative analysis of the integration of benefits and services in different welfare regimes.

Engagement and Dissemination

Throughout the process, the partners worked together and in parallel on papers and documents on two Microsoft Teams platforms: one for the core team and the other for the foreign teams, to provide access to centrally held documents.

The project steering group enabled a fast and smooth information flow to different administrative services in Finnish ministries, thereby ensuring that the project findings contributed to the preparation of Finnish social security reform. Steering group meetings were held four times a year. They facilitated cross-fertilisation of ideas between policymakers and academics. For example, the policymakers made an input to the selection of cases for jobseekers to be investigated in vignettes. The meetings enabled frequent knowledge exchange between researchers and policymakers, who were also involved in planning the social security reform together with the parliamentary committee.

The group played an important role in the assessment of the progress reports. The core research team presented interim reports at their regular meetings. They also made (preliminary) findings available to a wider audience (through blogs and other outputs) at strategic milestones (start, middle and end of the project). The project team was able to make a direct input to the ongoing parliamentary process of social security reform and the work of several ministries by contextualising the situation in Finland in relation to other European societies. The research team members participated frequently in governmental committees and working groups.

In their final assessment of the project, VN TEAS agreed that the core research team had identified and provided acceptable responses to the issues relevant to social security reform planning. The high-level ministerial staff involved in planning the reform of the Finnish social security system deemed the impact of the research to be significant. They recognised that, in combination with other VN TEAS evaluations and research projects being funded, and other national and international projects on the topic, it contributed to a valuable corpus of information for policymaking. They acknowledged that the POLKU project would directly impact on the future development of the Finnish welfare state by providing research-based knowledge in an area of policymaking marked by political complexity.

VN TEAS projects are required to be transparent, and the outcomes are expected to be as widely applicable as possible within the Finnish context. Dissemination of findings was ongoing throughout the project in blogs and publicly available outputs targeting the general public, policymakers, academics and other stakeholders, as well as active participation in public consultations about the social security reform.

The project assessors ensured that all the dissemination plans and strategies embedded in the research proposal were implemented by the project management team. The University of Helsinki and THL took the main responsibility for dissemination in Finland, and the prime minister's office assisted with public dissemination of project progress reports and findings. Although the purpose of the project was to provide evidence-based support for the Finnish reform, the research also led to knowledge exchange and dissemination between collaborating countries. For example, the vignette surveys led to bilateral discussions and mutual learning between the Finnish and Dutch policymakers. During the project, no disagreements or incompatibilities emerged over authorship of reports and academic outputs. The core team remained in charge of activities, and approached partners with requests for their input where necessary.

Comparative outputs for academic outlets were planned with the other project partners after the end of the project for publication in high-ranking (international) journals in the field of social policy, and in influential blogs and policy briefs at national and European levels: the *Tieto käyttöön VN TEAS blog* and THL dissemination series such as *Tutkimuksesta tiiviisti*; and European journals such as *Social Europe*. All partners contributed to the academic outputs insofar as their other work commitments and investment of time allowed. Since academic publications were not required by the funder, they were produced in English and/or Finnish as appropriate.

BOX 11.2 LESSONS LEARNT (POLKU)

The VN POLKU project affords a good example of how to manage integrated international evidence-based policy research with limited national government funding and a relatively small but committed research team.

- At the outset, the project manager needs to be conversant with, and prepared to work within, the constraints involved in low-cost short-term national government funding programmes.
- Research coordinators need to observe closely the terms and conditions laid down in the funding call and be confident that they can achieve the funder's aims and objectives within the time frame and provide value for money.
- If the core research team is unable to negotiate a larger budget or a reallocation of the tasks prescribed in the call, they must be prepared either to seek co-funding from elsewhere, or to have recourse to in-kind (and in-house) resources to enable them to meet the requirements of the programme.
- In building the project team, they need to recruit members with previous experience of working with the government department in question and of contributing to policy formation.
- To ensure the success of the collaboration, project managers must build on and maintain good working relationships between coordinators, funders and partners through meetings, different forms of knowledge exchange, and regular monitoring, reporting and assessment.
- In a comparative study involving new empirical research and with a limited budget, it is essential to be able to draw on a well-established international network of collaborators in disciplines that are relevant to the funder's topic, and who understand the importance of contextualising the findings.
- Depending on the project design and methods, team members must possess complementary data collection and analytical skills, and have ready access to data sources and potential respondents in relevant policy areas in the comparator countries.
- Engagement with team members, funders and other stakeholders should be scheduled throughout the process.
- In designing a dissemination strategy, project managers need to remain aware that the expectations of academic institutions are different from those of government departments, which means that scholarly outputs will not be catered for in the budget.

REFERENCES

Björklund, L., Kyröläinen, A., & Hilli, P. (2020, 2 September). *Osatyökykyisten työllistymisen edistäminen – yhteiskunnallisen hyödyn mallinnus – yhteenvetoa* [*Promoting employment of persons with impaired capacity to work – the modelling of social benefits – conclusions*]. Työ-ja elinkeinoministeriö. Vaikuttavuusinvestoimisen osaamiskeskus. https://tietyoelamaan.fi/julkaisut/

Esping-Andersen, G. (1990). *The three worlds of welfare capitalism.* Princeton University Press.

Heidenreich, M. & Aurich-Beerheide, P. (2014). European worlds of inclusive activation: The organisational challenges of coordinated service provision. *International Journal of Social Welfare, 23,* S6-S22. https://doi.org/10.1111/ijsw.12098

Heidenreich, M. & Rice, D. (2016). *Integrating social and employment policies in Europe: Active inclusion and challenges for local welfare governance.* Edward Elgar Publishing.

Minas, R. (2016). The concept of integrated services in different welfare states from a life course perspective. *International Social Security Review, 69*(3–4), 85–107. DOI: 10.1111/issr.12113

Organisation for Economic Cooperation and Development (OECD). (2020). *Faces of joblessness in Finland: A people-centred perspective on employment barriers and policies.* OECD. https://stm.fi/documents/1271139/0/Finland+FOJ.pdf/9834c041 -b47c-d48f-e5dd-c91dca648af4?t=1602073692563

12. Promoting integrity in the use of research results (PRO-RES)

Emmanouil Detsis and Ron Iphofen

BOX 12.1 PROJECT DESCRIPTORS (PRO-RES)

Duration: 1 May 2018–30 April 2021 (3 years, plus 6 months no-cost extension)

Web Link: https://prores-project.eu/

Project Manager: Emmanouil Detsis, European Science Foundation, Strasbourg, France (astronomy and space science)

Principal Investigator: Ron Iphofen, Academy of Social Sciences (AcSS), UK (sociology, health sciences)

Co-Investigators: Academy of Social Sciences (AcSS), UK – Robert Dingwall (research ethics); Helen Kara (research ethics); John Oates (psychology)

Partners: Belgium, European Alliance for Social Sciences and Humanities (EASSH) – Gabi Lombardo (international relations); European Policy Centre (EPC) – Fabian Zuleeg, Johannes Greubel (economics, policy analysis); Innovation in Research & Engineering Solutions (IRES) – Niki Kokkinaki (physics)

Croatia, Catholic University of Croatia (CUC) – Zvonimir Koporc, Hrvatsko Katolicko Sveuciliste (life sciences)

Estonia, University of Tartu (UTARTU) – Mari-Liisa Parder, Kadri Simm, Margit Sutrop (philosophy); Dietmar Pfahl (computer sciences)

France, Institut des Hautes Etudes Economiques et Commerciales (INSEEC) – Caroline Gans Combe (business ethics, economics)

Germany, Steinbeis 2i GmbH (S2i, non-profit organisation) (project and innovation management)

Greece, National Technical University (NTUA) – Costas Charitidis,

Panagiotis Kavouras, Eleni Spyrakou (nanotechnology); Hellenic Centre for Marine Research (HCMR), Popi Pagou, Nikos Streftaris (marine biology)

Ireland, Dublin City University (DCU) – Dónal O'Mathúna (disaster ethics, research ethics)

Italy, Conoscenza e Innovazione a Responsabiltà Limitata Simplifiât (K&I) – Alfonso Alfonsi, Maria Berliri, Giovanna Declich (social sciences); Consiglio nazionale delle Ricerche (CNR-ISTI) – Francesca Pratesi, Roberto Trasarti (computer science)

Funding Organisation: European Union's Horizon 2020 (FP8) research and innovation programme, award number 788352, amount €2.8 million.

THE PRO-RES CASE STUDY

This case study describes the different stages in the PRO-RES project, 'Promoting ethics and integrity in non-medical research', in the form of a coordinating and support action (CSA), from the application for funding to the EU's Horizon 2020 Framework Programme (FP8), through the formation of the project team and implementation of the project design, to its completion and dissemination activities.

Aims and Objectives

The broad aims of the project were to produce a guidance framework for responsible research and innovation in the non-medical sciences; to balance political, institutional and professional contradictions and constraints; and to provide practical solutions for all stakeholders enabling them to comply with the highest standards of research ethics and integrity.

Specific objectives were mapped onto the work packages (WPs):

1. To identify and categorise stakeholders, guidelines and codes, across the EU area and across non-medical disciplines, and to ensure that the organisation and channelling of expertise, in the context of policy advice, are well understood (WP1)
2. To activate and engage stakeholders across the EU and across disciplines (WP2)
3. To construct a normative framework for evidence-based policy originating from cutting-edge research responses to ethical challenges (WP3)
4. To understand the implications and pragmatic issues entailed in the implementation of such a framework at a national level and analyse the relationship between science-based policy advice, responsible conduct of research and research ethics (WP4)

5. To ensure that the framework produced is sustainable and adaptive and can anticipate future needs that may arise from new scientific discoveries and new technologies as they become available (WP5)
6. To provide a toolbox for policymakers to enable them to monitor ethical use of research results, perform impact assessments and gauge the socio-economic impact of not conducting responsible research (WP6)
7. To ensure that the needs of society are fully encapsulated by the framework, by threading this objective into the consultation phase (WP2) as well as the communication and dissemination actions (WP7)

Themes and Research Questions

As a coordinating and support action (CSA), the project set out to capture the entire spectrum of non-medical sciences. The selection of topics was not intended to be exhaustive. Rather, it included communities and areas with important ethical concerns and problems when it comes to policy advice. All the topics addressed in the interactive workshops were 'contemporary issue areas' that the Commission felt needed exploring. To delimit the scope to certain communities and to facilitate the research, the workshop themes focussed on the main areas identified in the funding call: covert research, surveillance and privacy; working in dangerous areas/conflict zones and crisis/disaster research; and behavioural research. This list of themes was extended in the PRO-RES project to include environmental issues and climate change; ethics in finance and economics; technological innovation (cutting-edge research such as nanotech and biotech); research innovation; ethical frameworks and research funding organisations; and think tanks and their role in policy advice.

The project team addressed the overarching research question: How should the non-medical research community promote ethics and integrity in the use of research results?

THE RESEARCH PROCESS

The project's key objectives were determined essentially by the funder's requirements as laid down in the formal call for proposals. The composition of the project team was the result of discussions and suggestions from an initial core group, including the principal and co-investigators, the project manager, and the Estonian and German partners. The consortium was subsequently enlarged to cover a wider range of relevant research communities. The research design and methodology were decided after discussions between partners in the proposal submission phase, as were plans for engagement and dissemination. The proposal phase lasted about six months, during which the final composition of the consortium was decided (about four months), the methodology was outlined (about one month), and the proposal was finalised (about one month). This section of the case study describes the different stages in the research process, identifies the issues that arose at each stage, and explains the ways in which the coordinators sought to resolve them.

Meeting the Funder's Requirements

The central requirement of the funder was that the project should seek to emulate the Oviedo/Helsinki medical frameworks for non-medical sciences. The Oviedo Convention on biomedical research and the Helsinki Framework on health policies were originally established to protect the dignity and identity of all human beings and guarantee, without discrimination, respect for their integrity and other rights and fundamental freedoms in the areas of biomedical and health research. The European Commission's call for proposals required successful applications to produce a framework that could be applied to the full range of non-medical sciences.

The project coordinator from European Science Foundation (ESF) – Science Connect, who managed the budget, was fully aware of the rules and regulations governing EU funding arrangements. The EU's General Data Protection Regulation (GDPR) was the main legislation that was pertinent to the consortium actions, and the research team took action to respect and apply it fully in all their processes.

The level of funding was adequate to carry out the required research in terms of its overall structure. But the project partners were constrained by the fact that 'non-medical' could be construed to cover such a large number of disciplines that it would be almost impossible to deal with all areas, while achieving wide acceptance of the prescribed framework from so many stakeholders. The initial funder's requirements requested that applicants covered a minimum of three specified aspects: covert research, surveillance and privacy; working in dangerous areas/conflict zones and crisis/disaster research; and behavioural research collecting data from social media/internet sources. The consortium included other areas to provide wider coverage and understanding, reflecting the available resources, while leaving a margin for extending coverage during the project's execution phase. Another area – non-academic scientific advice focussing mainly on think tanks – was added at the end of the first year of the PRO-RES project.

The proposal agreed with the funder provided for two sets of workshops scheduled to take place during the period of the award. Due to the onset of the COVID-19 pandemic, the second set was replaced by remote interviews, which resulted in a reduction in the travel budget. The funder allowed the savings to be transferred to the personnel budget for the partners involved in preparing and analysing the online interviews to account for their increased workload.

Budget distribution at proposal stage was dictated by the workload of participants and the workshop planning. Given the large number of workshops and travel claims for participants, the budget allocation was significant (12% of project total). Initial budget estimates needed adjustment at the project mid-point. Three of the fourteen partners had underestimated their input, and three had overestimated the effort needed for their WP involvement. All but two workshops underspent their budgets due to the recruitment of a smaller number of participants than expected. Initially, more effort was devoted to enlarging the pool of potential workshop participants. As the COVID-19 pandemic took hold, and physical workshops were no longer possible, funds were diverted to extending the pool of interviewees.

Building the Project Team

In response to a recommendation from common contacts, the principal investigator (PI) contacted the ESF to seek their collaboration in managing the project. ESF specialises in coordinating European-funded projects, leaving scientific leads to focus on the research. Discussions between ESF and the PI concentrated on the selection of non-medical disciplines that are facing ethical issues and dilemmas, on who could represent each discipline, and which EU countries could be covered within the limits of the available resources. ESF proposed several possible disciplines and countries, and others were suggested by core team members. Final decisions were taken in conjunction with the project's steering committee, whose members were drawn from consortium partners. Project team members were proposed by each partner organisation. In some cases, individual researchers were contacted with the requisite knowledge and skills, who then brought their organisations into the project.

Members of the consortium were chosen to fill three main roles. Firstly, they needed ethics code-building skills and expertise in guidance frameworks, ethics and integrity, as well as cross-cultural knowledge of ethics. Secondly, the consortium was looking for community network representatives embedded in specific disciplines as researchers, or as part of umbrella institutions, who could serve as 'nodes' in various communities in Europe and could mobilise links to stakeholders by promoting the project and attracting a critical mass of representatives to the work packages for which they would be responsible. Thirdly, partners were sought who would bring essential and complementary skills in project management and communication.

In choosing the partners, consideration was given to the need for them to be able to carry out national case studies in different policy contexts. The case study countries (and suitable partners) were selected for the range of research-related activities that they covered, from government research to independently commissioned research bodies able to broker evidence-based policymaking. Since the purpose of the project was to be 'acceptable by all', particular attention was paid to the institutional and personal demands and expectations of a wide range of stakeholders. Representatives were sought in public and private agencies, think tanks, NGOs and among policy advisers.

The partners chosen to lead the workshops and WPs were either academics who were studying the topic or research institutions widely recognised in their fields. Experts from these institutions were chosen for their experience of the policy advice 'chain', responsible for liaising between policymakers, local authorities and the public, or for soliciting their participation in policy discussions. In 2020, the Dublin City University (DCU) representative relocated to Ohio State University in the United States. DCU fulfilled its contributions to WPs 1, 2 and 3, and its representative continued to contribute to the project publications.

The disciplinary mix of the partners proved to be vital in examining the full chain of policy advice, in gaining access to insights from actors outside academia and, ultimately, to achieving the project's objectives. Specifically, the disciplinary mix added valuable interpretations to the analysis that were then digested and enabled the project coordinators to take decisions that facilitated the outcomes. These achievements came at the price of longer interactions than anticipated at consortium level to ensure understanding and agreement.

Although English was the main language, two instances arose when it proved necessary to switch to Estonian, Croatian and Italian in workshops at local level to integrate national stakeholders. When a workshop took place in a different language from English, the partner conducting the workshop was responsible for providing adequate material for the event in English, either in the form of notes or transcripts.

Examples of difficulties in reaching agreement between disciplines are illustrated by the prolonged discussions over the key concept of 'independent research', and the way that the final framework should address the positioning of policymakers. While academics championed the independence of research, this approach was not supported by think tanks. Given their funding source, several of the research establishments did not have complete freedom when selecting their research topics or making their research output relevant to certain regions, which was the case for a more academic research institute funded by a European region. Divergent opinions were voiced regarding the status of policymakers: as clients who would use the framework as a regulatory instrument, as a group to be advised and informed, or as a consultative resource. This last option seemed most prudent, given the extensive experiences of consortium partners in working closely with policymakers.

Issues arose concerning the disciplinary composition of the consortium when the work programme was being assessed, because the reviewer came from a theoretical and philosophical background and had different expectations about the form that an ethical framework should take from those of the consortium. Their interpretation was informed more by their interest in the practical application of the work. Several discussions ensued until a compromise could be reached. In the final analysis of the results, disciplinary perspectives became irrelevant for a policy audience, since the aim was to ensure that the framework could be applied to all non-medical sciences irrespective of cultural or professional differentiation.

Research Design and Methods

The research design and methodology were decided following discussions between partners in the proposal submission phase. The research was structured around 13 institutes, 11 workshops and 9 work packages across 9 EU member states and the UK. Together, they were designed to deliver the PRO-RES framework for ethical evidence in consultation with a variety of stakeholders. Different partners hosted and led the work packages, most of which were conducted concurrently throughout the period of the award in conjunction with the workshops. All except WP8 and WP9 involved most of the partners. During the first two years of the project, in-person workshops were held to discuss concepts and practices central to the aim of constructing an ethical framework for research in non-medical disciplines. These discussions subsequently moved online during the pandemic and took the form of virtual interviews.

The partners selected to lead the workshops were either academics who were studying the topic (K&I, DCU, UT, NTUA) or research institutions widely recognised in their fields. They were part of the policy advice 'chain' (CNR-ISTI); responsible for liaising between policymakers, local authorities and the public for implementing policy (HCMR); or they served a widely recognised forum (EPC) for policy discussions. The workshops had a European audience, with one workshop focussing on a specific region (the Baltics).

WP1: Existing policies, projects, networks and practices
UTARTU (lead), ESF, AcSS, NTUA, CUC, EASSH, INSEEC, K&I, S2i, DCU, HCMR, EPC

WP1 sought to fulfil objective 1, with preparatory elements regarding objectives 2 and 3. WP1 mapped existing codes and guidelines on ethics and integrity across disciplines based on evidence from existing literature, codes and documentation, enabling the project team to produce provisional framework elements. The disciplinary backgrounds and experience of the consortium partners allowed them to frame an initial set of conceptual and substantive issues relevant to their communities.

WP2 Consultation
S2i (lead), ESF, AcSS, NTUA, UTARTU, IRES, EASSH, K&I, DCU, HCMR, CNR-ISTI, EPC

WP2 laid the ground for the wider consultation process, which continued throughout the project. As a starting point the consortium built up a core group of stakeholders, and then enlarged it with the aim of promoting a wider consensus and engagement with the project issues. The agreed process of consultation was for the coordinator to prepare for the workshops by an initial sounding of opinions about possible pathways to adopt. If a consensus could not be reached, a time period of one to two weeks was scheduled for further discussion and re-examination of the issues offline. If a unanimous decision could still not be reached, final arbitration rested with the PI and coordinator. An online consultation was carried out as part of the same WP with stakeholder groups to seek their agreement on appropriate values, principles and standards to be incorporated in the framework.

WP3: Framework
AcSS (lead), ESF, UTARTU, CUC, INSEEC, K&I, S2i, DCU, EPC

WP3 focussed on building the framework for delivery using an interactive virtual platform in the form of advice and 'guidelines' rather than a prescriptive code with sanctions. WP3 addressed the ethical fault lines in societal, organisational and political structures that make it impossible for individual researchers to act ethically. Potential solutions were proposed within a value- and standards-based framework of ethical principles. The project team recognised that the framework would work only if it was seen as educational, informative and aspirational, and served as a stimulus and guide to achieving integrity in research.

Since principles do not always easily carry across different cultures, the framework was built on underlying values such as beliefs in democratic practice, inclusivity, freedom of action, a right to privacy, shared benefits from research and harm minimisation. This WP produced draft discussion and commentary papers. A draft statement on ethical principles was circulated to broader stakeholders and other interested parties for comment and amendment before being presented at the mid-term conference. It was used subsequently as input to the consultation process and the second series of workshops that dealt with validation of the framework by stakeholder communities.

WP4: Framework at the national level: Case studies
AcSS/ESF (lead), NTUA, UTARTU, CUC, EASSH

WP4 was designed to test the framework in national contexts, its application to overarching themes, and its relevance to a range of the communities of interest using case studies derived from WP3. 'Bench testing' of the framework (in vitro) was conducted in 'thought experiments' with working groups selected from the partners, using their contacts. Questions asked in the thought experiments included: 'How will this work for "x" agency or research institution? How can the framework be applied in "x" case or "y" research site?'

The case studies in WP4 provided an opportunity to examine best practices or investigate in a practical way the issues that arise in implementation of ethical frameworks in research. The approach also offered a means of addressing the national aspect of the call.

WP5: Sustainability of the framework/Road-mapping
NTUA (lead), ESF, AcSS, IRES, INSEEC, K&I, S2i, HCMR

WP5 concerned the sustainability of the framework and reaction to future technological developments (objective 5). It incorporated the feedback from the consultation process (WP2) as well as the test cases (WP3, WP4). Partners sought endorsements for its implementation from key stakeholders.

WP6: Regulation monitoring and assessment
INSEEC (lead), AcSS, EASSH, K&I, HCMR

WP6 focussed on how cultures of high standards of integrity and ethics in research and usage of research results can be promoted and maintained by governing bodies; how adherence to explicit standards of ethics and integrity in research can be supported, monitored and managed; and how any breaches can be minimised. It provided the toolbox sought in objective 6.

WP7: Project communication, dissemination and exploitation
IRES (lead), ESF, AcSS, NTUA, UTARTU, CUC, EASSH, INSEEC, K&I, EPC

In addition to the ongoing process of consultation and feedback, the project's dissemination strategy ensured that the framework was made widely available. This task also included the creation of the project website, which was the central location of the PRO-RES framework.

WP8: Project management
ESF (lead), all other partners

WP8 managed the administrative and financial aspects of the project, as well as facilitating the work of the project team.

WP9: Ethics requirements
ESF

WP9 was included as a standard procedure from the funder. The ESF had oversight of the consortium's responsibility regarding the EU's GDPR, gender issues and the transfer of policy findings from the project.

Engagement and Dissemination

Communication was a core feature of the PRO-RES project, both between project partners and with stakeholders, using in-person and virtual forms of contact. At the outset, the consortium had proposed an ambitious communication and dissemination strategy. The project manager and PI remained in frequent contact to prepare and deliver the consortium's internal and external communications concerning management. The partners liaised constantly with various national associations and agencies to understand, in practical terms, what the implementation of frameworks, codes and guidelines entails.

Interactions between WP1, WP2 and WP3 were built into the project design, and all the WPs utilised elements from previous packages. WP7 was dedicated to project communication, dissemination and exploitation. The project's website and consultation process targeted a wide range of stakeholders, including representatives of civil society (journalists, local authorities, NGOs), as well as responsible research and innovation constellations of actors. The workshop focussing on the Baltic and Nordic countries used data from social media and other internet sources in organising an event on data mining and social media.

For the duration of the project, contact and cooperation was maintained with the selected cases, and their responses were 'fine-tuned' as the framework and resource platform developed. WP4 exemplified engagement with a range of stakeholders specialising in ethical issues: the UK Social Research Association (SRA) on updating of their research ethics guidelines for independent and government researchers as well as academics; the UK Research Integrity Office on updating the integrity compliance framework across the scientific spectrum; data protection at the national level (AZOP), and research ethics review at institutional levels in Croatia on implementation; and the Centre for Ethics (University of Tartu) and other national partners and agencies on the elaboration of national codes of conduct for research integrity.

Within WP4, the European Alliance for Social Sciences and Humanities (EASSH) organised four to six dialogue workshops over the three years of

PRO-RES to test the results during its different phases with a significant stakeholder community of government science advisers. EASSH engaged with the wider International Network for Government Science Advice (INGSA) as well as national research councils. The vice-chair of INGSA was a member of the PRO-RES advisory board. INGSA provides a forum for policymakers, practitioners, academies and academics to share experience, build capacity and develop theoretical and practical approaches to the use of scientific evidence in informing policy at all levels of government.

A wide range of dissemination activities were implemented both during the lifetime of the PRO-RES project and at the end of the project to achieve the highest possible visibility, which was considered to be essential in ensuring take-up by policymakers. The vehicles of dissemination included: the website interactive platform, internet and social media presence, an electronic newsletter, public conferences transmitted via the project's website, press releases and partners' participation in scientific conferences.

At the launch event in Brussels in 2018 and mid-term conference in 2019, the PRO-RES team presented the goals of the project and the initial design of the website to a wide range of stakeholders. At a dedicated session during the mid-term conference, key actors from the European Commission, ethics experts and public and industry researchers from various disciplines, together with science advisers, chief scientific officers, civil society leaders and science journalists, explored how to ensure robust science-led policymaking. A short report outlining project policies for these areas was delivered to the funder in the first official review.

The European Policy Centre (EPC) led the task of testing the emerging framework with policymakers, by engaging in an online dialogue and workshops with networked policymakers to assess the draft framework. Resources and a framework that are practically applicable to non-medical research were delivered to a variety of levels from undergraduates to funded professional research agencies. The EPC organised the PRO-RES end-of-award conference where the final framework was presented to, and validated by, policymakers, funding agencies and public figures.

The project partners, in conjunction with several external collaborators produced three books for open access publication, co-edited by the PI and one of the original consortium partners, who both had extensive editorial experience (Iphofen & O'Mathúna, 2022a, 2022b; O'Mathúna & Iphofen, 2022). The chapter authors comprised consortium partners and stakeholder associates with expertise in the relevant fields.

BOX 12.2 LESSONS LEARNT (PRO-RES)

Given the scope of the PRO-RES project and the importance of engagement and communication, most of the lessons drawn focus on the practical management issues of coordinating a diverse team and ensuring effective discussions in meetings between team members and with external organisations.

- The appointment of a professional research manager with a scientific background, who understands and can handle the priorities of funders, manage budgets and deal with day-to-day practical issues as they arise, allows project coordinators to concentrate their time and efforts on the scientific objectives.
- Professional project managers need to be able to deal with internal and external disruptions to ensure that funder's objectives and schedules are met, the research remains within budget, and work packages are efficiently coordinated.
- In multidisciplinary projects, where no one participant can be an expert on all topics and disciplinary approaches differ, for example moral philosophy and IT, project managers need to take account of the working practices associated with different disciplines.
- With very large teams and complex research projects, team members need to be kept engaged by organising the research process in such a way that not everyone needs to attend all meetings to ensure that their time is used productively.
- To allow experts from different disciplines to collaborate efficiently, a solution is to split the discussion between theoretical concerns and implementation to allow some participants to explore issues at depth, while others focus on actionable information.
- Online synchronous project meetings are important as well as in-person meetings, especially to encourage the participation of busy stakeholders.
- Online discussion using email or other forums can be used when matters arise in the course of the research between scheduled meetings.
- Ad hoc offline discussions can be summarised and fed into scheduled meetings as action points, giving the opportunity for other team members to follow the discussion at their own pace, and to relieve time pressure from project meetings.
- Dissemination strategies should be agreed at the outset to ensure that participants meet their own and their institutions' expectations in terms of outputs and impact.

REFERENCES

Iphofen, R. & O'Mathúna D. (Eds). (2022a). *Ethical issues in covert, security and surveillance research*. Vol. 8. Series: Advances in Research Ethics and Integrity. Emerald.

Iphofen, R. & O'Mathúna, D. (Eds). (2022b) *Ethical evidence and policymaking: Interdisciplinary and international research*. Policy Press.

O'Mathúna, D, & Iphofen, R. (Eds). (2022) *Integrity and policymaking: The value of the case study*. Springer Nature.

13. Transforming into open, innovative and collaborative governments (TROPICO)

Tiina Randma-Liiv

BOX 13.1 PROJECT DESCRIPTORS (TROPICO)

Duration: 1 June 2017–30 November 2021 (4.5 years)

Web Link: https://tropico-project.eu/

Principle Investigator/Coordinator: Lise Rykkja, University of Bergen, Norway (public administration, organisation studies)

Partners: Belgium – Koen Verhoest (WP7 lead), University of Antwerp (public administration); Claire Dupuy, University of Louvain (political science, public policy); Steven van de Walle (WP3 lead), KU Leuven (public administration)

Denmark – Peter Triantafillou (WP8 lead), Roskilde University (political science, public administration, welfare state)

Estonia – Tiina Randma-Liiv (WP5 lead), Tallinn University of Technology (public administration)

Germany – Julia Fleischer (WP4 lead), University of Potsdam (public administration); Gerhard Hammerschmid (WP6 lead), Hertie School, Berlin (public management)

Hungary – Agnes Batory (WP2 lead), Central European University, Budapest (political science, European studies)

Netherlands – Erik Hans Klijn, Erasmus University Rotterdam (public administration)

Spain – Lourdes Torres, University of Zaragoza (public administration, finance)

Wales, UK – James Downe (WP9 lead), Cardiff University (public administration)

Funding Organisation: European Union's Horizon 2020 (FP8) Research and Innovation Programme, award number 726840, amount €4.9 million.

THE TROPICO CASE STUDY

This case study describes the different stages in the TROPICO project, 'Transforming into open, innovative and collaborative governments', from the application for funding and formation of the research team through to its final year, with a specific focus on the fifth work package (WP5), which was led by the author. The project was funded under the European Commission's Horizon 2020 Framework Programme (FP8). The Directorate-General for Research and Innovation (DG RTD) worked in conjunction with the Directorate-General for Communications Networks, Content and Technology (DG Connect) in managing the call for proposals. The programme was coordinated by the Department of Administration and Organisation Theory, at the University of Bergen in Norway. The research was conducted by a consortium composed of 12 partners in 9 countries and more than 40 team members. A different team was responsible for each of the WPs.

Aims and Objectives

Based on the conviction that the development of information and communication technologies (ICTs) and the process of digitalisation offer new prospects for such a transformation, and for more efficient, transparent and effective government, the overall aim of the TROPICO project was to investigate how public administrations are transformed into open, innovative and collaborative governments. The research team sought to improve understanding of how this transformation, together with collaboration in policy design and service delivery, can be achieved by advancing the participation of public, private and societal actors. The project aimed to compare collaborations in, and by, governments in ten countries representing different administrative traditions and uses of ICTs.

WP5 set out to evaluate the influence of e-participation initiatives on policy design and external collaboration, and to develop policy recommendations for further improvement of the functioning and administration of e-participation initiatives. Two specific objectives were pursued:

•   To examine the conditions and practices of innovative collaboration in policy design involving public, private and civil society actors, and to ascertain how user knowledge is integrated in the process

• To focus on e-participation practices in external collaboration for policy design with the aim of identifying critical success factors for such practices

Themes and Research Questions

WP5, the focus for this case study, investigated governmental initiatives establishing novel government-to-citizen platforms for participation and consultation processes with stakeholders in policy design. This part of the project concentrated on the 'non-technical' aspects of e-participation, more specifically the 'supply-side', by focussing on how governments organise and administer e-participation initiatives. The WP5 research team examined the national and organisational contexts of e-participation adoption and identified the individual epistemologies of key players in these initiatives.

Four questions guided the research in WP5:

1. How are e-participation initiatives launched and institutionalised?
2. How are e-participation initiatives organised and managed?
3. Which national, organisational and individual level factors are particularly important in explaining the implementation of e-participation initiatives?
4. What lessons can be drawn for organising and managing these initiatives?

THE RESEARCH PROCESS

The project's key objectives and the composition of the project team were determined by the grant agreement signed by the European Commission and the TROPICO consortium. The TROPICO case study examines to what extent the Commission's requirements for the conduct of the research funded under the Horizon 2020 Framework Programme (FP8), and the level of funding awarded, determined the research design and the integration of international and multinational dimensions.

Meeting the Funder's Requirements

The proposal submitted by the TROPICO team in response to the funding call was originally placed on the reserve list but was eventually granted funding six months later. In the negotiations of the grant agreement, the funder required more emphasis to be given to ICT, which had been presented as a relatively marginal element in the original TROPICO proposal. Funding was granted to the project on the condition that ICT became a central horizontal topic across the WPs.

The grant agreement specified the obligations of the partners, the tasks to be carried out in each WP, the estimated work effort for each partner in the different WPs, and the corresponding estimated amount of funding to be allocated to each of the partners. The funds were allocated between the partners to cover eligible costs related to the specified tasks in the grant agreement, enabling the appointment of postdocs as research fellows, and postgraduate students as research assistants. In the case of WP5, the funder specified the empirical country case studies that were to be conducted by the team members. Funding did not explicitly cover buy-out from teaching and administration, but these issues were resolved by the internal procedures in each participating university.

Due to the COVID-19 pandemic, the original work plan had to be adapted, for example by moving meetings, dissemination activities and parts of the fieldwork online. All changes to the work plan were negotiated in a contract amendment process, resulting in adjustments to the grant agreement.

Building the Project Team

Norway, where the coordinator of the TROPICO project is based, is not an EU member state. Norway and Norwegian researchers participated in the Horizon 2020 programme on the same basis as the EU member states through the European Economic Area Agreement. The coordinator's expertise in public administration and organisation studies, and the experience gained from participation in previous EU-funded research projects and from leading other (national) research grants, meant that she had acquired the necessary skills for coordinating a large-scale international project. The lead of WP5 also had experience in managing cross-national research in previous EU-funded projects.

During the grant application process, the coordinator together with a core group of international partners chose the lead researchers and partners for each of the work packages on the basis of prior knowledge about their research expertise and leadership credentials. The rationale for selecting partners from nine countries for the TROPICO project was to include representatives in the consortium from different administrative traditions in Europe: Belgium, Denmark, Estonia, France, Germany, Hungary, the Netherlands, Norway, Spain and the UK.

The partners assigned to WP5 in the grant agreement were from Estonia, France, Germany, the Netherlands, Norway and the UK. Although the WP5 lead did not personally know all the partners assigned to her team, they were able to establish easy working relations due to their shared expertise in public administration, interest in the topic, experience of working in international settings, and their ability to communicate effectively in English. Subsequently, three other partners within the TROPICO consortium, representing Belgium, Hungary and Spain, agreed to participate in WP5 without being formally allocated person months. The WP5 lead then recruited researchers from Austria, Croatia, the Czech Republic, Ireland, Latvia, Lithuania, Slovakia and Sweden to join the project and to extend the mix of countries for cross-national comparison even further.

The WP5 lead used her own academic network to approach potential partners from among contacts who had previously been conducting similar research. Negotiations were also undertaken with researchers from Finland, Italy, Romania and Switzerland, but were discontinued due to the lack of relevant cases in these countries or the unwillingness of the researchers to engage in the project. While WP5 was being developed, and especially after dissemination of its early results in conferences, the level of interest raised by WP5 was such that researchers who had not hitherto been involved in the project team welcomed the opportunity to be associated with a European-funded project by offering to contribute voluntarily to the outputs.

Individual members in the TROPICO consortium were selected because they belonged to cognate disciplines in public administration, political science and management studies, and had previously worked together in larger research collaborations and projects. They had maintained regular contact through relevant academic and practitioner-oriented conferences, collaborated on European funded projects and published in many of the same journals. As a result, the composition of the consortium was essentially monodisciplinary insofar as its members were all social scientists with backgrounds in public administration and political science, based in university departments.

Previous research has shown, however, that different state traditions within Europe have led to disparate identities for scholars studying public administration, and to different approaches to its disciplinary, multidisciplinary or interdisciplinary character (Randma-Liiv & Connaughton, 2005). As recently as the 1990s, in some European states, public administration did not exist as an independent institutionalised field of study, and was taught as a specialisation in departments of law, political science, economics or business administration programmes. Today, public administration is recognised as a hybrid or chameleon field of study integrating a variety of disciplines (Hustedt, et al., 2020).

Although the TROPICO consortium did not include ICT specialists, and most of the WP5 team members had not previously worked specifically on e-governance or e-democracy, due to their training in public administration, political science or sociology, the TROPICO team members possessed the necessary interdisciplinary expertise to address collaborative governance through the use of ICT. The project's academic advisory board included several experts on digital governance, who were able to make a useful input to the project throughout the research. The mid-term reviewers, who were experts in political science, public administration and digital governance, reported positively on the way team members were working together and the project was progressing.

Despite the proximity of the disciplinary backgrounds of the team members, lengthy discussions were held in meetings about the various understandings of central concepts such as 'collaborative governance', 'digitalisation', 'efficiency' and 'effectiveness', and how to measure them. In some national contexts, collaboration has very different connotations, which was critical when the consortium was producing its 'collaboration monitor' as an innovative online self-assessment tool enabling practitioners to compare their collaborative practices (TROPICO, 2021).

The problem of finding experts in ICT interested in being centrally engaged with the WP5 research was only partially remedied in the recruitment of stakeholders in national and local government departments to participate in the empirical work, since few of the interviewees involved in delivering e-participation platforms were ICT experts. In addition to the academics from a variety of disciplines, including ICT, on the academic advisory board, government and private sector stakeholders had an opportunity to comment on findings and provide feedback to the consortium via a practitioners' advisory board. During the project dissemination phase, the team members were also able to benefit from direct input from experts in ICT, who agreed to participate in the two project 'summits' and the final conference.

Research Design and Methods

Decisions about the TROPICO project design were taken by a core group of four to five members during the preparation of the grant application. The proposal was subsequently endorsed at a meeting of all partners. Eleven parallel WPs were organised, three of which covered administrative matters: WP1 dealt with ethics and data, WP10 with communication and dissemination, and WP11 with management and coordination.

The eight scientific WPs (WP2 to WP9) followed a four-step sequential design. The first pillar (WP2 and WP3) studied the institutional conditions and individual drivers and barriers to collaboration. The second pillar (WP4 and WP5) investigated the practices of open and innovative collaboration in and by governments in policy design. The third pillar (WP6 and WP7) examined service delivery, inside and between governments, with external actors including stakeholders and citizens. The final pillar (WP8 and WP9) focussed on the consequences and effects of innovative collaboration based on ICT for legitimacy and accountability as well as government efficiency.

WP5 concentrated on empirical analysis of recent e-participation initiatives, fostering collaboration between governments and citizens in policy design from a politico-administrative perspective, to determine how these initiatives are organised and managed, and to identify the contextual challenges associated with the implementation of e-participation. The study employed both exploratory and explanatory approaches to investigate the functioning of e-participation practices, and to identify drivers and barriers that contribute to their success or failure. In doing so, the team explored the contextual factors surrounding e-participation platforms, including national contexts, organisational and individual-level characteristics.

The empirical work was designed to gauge how governments with different administrative characteristics contextualise and deal with the issues that arise in designing and implementing e-participation. The WP5 team was also tasked with evaluating the influence of e-participation practices on external collaboration and participation in wider policy processes from a normative viewpoint, by juxtaposing the research results with aspects regarding accountability and democratic practices.

The case study method adopted in WP5 was organised in three phases:

1. Mapping of e-participation initiatives based on the case selection strategy and the choice of a relevant case in each country
2. Preparation of the case studies based on a joint case study protocol
3. Development of cross-national research deliverables on e-participation based on the case studies

The desk research, conducted by the WP5 partners, provided an overview of relevant public sources on a selected e-participation platform in each of the countries, including websites and publications on e-participation schemes, as well as legal and other government policy documents, such as codes of collaboration, relevant reports by third parties and international organisations, and available statistics about ICTs at local and national levels.

The case selection was based on four criteria:

- Cases representing different administrative levels (national, regional, local)
- Cases connecting stakeholders with the public sector via an online platform that is open and transparent
- Cases designed for long-term or permanent collaborations and in operation for long enough to enable their impact to be evaluated
- Cases set up with the aim of informing and influencing policymaking rather than delivery of public services

The empirical work in the second phase was guided by a joint case study protocol based on a comprehensive literature and documentary review of existing studies of e-participation. The purpose of the protocol was to provide a common conceptual framework for the comparative case studies and to streamline the process using mutually agreed procedures and timelines. The protocol was agreed by the WP5 partners in meetings and online discussions. Partners were required to develop in-depth case studies for the selected e-participation initiatives, including thick description elaborating on the influence of contextual factors on the functioning of platforms, leading to an assessment of the impact of e-participation on policy decisions.

As prescribed in the protocol, interviews were used for specifying and triangulating information collected through desk research. Between eight and twelve semi-structured interviews were conducted in each of the countries, with individuals officially involved in the administration of the platform (except for purely technical staff), senior managers of the public sector organisations where the e-participation initiative was being administered, and representatives of policymakers and other stakeholders who had been using the platforms. TROPICO's data management plan required written consent from all respondents and approval by respective ethical committees in each country/ university. Although various partner universities had different practices of ethical approvals, this did not cause problems for the WP5 research. Interviews were anonymous, although it was acknowledged that some respondents might be indirectly identifiable through a combination of background information.

The case studies were composed according to a common analytical model, relying on information collected from desk research and semi-structured interviews. Each interview lasted between an hour and an hour and a half, and was recorded and transcribed by the case study authors. Partners were asked to provide background information relevant to their specific national contexts, in particular identifying features distinguishing a specific country from other European member states. Information was collected about cultural, historical, socio-economic, politico-administrative and legislative contexts of e-participation schemes, as well as organisational aspects influencing the e-participation initiative and the individual backgrounds and epistemologies of actors administratively associated with the initiatives.

The interviews were not translated into English, but the in-depth analyses, each of 8–10,000 words, were prepared in English. The WP5 lead edited the case studies and made sure that all the information required by the protocol was included. In most cases, partners had to provide two or three revised versions. The respective TROPICO partners who had conducted the case studies presented their findings in reports that were circulated among the team members for comment.

The cross-country comparative analysis was carried out by the WP5 lead partner with assistance from her research fellows. A two-step approach was used for content analysis. First, individual case studies were scrutinised, and their descriptive content was classified into specific thematic codes such as ownership, organisational structure, participatory process, technical solutions, internal partners, external partners, coordination mechanisms, accountability relations, funding and human resources. Second, the analytical and explanatory parts of the case studies were examined and ordered according to the interpretative codes. The information gathered through the thematic and interpretative codes was then integrated and compared.

When conducting the analysis, it was acknowledged that the effects of electronic tools were highly dependent on their context. Although the cases had been carefully selected, the e-participation platforms had been implemented in different national and institutional contexts, and were in different developmental stages; they represented diverse levels of government and targeted either legislative or executive branches of government. Despite the variety of cases, the inductive approach allowed the detection of certain organisational patterns and challenges across the cases. The comparative analysis of the data focussed on the explanation of drivers and barriers to e-participation initiatives in an attempt to capture and evaluate critical contextualised factors contributing to the success or failure of different initiatives that need to be given systematic attention in the development of new initiatives or improvement of existing e-participation platforms.

Across the cases, the analysis showed how the impact of technology on policymaking is mediated by the institutional context that frames how the public sector interacts with citizens and other governmental and non-governmental units. Cases were identified that offered examples of good practice based on quality and quantity of citizen participation, transparency of the participatory process and impact of citizen engagement on policymaking. After citizens have given their voice, whether and how that voice affects the actual policymaking process were found to depend on characteristics of the organisation, process and management which, in turn, are influenced by their national contexts. Citizen involvement was shown to be embedded in existing institutional arrangements and constrained by political, administrative, organisational and procedural factors. If the participatory process is not carefully designed or implemented, decisions are likely to be delayed resulting in increased conflict, disappointed participants, and more distrust of service providers.

Analysis of the empirical material revealed how multifaceted organisational structures and processes combined with the complexity of the surrounding societal and political context to make e-participation systems prone to fail, requiring them to be managed as a process of learning and adaptation rather than as a static technological product. The French and German case studies showed, for example, that due to barriers in the institutional framework and relevant processes, e-participation systems may end up struggling with low demand and acceptance. Where e-participation schemes were tailor-made for one organisation, for example local government as in the Dutch and Spanish cases, they tended to be more successful than in countries where they were developed centrally and imposed on other administrative units. Countries and organisations where traditional (offline) participation had previously been successfully implemented were found to be more likely to benefit from e-participation.

Engagement and Dissemination

Throughout the project, given the importance of the findings for policy formation and development, the TROPICO consortium engaged with government (policymakers, civil servants, public managers) and non-government stakeholders (practitioners across public, private and civil society sectors). In addition to the internal reports produced by the WP leaders, and the regular reports required by the European Commission, the funding proposal included a budget for meetings with stakeholders, conferences and public events. Partners presented papers and condensed research results at events not only in the countries where the research was being carried out but also elsewhere in the world, including Brazil, Canada and the United States.

The WP5 lead was committed to providing a comparative research report and a policy brief. Project findings were presented at a TROPICO summit meeting in Tallinn in 2019, at the project's final conference in 2021, and at two annual conferences of the European Group for Public Administration, in Belfast in 2019 and in Brussels in 2021. In addition, WP5 results were introduced in 'road-shows' and meetings with government practitioners in participating countries. For example, in Estonia a practitioners' conference was organised jointly by the WP5 lead, the Government Office and Estonian Cooperation Assembly to discuss opportunities for developing e-participation in local government services.

The TROPICO end-of-award conference in November 2021 included a session on the involvement of citizens in policy design through e-participation. Other sessions addressed questions about the relative merits of centralised or decentralised organisation of digitalisation, and how to assess the efficiency and legitimacy of collaborations. The final session focussed on 'Understanding the transformation of public administrations: Research, achievements and perspectives'. Here, team members summarised the impact of the project, identifying steps towards a research agenda that will be relevant for academics and the scientific community more widely. The session involved debate, an interactive workshop, roundtables, open discussions and experience sharing with other research projects in receipt of funding under the same call, and short research presentations, as well as opportunities for virtual social interaction.

Contributions from early career researchers at the dissemination conference demonstrated the value for them of having been associated with a large international multidisciplinary project. They were able to expand their network of contacts with both senior scholars and other early career researchers, as well as practitioners and stakeholders at different levels. They learnt about the challenges of working in different countries, whether it be in data collection or in negotiating ethical regulations. They became aware of the importance of effective communication in a variety of settings using different media, and of issues to be addressed in disseminating findings. All in all, they felt that they had acquired solid skills and competences that would serve them well in their careers.

Although team members were mostly left to decide where and with whom to publish academic outputs, their preferences were often dictated by previous experience and their knowledge of institutional expectations, which varied from one country to another. The WP5 team members found that the articles they wrote on e-participation were more likely to be accepted for publication in public administration than in ICT journals due to the persistence of disciplinary silos and requirements for research assessment in their institutions. Comparative findings from the project were published in two academic articles (Randma-Liiv 2022a; Randma-Liiv, 2022b), and several multi-country comparative articles were already in preparation when the present case study was being drafted.

An edited book was published by Edward Elgar containing fifteen WP5 case studies, as well as a chapter devoted to the theoretical background of the study, research methodology and analytical framework, and the lessons learnt from the exercise (Randma-Liiv & Lember, 2022). The expectation that publications from European-funded research should be open access turned out to be a constraining factor for some partners, given that the associated publishing costs had not been specified in detail in the original project budget. WP5's commitment to publish an open access edited volume was made possible due to negotiations between the consortium partners resulting in a reallocation of funds through a grant agreement amendment during the project.

BOX 13.2 LESSONS LEARNT (TROPICO)

The most important lessons learnt from the TROPICO project for mid-career researchers are the value of being able to call on an established network of like-minded researchers and of being involved in managing sub-projects within a larger international multidisciplinary consortium.

• Project coordinators must be familiar with the expectations of the funders in terms of application procedures, and they must be prepared to develop their competences and skills in financial and data management; in communication across cultures, disciplines and sectors; and in coordination and dissemination.

- Project coordinators need to be supported by professional administrators and institutional research offices who are familiar with the funding application and research process, as well as being well qualified in terms of project management, implementation, reporting and communication.
- Project managers who also have academic responsibilities must be able to negotiate their time management within their institutions and be realistic about the demands that they make on team members.
- Mid-career researchers should take advantage of the opportunity to engage in international multidisciplinary research and to lead a work package or sub-project within a larger cross-national consortium.
- In building a project team, research project managers need to recruit researchers who share the same interests in the topics concerned, have complementary and compatible skills, and have experience of working in international multidisciplinary contexts.
- Coordinators and WP leaders of cross-national projects must possess good people skills, and be adaptable and able to deal with changing circumstances both in their own lives and in those of their team members.
- All project team members need to be trained in international comparative and interdisciplinary research methods, and project managers should contribute to the training of postgraduate and postdoctoral assistants associated with the research by organising training sessions and providing feedback and encouragement to assist them in their career progression.
- Project managers need to pay attention to the different needs and expectations of team members and ensure that agreement is reached about the arrangements for communicating findings to a wide range of stakeholders.

REFERENCES

Hustedt, T., Randma-Liiv, T., & Savi, R. (2020). Public administration and disciplines. In G. Bouckaert & W. Jann (Eds), *European perspectives for public administration: The way forward* (pp. 129–146). Leuven University Press.

Randma-Liiv, T. (2022a). Organizing e-participation: Challenges stemming from the multiplicity of actors. *Public Administration*. Early view: http://doi.org/10.1111/padm.12788

Randma-Liiv, T. (2022b). Adoption is not enough: Institutionalization of e-participation initiatives. *Public Policy and Administration*. [Accepted for publication on 22 November 2021]

Randma-Liiv, T. & Connaughton, B. (2005). Public administration as a field of study: Divergence or convergence in the light of 'Europeanization'? *TRAMES: A Journal of the Humanities & Social Sciences, 9*(4), 348–360.

Randma-Liiv, T. & V. Lember (Eds). (2022). *Engaging citizens in policy-making: e-participation practices in Europe*. Edward Elgar Publishing.
TROPICO (2021). *Collaboration Monitor*. https://tropico-project.eu/collaboration-monitor/

References

Agence nationale de la recherche (ANR). (2021). *Generic call 2021: Research themes.* https://anr.fr/en/call-for-proposals-details/call/generic-call-2021/

Akrich, M., Callon, M., & Latour, B. (1988). A quoi tient le succès des innovations? *Annales des Mines.* https://halshs.archives-ouvertes.fr/file/index/docid/81741/filename/SuccesInnovation.pdf

Armer, M. & Grimshaw, A.D. (Eds). (1973). *Comparative social research: Methodological problems and strategies.* John Wiley & Sons.

Benjamin, R. (1982). The historical nature of social-scientific knowledge: The case of comparative political inquiry. In E. Ostrom (Ed.), *Strategies of political inquiry* (pp. 69–98). Sage.

Brannen, J. (1992). Combining qualitative and quantitative approaches: An overview. In J. Brannen (Ed.), *Mixing methods: Qualitative and quantitative research* (pp. 3–37). Avebury.

Brannen, J. (2005). Mixing methods: The entry of qualitative and quantitative approaches into the research process. *International Journal of Social Research Methodology, 8*(3), 173–184. DOI: 10.1080/13645570500154642

Brannen, J. (2021). *Social research matters: A life in family sociology.* Bristol University Press.

Brannen, J. & Nilsen, A. (2011). Comparative biographies in case-based cross-national research: Methodological considerations. *Sociology, 45*(4), 603–618. DOI: 10.1177/0038038511406602

Brosan, G. S. (1972). The development of polytechnics in the United Kingdom. *Paedagogica Europaea, 7,* 41–53. https://www.jstor.org/stable/1502485

Brown, E., Campbell, B., Cloke, J., Seng To, L., Turner, B., & Wray, A. (2018). Low carbon energy and international development: From research impact to policymaking. *Contemporary Social Science, 13*(1), 112–127. DOI: 10.1080/21582041.2017.1417627

Bryman, A. (2008). The end of the paradigm wars? In P. Alasuutari, L. Bickman, & J. Brannen (Eds), *The SAGE handbook of social research methods* (pp. 13–25). Sage.

Centre Européen pour la Recherche Nucléaire (CERN). (2021). Where did it all begin? https://home.cern/about/who-we-are/our-history

Centre National de la Recherche Scientifique (CNRS). (2021a). *History.* https://histoire.cnrs.fr/

Centre National de la Recherche Scientifique (CNRS) (2021b). *Assessing researchers' activities.* https://www.cnrs.fr/comitenational/english/cn_eval_acc.htm

Centre for Postdoctoral Development in Infrastructure Cities and Energy (C-DICE). (2021). *Sandpits.* https://www.cdice.ac.uk/programme/sandpits/

Chou, M-H. & Gornitzka, Å. (Eds). (2014). *Building the knowledge economy in Europe: New constellations in European research and higher education governance.* Edward Elgar Publishing. DOI: https://doi.org/10.4337/9781782545293

Clark, T., Wright, M., & Kitchen, D. J. Jr. (Eds). (2016). *How to get published in the best management journals.* Edward Elgar Publishing.

Cogswell, G. A. (1899). The classification of the sciences. *The Philosophical Review,* *8*(5), 494–512. https://www.jstor.org/stable/2176887

Commission of the European Communities (2003). *The role of universities in the Europe of knowledge.* Communication from the Commission of 5 February 2003, COM(2003) 58 final. https://eur-lex.europa.eu/LexUriServ/LexUriServ.do?uri=COM:2003:0058:FIN:en:pdf

Daunt, K. L. & McDermott, A. M. (2018). Authorship in action. In K. Townsend & M. N. K. Saunders (Eds). *How to keep your research project on track: Insights from when things go wrong* (pp. 149–156). Edward Elgar Publishing.

Desrosières, A. (1993). *La politique des grands nombres: Histoire de la raison statistique.* La Découverte.

Deutsche Forschungsgemeinschaft (DFG). (2016). *Germany's excellence strategy: Call for proposals in the clusters of excellence funding line.* https://www.dfg.de/en/research_funding/announcements_proposals/2016/info_wissenschaft_16_59/index.html

Deutsche Forschungsgemeinschaft (DFG). (2021a). *Individual grants programmes – A how-to guide.* https://www.dfg.de/en/research_funding/individual_grants_programmes/index.html

Deutsche Forschungsgemeinschaft (DFG). (2021b). Mission statement. https://www.dfg.de/en/dfg_profile/mission/index.html

Deutsche Forschungsgemeinschaft (DFG). (2021c). *What is the DFG.* https://www.dfg.de/en/dfg_profile/index.html

Economic and Social Research Council (ESRC). (2021a). *How to write a good proposal.* https://www.ukri.org/councils/esrc/guidance-for-applicants/how-to-write-a-good-proposal/

Economic and Social Research Council (ESRC). (2021b). *Impact, innovation and interdisciplinarity expectations.* https://www.ukri.org/councils/esrc/guidance-for-applicants/impact-innovation-and-interdisciplinarity-expectations/

Engineering and Physical Sciences Research Council (EPSRC). (2021). *Sandpits.* https://beta.ukri.org/councils/epsrc/guidance-for-applicants/types-of-funding-we-offer/transformative-research/sandpits/

EUR-Lex (2021). *Trade and Cooperation Agreement between the European Union and the European Atomic Energy Community, of the One Part, and the United Kingdom of Great Britain and Northern Ireland, of the Other Part. OJ* L 149, 30.4.2021. https://eur-lex.europa.eu/legal-content/EN/TXT/?uri=uriserv:OJ.L_.2021.149.01.0010.01.ENG

European Alliance for Social Science and Humanities (EASSH). (2019a). *Improving research impact assessment in Horizon Europe: A perspective from the social sciences and humanities.* https://eassh.eu/Position-Papers/easshimpactfnl.pdf

European Alliance for Social Science and Humanities (EASSH). (2019b). *Interdisciplinary perspectives for Horizon Europe: Lessons from the 4th SSH integration monitor report.* https://eassh.eu/Position-Papers/easshsshintegration4threportfnl.pdf

European Alliance for Social Science and Humanities (EASSH) (2019c). *Mission.* https://eassh.eu/About/Mission

European Commission (n.d.). Applying for funding. *Horizon 2020 online manual.* https://ec.europa.eu/research/participants/docs/h2020-funding-guide/grants/applying-for-funding_en.htm

European Commission (1999). *Specific programme of targeted socio-economic research, 1994–1998.* https://cordis.europa.eu/programme/id/FP4-TSER

European Commission (2000). *European Research Area (ERA).* https://ec.europa.eu/ info/research-and-innovation/strategy/strategy-2020-2024/our-digital-future/era_en

European Commission (2007). *European Research Council: Mission.* https://erc .europa.eu/about-erc/mission

European Commission (2014). *Horizon 2020 online manual: Social sciences and humanities.* https://ec.europa.eu/research/participants/docs/h2020-funding-guide/ cross-cutting-issues/ssh_en.htm

European Commission (2021a). *International cooperation.* https://ec.europa.eu/info/ research-and-innovation/strategy/strategy-2020-2024/europe-world/international -cooperation_en#Horizon-Europe

European Commission (2021b). *Q&A on the UK's participation in Horizon Europe.* https://ec.europa.eu/info/sites/default/files/research_and_innovation/strategy _on_research_and_innovation/documents/ec_rtd_uk-participation-in-horizon -europe.pdf

European Commission Press Corner (2020). *A new European Research Area: Commission sets new plan to support green and digital transition and EU recovery* [Press release]. https://ec.europa.eu/commission/presscorner/detail/en/IP_20_1749

European Cooperation in Science and Technology (COST). (2017). *COST FP9 position paper, 047/17.* https://www.cost.eu/uploads/2018/08/COST_FP9_position_paper .pdf

European Parliament (2000). *Presidency Conclusions.* Lisbon European Council 23 and 24 March 2000. https://www.europarl.europa.eu/summits/lis1_en.htm#:~: text=PRESIDENCY%20CONCLUSIONS&text=The%20European%20Council %20held%20a,of%20a%20knowledge%2Dbased%20economy.

European Research Advisory Board (EURAB). (2005). *The social sciences and humanities in the 7th framework programme.* Rapporteur C. Caswill. EUR 22004. European Commission.

European Research Council (ERC). (2021). *Statistics: ERC projects and figures.* https://erc.europa.eu/projects-figures/statistics

European Science Foundation (ESF). (1974). *Archives.* https://archives.eui.eu/en/isaar/ 646

European Science Foundation (ESF). (2015). *EUROCORES (EUROpean COllaborative RESearch) Scheme.* European Science Foundation Archives. http://archives.esf.org/ coordinating-research/eurocores.html

European Science Foundation (ESF). (2021). *The new ESF.* http://archives.esf.org/esf -today/the-new-esf.html

European Strategy Forum on Research Infrastructures (ESFRI). (n.d.). *About ESFRI.* https://www.esfri.eu/about-esfri

European Strategy Forum on Research Infrastructures (ESFRI). (2020). *Making science happen: A new ambition for research infrastructures in the European Research Area* [White Paper]. https://www.esfri.eu/sites/default/files/White_paper_ESFRI-final .pdf

Galtung, J. (1982). On the meaning of 'nation' as a variable. In M. Nießen & J. Peschar (Eds), *International comparative research: Problems of theory, methodology and organisation in Eastern and Western Europe* (pp. 17–34). Pergamon Press.

Gilbert, N. (2016). More than the sum of its parts: Social science and technologi-cal development. *University of Surrey blog.* https://blogs.surrey.ac.uk/sociology/ 2016/10/31/more-than-the-sum-of-its-parts-social-science-and-technological -development/

Graves, N. J. (1965). The 'Grandes Ecoles' in France. *The vocational aspect of secondary and further education, 17*(36), 40–49. DOI: 10.1080/03057876580000041

Grootings, P. (1986). Technology and work: A topic for East–West comparison? In P. Grootings (Ed.), *Technology and work: East–West comparison* (pp. 275–301). Croom Helm.

Guy, K. (Ed.). (2004). *Policy issues and research directions in the social sciences* [A report prepared for DG Research of the European Commission].

Hantrais, L. (2006). *Pour une meilleure évaluation de la recherche publique en sciences humaines and sociales* (Vol. 2). La Documentation Française.

Hantrais, L. (2009). *International comparative research: Theory, methods and practice.* Palgrave Macmillan.

Hantrais, L. & Thomas Lenihan, A. (2016). *The implications of the EU referendum for UK social science: Post-referendum options for UK social scientists.* LSE Centre for International Studies Working Paper CIS/2016/03. http://www.lse.ac.uk/international-relations/assets/documents/cis/working-papers/cis-working-paper-2017-04-hantrais.pdf

Hantrais, L. & Thomas Lenihan, A. (2021). Social dimensions of evidence-based policy in a digital society. *Contemporary Social Science, 16*(2), 141–155. DOI: 10.1080/21582041.2021.1887508

Hantrais, L., Thomas Lenihan, A., & MacGregor, S. (2015). Evidence-based policy: Exploring international and interdisciplinary insights. *Contemporary Social Science, 10*(2), 101–113. DOI: 10.1080/21582041.2015.1061687

Hustedt, T., Randma-Liiv, T., & Savi, R. (2020). Public administration and disciplines. In G. Bouckaert & W. Jann (Eds), *European perspectives for public administration: The way forward* (pp. 129–146). Leuven University Press.

Info Swiss (2017). European Leadership: CERN, in search of the secrets of the universe. *Info Swiss,* March 2017. https://www.swissbiz.ca/is_article.php?articleid=48

Iphofen, R. (Ed.). (2020). *Handbook of research ethics and scientific integrity.* Sage. https://link.springer.com/referencework/10.1007/978-3-030-16759-2

Joint Research Centre (JRC). (2007). *Highlights of the JRC: 50 years in science.* European Commission. https://ec.europa.eu/jrc/sites/default/files/jrc_50_years_brochure_en.pdf

Kania, K. & Bucksch, R. (2020). *Integration of social sciences and humanities in Horizon 2020: Participants, budgets and disciplines* (5th monitoring report on projects funded in 2018 under the Horizon 2020 programme). European Commission. DOI: 10.2777/141795

Kritikos, M. (2020). *Ten technologies to fight Coronavirus: In-depth analysis.* Scientific Foresight Unit, European Parliamentary Research Services. https://www.europarl.europa.eu/thinktank/en/document.html?reference=EPRS_IDA(2020)641543

Marchipont, J-F. (2003). Preface. In L. Hantrais (Ed.), *Policy relevance of 'Family and welfare' research* (p. vi). [Dialogue workshop, Brussels]. Office for Official Publication of the European Communities.

Max-Planck-Gesellschaft (2021). *Our history.* https://www.mpg.de/183298/history

Meyerhardt, M. W. (1915). Wandering scholars. *The Pedagogical Seminary, 22*(3), 401–412. DOI: 10.1080/08919402.1915.10533971.

Mohler, P. (2007). What is being learned from the ESS? In R. Jowell, C. Roberts, R. Fitzgerald, & G. Eva (Eds), *Measuring attitudes cross-nationally: Lessons from the European Social Survey* (pp. 157–168). Sage.

Moulier-Butang, Y. (2015). Sorbonne Université et l'interdisciplinarité. *Interactions,* No. 34. https://interactions.utc.fr/thematiques/pluridisciplinarite/34-sorbonne -universite-et-linterdisciplinarite/

National Centre for Research Methods (Restore). (2014). *International social research methods training workshops.* https://www.restore.ac.uk/ISResMeth/Project%20info/

National Science Foundation (NSF). (2021). *Research areas.* https://www.nsf.gov/ about/research_areas.jsp

Natural Environment Research Council (NERC). (2021a). *Funding for international collaborations.* https://www.ukri.org/councils/nerc/guidance-for-applicants/types -of-funding-we-offer/

Natural Environment Research Council (NERC). (2021b). *Handbooks, guidance and forms.* https://www.ukri.org/councils/nerc/guidance-for-applicants/handbooks -guidance-and-forms/

Natural Environment Research Council (NERC). (2022). *Consultation and engagement.* https://www.ukri.org/about-us/nerc/who-we-are/consultation-and-engagement/

Nießen, M. & Peschar, J. L. (Eds). (1982). *International comparative research: Problems of theory, methodology and organisation in Eastern and Western Europe.* Pergamon Press.

Organisation for Economic Co-operation and Development (OECD). (2015). *Frascati manual 2015: Guidelines for collecting and reporting data on research and experimental development.* OECD Publishing. https://www.oecd.org/sti/frascati-manual -2015-9789264239012-en.htm

Percy, E. (1945). *Higher technological education* (Report of a Special Committee appointed in April 1944. Ministry of Education). His Majesty's Stationery Office. http://www.educationengland.org.uk/documents/percy1945/percy1945.html#07

Petrella, R. & Schaff, A. (1974). *A European experiment in cooperation in the social sciences: Ten years activities at the Centre, 1963–1973* [trans. C. Strange]. European Coordination Centre for Research and Documentation in Social Sciences.

Pohoryles, R. J. & Sors, A. (2017) On the future of social sciences and humanities – a pragmatic perspective. *Innovation: The European Journal of Social Science Research, 30*(1), 1–4. DOI: 10.1080/13511610.2016.1230491

Randma-Liiv, T. (2021). *Academician Tiina Randma-Liiv: Real life problems are interdisciplinary* (Tallinn University of Technology). https://taltech.ee/en/news/ academician-tiina-randma-liiv-real-life-problems-are-interdisciplinary

Research England (2021). *Connecting Capability Fund (CCF).* https://re.ukri .org/ knowledge-exchange/the-connecting-capability-fund-ccf/

Research Excellence Framework (REF). (2021). *REF2021: Interdisciplinary research.* https://www.ref.ac.uk/about/interdisciplinary-research/

Rose, R. (2003). When all other conditions are not equal: The context for drawing lessons. In C. J. Finer (Ed.), *Social policy reform in China: Views from home and abroad* (pp. 5–22). Routledge.

Rothblatt, S. & Wittrock, B. (Eds). (1993). *The European and American university since 1800: Historical and sociological essays.* Cambridge University Press.

Royal Society (2016a). UK research and the European Union: The role of the EU in funding UK research. https://royalsociety.org/~/media/policy/projects/eu-uk-funding/uk-membership-of-eu.pdf

Royal Society (2016b). UK research and the European Union: The role of the EU in international research collaboration and researcher mobility. https://royalsociety.org/ ~/media/policy/projects/eu-uk-funding/phase-2/EU-role-in-international-research -collaboration-and-researcher-mobility.pdf

Russell Group (2021). *About*. https://russellgroup.ac.uk/about/

Social Sciences and Humanities Research Council of Canada (SSHRC). (2021). *How to apply*. https://www.sshrc-crsh.gc.ca/funding-financement/apply-demande/index-eng.aspx

Statistical Office of the European Communities (Eurostat). (2021). *History*. https://ec.europa.eu/eurostat/about/overview/history

Stern, N. (2016). *Building on success and learning from experience: An independent review of the research excellence framework*. Crown Publishing. https://assets.publishing.service.gov.uk/government/uploads/system/uploads/attachment_data/file/541338/ind-16-9-ref-stern-review.pdf

Szalai, A. (1977). The organization and execution of cross-national survey research projects. In A. Szalai & R. Petrella (Eds), *Cross-national comparative survey research: Theory and practice* (pp. 49–93). Pergamon Press.

Tennom, J. (1995) European research communities: France vs. the United Kingdom. *European Yearbook on Youth Policy and Research* (CYRCE). Vol. 1, *The puzzle of integration*, 269–281.

Torstendahl, R. (1993). The transformation of professional education in the nineteenth century. In S. Rothblatt & B. Wittrock (Eds), *The European and American university since 1800: Historical and sociological essays* (pp. 109−141). Cambridge University Press.

Treaty on the Functioning of the European Union (TFEU). (2012). *Title XIX: Research and technological development and space. OJ* C 326. https://eur-lex.europa.eu/legal-content/EN/TXT/HTML/?uri=CELEX:12012E/TXT

UK Energy Research Centre (UKERC). (2021). *About*. https://ukerc.ac.uk/

UK Government (2016). *Higher education: Success as a knowledge economy* [White Paper]. https://www.gov.uk/government/publications/higher-education-success-as-a-knowledge-economy-white-paper

UK Research and Innovation (UKRI). (2021a). *About us*. https://www.ukri.org/about-us/

UK Research and Innovation (UKRI). (2021b). *Get support for your project: If your research spans different disciplines*. https://www.ukri.org/apply-for-funding/before-you-apply/preparing-to-make-a-funding-application/if-your-research-spans-different-disciplines/

University College London (UCL). (2021). *Financial management*. Research and Innovation Services. https://www.ucl.ac.uk/research-innovation-services/research-services/managing-funding/financial-management

Warwick, D. P. & Osherson, S. (1973). Comparative analysis in the social sciences. In D. P. Warwick & S. Osherson (Eds), *Comparative research methods* (pp. 3–41). Prentice-Hall.

Wordvice K. H. (2021, 5 December). How to order author names and why that matters. *Wordvice blog.* https://blog.wordvice.com/journal-article-author-order/

Index